COLOMBIA JAIL JOURNAL

JAMES MONAGHAN

COLOMBIA
JAIL JOURNAL

BRANDON

A Brandon Original Paperback

First published in 2007 by Brandon
an imprint of Mount Eagle Publications
Dingle, Co. Kerry, Ireland, and
Unit 3, Olympia Trading Estate, Coburg Road, London N22 6TZ, England

www.brandonbooks.com

ISBN 9780863223761

2 4 6 8 10 9 7 5 3 1

Cover design: www.designsuite.ie
Typesetting by Red Barn Publishing, Skeagh, Skibbereen
Printed in the UK

Contents

Prologue: Arrest   9

Chapter 1
A Time of Hope   11

Chapter 2
Army Interrogation Centre   17

Chapter 3
La Modelo   25

Chapter 4
*Police Holding Centre DIJIN (Dirección Central de
Policía Judicial y Inteligencia)*   42

Chapter 5
La Picota Prison   57

Chapter 6
The DIJIN Once Again   61

Chapter 7
La Picota Again   75

Chapter 8
Collapse of the Peace Talks   84

Chapter 9
Three Days in October   107

Chapter 10
La Modelo Again   118

Chapter 11
Into the Mountains: Cómbita   133

Chapter 12
Prison Reception   142

Chapter 13
Pabellón 6   157

Chapter 14
Raids, Conditions, and a New FARC Leader   177

Chapter 15
Our Trial Resumes   199

Chapter 16
The Law's Delay   216

Chapter 17
Our Trial Resumes Again   241

Chapter 18
Waiting for the Verdict   250

Chapter 19
The Verdict at Last   259

Chapter 20
Freedom Ride?   272

Acknowledgements and thanks   275

The views expressed in this book are my own and are not to be taken as the views of any other person or organisation.
– James Monaghan

Prologue: Arrest

ON SATURDAY, 11 August 2001, Niall Connolly, Martin McCauley and I flew into Bogotá Airport on an internal flight from San Vicente del Caguan. We were travelling using passports in different people's names to hide our real identities. Niall, who used the name David Bracken, was about thirty-six, tall, well-built and had a well-trimmed black beard. Martin, who used the name John Joseph Kelly, was around forty and was small and stocky; he had short brown hair and was clean-shaven. My passport said Edward Joseph Campbell; I was fifty-six and of medium height and my hair, which was almost white, was cut short. All of us wore jackets, jeans and hiking boots and carried our things in haversacks.

We collected our haversacks and made our way to the nearby International Airport to book our flight. We had been on the holiday of a lifetime, to visit the FARC guerrillas who were holding peace talks with the Colombian government. However, the story of what happened to us started long before this.

The airport was crowded but cool compared to the heat outside. I adjusted my haversack to make it more comfortable and hefted the case of video equipment in my left hand. We were looking for the Air France check-in to find out about the times of flights to Paris for the homeward leg of our long journey. 'David' spoke.

"I can see the check-in, it's the fourth one on our right."

The three of us made for it through the crowd, 'David' leading, then 'John' and I bringing up the rear.

Security was heavy. There were soldiers standing near the entrance door and more further down the line of check-ins. I barely noticed them at the time. We reached the Air France desk and 'David' asked the girl about flights.

I put my haversack down and straightened up to find lots of soldiers, dressed in dark-green uniforms and steel helmets, moving towards me. I felt a shock of fear and the blood draining from my stomach. These were the soldiers whose fearsome reputation we had recently been hearing about. In front of the soldiers there was a civilian in a long black leather coat. He said:

"Do not be alarmed, this is a routine check!"

I felt very, *very* alarmed.

Chapter 1

A Time of Hope

MANY PEOPLE SAW the millennium as a time of hope for the world. The cold war was over and there were moves towards peace in a number of long-running conflicts: in Ireland, in South Africa, in Palestine /Israel and in Colombia. In the year 2001 the peace process in Ireland was well under way. People who had been in prison as a result of the conflict were being released as part of the Good Friday Agreement between the British and Irish parties to the war.

I had fought in the long war as an IRA volunteer. I was a prisoner in England from 1970 to 1972, and again in the Irish Republic, from 1976 to 1985. While in Portlaoise prison I had spent some years as Education Officer for the IRA prisoners there. That involved organising political discussions and setting up classes for education in languages, computers and art, and an Irish speaking part of the jail. I had organised regular political discussions among the prisoners who were interested in contributing to what was happening outside. At the time there were intense feelings both for and against supporting a move into political involvement in the general elections in the Republic.

During the Civil War (1921-1923), both the IRA and the Sinn Féin political party had opposed the treaty setting up the Irish Free State (later the Irish Republic) and so refused to recognise its authority ever since. I argued that we should contest the elections and take any seats that we won, because with the passage of time most of the people in the state had come to accept it as their own state. The outcome of that argument was to profoundly change Irish history.

I was OC (officer commanding) of the prisoners for a year or so. On my release I joined Sinn Féin and as a result of my prison experience, I was asked to take the position of director of education when it became vacant. As director of education I had a seat on the Ard

Comhairle, which is the ruling body, and I used it to advance the moves towards taking any seats that we won in elections. The Irish peace process began to take shape a few years later as a result of the party decision in 1986 to take seats and really become involved in electoral politics.

In the year 2000 I was asked to take the job of managing *Tar Isteach*. In Irish, the words *tar isteach* mean 'come inside' and the office was to help reintegrate IRA ex-prisoners into work and social life. Many IRA prisoners went into jail as teenagers and came out without some of the basic skills for work or life in peacetime. Being in prison is in itself a traumatic experience that takes years to get over. No one had experience in how best to handle such complex problems, but at least the ex-prisoners trusted other ex-prisoners such as me. *Coiste na nIarchimí* (committee of ex-prisoners) was the umbrella group covering the whole of Ireland, while *Tar Isteach* was for ex-prisoners from the Dublin region.

Tar Isteach held weekly discussions which usually centred on questions and answers after an ex-prisoner told their experiences in prisons abroad or in Ireland. As part of a separate project to make an archive of first-hand historic sources on the war, we video recorded these meetings. For variety we sometimes invited other interesting speakers, and at one meeting two women from Atlantis, an ecological commune in Huila, in the south of Colombia, had talked about the killing of two of the commune members by the FARC-EP (*Fuerzas Armadas Revolucionarias Colombianas-Ejército del Pueblo*) (Revolutionary Armed Forces of Colombia-People's Army) in Colombia. The Atlantis commune had once been based on Innisfree Island off the coast of Donegal, where they had been known as 'The Screamers'. One of the women, Beckey Murray, was the mother of one of the victims, Tristan Murray; the other victim was an eighteen-year-old Colombian friend called Javier Nova. They also talked about what was happening in Colombia regarding the guerrilla war and the problem of drugs.

Members of *Coiste na nIarchimí* had travelled abroad to learn from the experience of other countries that had recently had peace processes. Niall and I had gone to Nicaragua; others had visited South Africa, Palestine and the Basque Country. There was a peace process going on in Colombia at the time and Niall, Martin and I decided to go there. Colombia was much more dangerous than almost anywhere else on the planet, and we decided to take extra precautions.

We arranged to travel using other people's passports and were very discreet about our plans, because we had every reason to believe that we would be risking our lives if we fell into the hands of the Colombian army or their paramilitary allies. British and Irish intelligence forces were intensely hostile towards Sinn Féin and were still in war mode in spite of the peace talks. They would tip off the Colombians if they knew that we were going to Colombia.

We arrived in Colombia towards the end of June 2001, taking a regular plane flight to San Vicente del Caguan, the largest town in the 16,000-square-mile demilitarised zone where the peace talks were taking place. A taxi took us from the small airport to the square in the centre of the town where the offices of the FARC-EP were (the name was usually shortened to FARC). The officials in the office were like any other officials, except that they wore military camouflage and were more cheerful. They had a queue of people arriving on their territory and there were forms to be filled and questions to be asked, such as the reason for visiting the zone. We had been told in the office that there was a steady stream of foreign visitors to observe the peace talks, which were open and welcoming to Colombians and interested people from any country. The foreign visitors had included various government envoys, ambassadors, parliamentarians, journalists, political activists from various countries and even a group from the New York stock exchange.

Niall spoke for the three of us as his Spanish was much better than ours. He explained who we were and that we would like to exchange views and ideas regarding the Colombian and the Irish peace processes. They were very interested. We were told to stay in one of the local guest houses and they would contact us.

The three of us booked in to a guest house near the town square. It was spartan but clean and tidy and the women working there were friendly and helpful. The food was well prepared. Our very favourable impression of the guest house later extended to the people of the town. I had wondered what it would be like to live in a town controlled by the

FARC, and it seemed to my eye that the people were in good spirits and the streets and small houses and shops were tidy and relatively prosperous. Niall spoke to local people who said that there were no paramilitary killings in the zone, unlike most of Colombia. There was not much ordinary crime either and what there was, the local municipal police dealt with, not the FARC.

We were waiting a few days before the FARC officials got in touch to arrange a lift on a truck to a small village nearer Los Poses where the talks were going on. We booked into a small guest house there.

Every few days we were invited to a house nearby where we talked with two or three FARC people who were connected with the negotiations as public relations personnel. We visited Los Poses with them, but found it much better to engage in face to face talks with the FARC where Niall could translate the Spanish and we could all take part. At Los Poses Martin and I found it very difficult to follow the rapidly spoken Spanish. Sometimes the FARC people took us to a café where we could eat and talk for two or three hours around tables in the open air.

The discussions ranged over the present talks and the history of both Colombia and Ireland that formed the background to the conflicts. They told us of the work that had been carried out by the FARC in the zone during the two years of its existence. They had performed the near miracle of bringing in heavy earthmoving machinery and constructed over 250 kilometres of new roads. They built over twenty bridges and paved the streets of many of the small towns. They installed running water and carried out public health works such as a massive vaccination programme. The zone had seen the arrival of thousands of refugees fleeing the terror imposed on the rest of Colombia by the powerful pro-government paramilitaries. As a gesture of goodwill the FARC had released 240 army and police personnel that they had held prisoner.

Like us, they were interested in ideas and methods that would be useful in the peace process. There was some similarity between the situation in Colombia and in the North of Ireland. In both cases there were ruling elites who had to appear to be democratic while manipulating their political systems to maintain their rule into the future. In Ireland it was done through a sectarian (Protestant) state, which maintained sectarian rule and divided the people. They used discrimination in jobs and housing to force the emigration of nationalists and encourage the loyalty of unionists, and so maintain a unionist majority over the long term. In Colombia it was done by the selective assassination of leaders of the opposition at all levels, so that no coherent alternative political force could be built. In both cases the elite contained more than one political party to represent different interests within it.

The FARC were sceptical that the government seriously wanted a political solution, pointing to the military build-up going on. Their main thrust seemed to be to get guarantees against systematic assassinations by the paramilitaries and armed forces so that they could fight elections on a level playing field, without being subject to a repeat of the thousands of assassinations that had wiped out the broad left Union Patriotica party in the 1980s. Given these conditions, they were confident that they could and would get into government. In government they would use the huge natural resources of Colombia for the benefit of the ordinary people.

They were intensely interested in our strategy of negotiation with the British. Instead of us trying to get a final settlement, a treaty, we spoke of the possibility of creating a framework of elected bodies and legally enforceable civil and political rights that all sides could accept. This would enable us to end discrimination and move politics on to the grounds of meeting the needs of ordinary people, and so remove the conditions for a permanent unionist majority.

Each different party to the agreement could then try to evolve society in the direction they favoured. For us this agreement would open a political road to a united Ireland, as the British had given a public commitment to accept the will of a simple majority in a referendum, to withdraw from Ireland if that was the outcome of the vote. Our armed struggle had brought about the conditions in which such a framework could be negotiated, even though we were never militarily strong enough to force a British withdrawal. If the FARC were able to get a similar framework, then they could also advance towards political power through elections.

As time went by other, more senior FARC people would drop by and take part in the exchange of ideas. We felt that real progress was being made for the future and we extended our time there until the last possible day.

When we were not involved in a discussion, which was a lot of the time, we explored the roads and forest. I had a video camera and we used it a lot for both film and still shots of the scenery and local people. That area was not jungle; it was hilly with open grassland and scattered forest areas. The local farmers were extending their grazing land bit by bit, burning small patches of forest. The land was covered with the remains of burnt trees from years gone by. I thought it was a pity to see the forest destroyed, but they had families to feed and little suitable land to farm. They grew maize and other crops and kept some cattle, usually white hump-backed cows.

A few days before we were to leave to return to Bogotá, I had an accident. We were crossing a river by wading through it. The dense trees overhead made it hard to see the bottom and I fell into a deep hole in the riverbed. One second I was up to my knees in water, the next I was up to my armpits! I climbed out of the hole still carrying the video camera, but all the film and equipment was saturated with dirty water. We tried to dry the video film but could not, although eventually the camera did work after a day or so of drying. Finally, having run a week over our intended holiday time, we reluctantly took the plane back to Bogotá.

Chapter 2

Army Interrogation Centre

THE MAN IN the long black leather coat ordered us to carry our haversacks and follow him. He had barely looked at our passports when he had asked to see identification. The fact that he spoke English and their general attitude made me think that they had been waiting for us to arrive.

"We want you to answer some routine questions," he said again.

The thirty or so heavily armed soldiers formed a line on each side of us and escorted us out of the airport to three waiting trucks. The soldiers, very young and very tense, said little to us and did not allow us say anything to each other. Their assault rifles looked far too big for them to manage, but I wouldn't have liked to test that idea.

I was thinking of all possibilities. They would have seen photo-copies of our passports, which were presented when booking our flight to San Vicente: mine and Martin's were British, while Niall's was Irish. Perhaps they wondered why we stayed for over a month in the zone.

We were all put into one army truck. A lot of soldiers sat along the sides while we stood up in the centre. I thought that they might be military police by the markings on their uniforms, but the letters were PM and not MP. The convoy of vehicles drove through the city and eventually entered a huge barracks, which had the logo over its gates: "13th Brigade Military Police". Soldiers were doing foot drill and a military band were practising marching with their instruments. Our truck drove to a part of the barracks where there were long, low, single-storey brick buildings with verandas along the sides, which looked like office buildings. We still had not been able to speak to each other.

We were ordered to dismount from the truck and go to the veran-da of a nearby building. We followed the man in black, who was clearly in charge, although he wore civilian clothes and was the interpreter. Each of us was put into a separate office. In my case the office was small and contained two desks and a few chairs and filing cabinets, and a door leading to another office adjoining it. There were three or four soldiers there, one of whom gestured to me to put everything in my pockets on the desk in front of me. They carefully examined each item.

Other armed soldiers stood just outside the door. When I had finished emptying my pockets they told me to take off my clothes and hand over each item for them to examine. I did as I was told. I had felt vulnerable since having been arrested, but never more so than standing there without clothes in front of those soldiers. Their numbers, their uniforms, their weapons and their reputation for brutality made the soldiers seem strong, while I felt we were few, each alone and without weapons or clothes or friends who could help. A soldier handed me back my trousers and when I had put them on, he ordered me to empty my haversack on the desk. Every item was carefully checked. Then we waited. Waiting proved a stressful experience in an army interrogation centre.

The man in black came in. He looked at my passport. "You are British?"

"No, I am Irish."

"Your passport is British!"

"My address on it is Belfast, that's a place in Ireland."

"What were you doing in San Vicente? Were you dealing in drugs?"

"Before I answer your questions, I want a lawyer present."

"You are in Colombia now, you do as we say."

"I won't answer questions until I have a lawyer present."

"Did you visit coca fields or laboratories?"

"I will answer your questions when I have a lawyer present."

"Did you see any FARC bases or transport vehicles while you were in the zone?"

"I will answer your questions when I have a lawyer present."

"We have an American expert from the Embassy; he will test your clothes for traces of drugs."

About an hour later a Caucasian man came into the room with a black briefcase. It looked to me to be the sort of case that would contain a rather large laptop. As soon as he spoke I realised that he was the American from the Embassy.

"The name is Molloy; I am here to do some forensic tests." I thought at the time that Molloy was an Irish name. He opened his briefcase and took out some small circles of white cloth. He laid out the contents of my haversack on the desk and used a cloth to wipe over each item, putting each cloth in a labelled plastic bag. He gave the impression to me that he was used to this routine and was familiar with the military officers and the soldiers. After about a half hour he left.

The man in black returned with a soldier who took two sets of my fingerprints. I figured that they would send one set to the British to see if I had any record there, which of course I did. They would also have Martin's prints.

When my prints were taken he went to the office next door. I could judge from the sounds that Martin was there, and was having his prints taken. Niall must have been in an office on the other side of Martin's because I could not make out any sounds that indicated his presence at all. The soldiers in the room with me made no objection when I put my things back in my haversack and took out warmer clothes to wear, now that it was getting colder.

It was dark outside when three plain-clothes men arrived at the door. I was told to go with them. My heart was hammering on my ribs as I walked out into the night. They had a car and told me to get in. *When you thought that there was a possibility that you were going to be shot, would you be better to make a desperate run for it or to proceed and hope that all would be well? Where was there to run to?* I got into the car. One of the men put his hand on my head and forced me down on the seat. I was on the verge of some desperate action but realised that the body language of the mysterious three was not threatening. I got down out of sight of anyone outside the car. I did not know what was happening. The car drove a few hundred metres and stopped.

I was let out at the doors of a hospital. The three escorted me inside and one of them spoke to a nurse at the reception desk, but I could not make out the meaning of the rapidly spoken Spanish. I was taken by the nurse to a room and given a thorough medical check and then returned to the waiting plain-clothes men. One of them had left with the car.

I walked back to the interrogation centre through the dark barracks with the two of them. They were very relaxed and joked among themselves, so much so that I thought they were making it easy for me to make an escape bid into the darkness. *And what might be waiting in the shadows?* We arrived back at the office building without incident. After I was given some coffee and takeaway food, one of the soldiers brought a foam rubber mattress and told me to sleep on the floor. I took my clothes out of the haversack and made a pillow from a pullover and pulled my jacket around myself for warmth. I was soon asleep.

The soldiers moving in the office woke me about daybreak. Saturday had been a long day; I wondered what today, Sunday, would bring. I was given a cup of coffee and two biscuits to start the day. I was suspicious that the coffee might be drugged but decided to chance it. Being hungry and thirsty would be almost as bad as being drugged, and that was a certainty if I did not eat, while being drugged was not very likely. I put away my things and waited to see what would happen.

The man in black came in and we repeated yesterday's performance about the lawyer and answering questions. He was waiting for the forensic report and the answer to his enquiries about our fingerprints, so he did not care whether I answered or not. I decided that he was building up a profile of each of us, based on carefully observing tiny reactions to different sorts of question. After a half hour my interrogator left me and went to Martin.

The American Embassy forensic report arrived. My interrogator slapped it down on the desk. Drugs! The Americans said that five different kinds of drug were found on our clothes, and for extra effect, several different types of explosives had also shown up. I looked in disbelief at the computer print-outs he showed me.

They are trying to scare us witless with this.

I replied that it was either false, to scare me, or was the result of contamination from the surroundings.

He said that we were going to be charged with rebellion and with possession of drugs. I had no idea of what a charge of rebellion entailed.

I had been worried when we were first arrested and put on a military truck going to an unknown destination. I thought it prudent to let someone know that three Irishmen were in the hands of the military. In the Irish civil war in 1921-23, prisoners were put on military trucks and driven to lonely roads in the Dublin Mountains to be shot. The Colombian civil war had gone on a lot longer than the Irish one and was even more vicious. The only witness that would have a chance of getting to meet us was someone from an embassy, and my passport was British, so when I was told that I could make a phone call, I phoned the British Embassy to say I wanted a visit. They sent a Mrs Pringle to see Martin and me. I did not have anything much to say to her, but the fact of her having seen us there made any disappearance more difficult for the army. I phoned them because the nearest Irish Embassy was in Mexico City, far away.

When the fingerprint reply arrived about mid-morning, the attitude of the soldiers changed noticeably. The man in black made a dramatic announcement that we were top explosives experts from the IRA, in Colombia to train the FARC! Further questioning was not necessary to establish our guilt!

I got a surprise when Martin was brought into the office where I was held, but the soldiers brought him on through the door to the office adjoining. They placed a guard on the door between the offices to stop us speaking to each other. It seemed that there was something important going on in the office where Martin had previously been held.

I was given some food and coffee and some more was taken into Martin. We were eating when we heard the sounds of a scuffle outside, followed by shouting and the sound of running feet. The guard on the door between us ran out the front and joined with my guard in the commotion outside. Martin appeared at the door beside me.

"What's happening?"

"Lean ar aghaidh ag caint" (continue talking), I said in Irish.

The two of us kept a conversation going while searching the furniture. Martin pointed to a hidden microphone under the table. He was able to tell me in Irish that Niall was okay and so was he. I asked was he told that he was going to be charged with drugs and rebellion and he said that he was. After a minute we heard the guards returning and made as if neither of us had moved since they left.

Late on Sunday night a large number of people arrived in my office. They included Molloy from the American Embassy, the British Embassy's Mrs Pringle, various military officers and a forensic man from the Security Service DAS (Department of Security Administration). There was a woman from *Fiscalía*, the civilian state prosecution agency. There was even a video camera crew who filmed everything going on. A note-taker worked busily in Spanish and English, as every word was translated. There were fourteen of us in the small room.

The woman from *Fiscalía* asked each of the forensic experts to state who they were, who they worked for and what were their qualifications to do forensic testing. The DAS expert had no problem answering, but Molloy had to admit that he "had taken a few lessons in the Embassy".

My haversack was emptied once again, and the contents were laid out on the table. The American used his cloth circles on each item and then the DAS man put a strip of adhesive tape on the same item. The tape was stuck to the material and then peeled off, carrying fibres, dust and hairs. It was sealed in labelled plastic bags. When both had taken around fifteen samples each, they packed their bags and moved into Martin's room. About a half hour later they all came out again through where I was and out the front door, going to where Niall was. I lay down and slept on the floor beside the desk again that night.

The next morning there was another interrogation session and I said the same about wanting a lawyer before answering questions. I was getting to know the interrogator and he was asking about things like what university had I attended and other general questions, just to break down the "I want a lawyer" routine from me. He told me a lot about his travels to Egypt and the discrimination he suffered in Israel. Then his patience snapped.

He took me outside in the company of two soldiers. The full-length black leather coat gave him a sinister look, and he delivered a sinister ultimatum.

"You have three minutes to make a meaningful statement, and unless you do, you will be sent to a prison controlled by the paramilitaries. They will consider you a friend of the FARC and an enemy of theirs. You are aware of what the paramilitaries will do to you?"

We stared into each other's eyes for the full three minutes. He did not blink once, and his eyes were dark and hard. He abruptly ordered the two soldiers to take me back to the interrogation room. I was glad I had not met him on a lonely jungle path, and I was annoyed with myself that I had let him lead me into playing mind games. Only a short time before I had been thinking that he seemed a fairly decent sort, a friendly face in a hostile crowd.

The army had finished with their interrogation; they took each of us to 'the bunker'. It was the home of the state security machine, and the place where *Fiscalía* carried out their interrogations. I was put in an army jeep and driven out of the barracks complex and across the city to this huge grey concrete building that the soldiers spoke about in awed voices. Bad things happened in the bunker, I was led to believe. I was taken from the army transport and into a basement cell where I waited in the company of some soldiers. After several hours I was ordered to accompany the soldiers upstairs to a large space that had plants and even small trees growing in it. The soldiers were formal and correct, but not openly hostile. They withdrew several metres and left me sitting alone for a long time, the tension growing.

A brisk, cheerful man suddenly appeared in front of me and said that he was my *abogado* – my lawyer. He gestured me to follow him into a corner among the plants, in case the seat area was bugged. He was about forty and going grey; his personality was lively and he gave off a strong feeling that he was on my side. He said that his name was Carlos Leon Camacho. I had difficulty following his Spanish but was able to grasp that a woman interrogator and several other people would question me. I was surprised at this turn of events and I wondered how was I to relate to this man who said that he was my lawyer. I was very suspicious of Carlos and yet he did seem to be giving some good advice.

He sat in on the interrogation and promised to visit me later in the army barracks, which he did. It turned out that he had been appointed to be *abogado* to all three of us.

Back in the army barracks afterwards, each of us was moved from our 'offices' to cells in a detention centre for soldiers. I was put in a fairly large cell which had passages from the bible written in large letters on the walls. Through a barred window I could see young soldiers resting outside, and some of them came over to the window. I tried to strike up a conversation in Spanish and they tried to help me with the words, but I could not cope with their accents and the speed of their sentences.

After a few days we were put together in a small cell in a detention block filled with soldiers awaiting military trials. There were five or six cells and a small area outside that all prisoners there used during the day when the cell doors were opened. The exercise area was surrounded by a high chain-link fence and there were always armed soldiers on guard outside the fence.

It was a huge relief to be there together – we even had our own coffee machine. Niall talked to the other prisoners in Spanish. Some were in for massacres of civilians and others for murders of fellow soldiers. Carlos came to visit with legal advice and Chinese takeaways. The life there was not too bad compared with the previous days in solitary or during interrogation. The other ten or so prisoners questioned us about why we had been arrested, as it was big on the radio and TV news. Niall fielded the questions for the three of us and he gave them no information.

Saturday evening came, and the prisoners were given *cerveza* (beer). As they got drunk some of them started to talk in loud voices about the need to kill the FARC and their 'collaborators'. It was quickly getting ugly and we decided to return to our cell and lock the door.

Next morning we went out among them again, because it was not good to appear intimidated by them. With no alcohol around, there were no more ugly incidents.

A few days later we were told to take our shopping bags with our clothes (our haversacks had been held as evidence) and get into a small lorry along with an escort of heavily armed soldiers. We left the barracks of the 13th Brigade Military Police in a convoy of vehicles, passing through a group of journalists and photographers at the gate. We sat between the impassive soldiers and looked at the city streets in the poorer areas as we travelled. Eventually we came to a street with a long, high brick wall and a big blue door. We had arrived at 'La Modelo' – the model prison.

Chapter 3

La Modelo

I LIFTED MY bag down from the army lorry. Three or four soldiers had jumped down before I moved and taken up positions around the lorry, rifles at the ready. An army jeep stood a few metres away. The soldiers from it had also taken up guard positions around their vehicle. An army officer spoke to the officer in charge of the INPEC (*Instituto National Penitenciario y Carcelario*) prison guards, handing us over to La Modelo prison, Bogotá. The prison guards, dressed in dark blue uniforms with peaked caps, were all armed to the teeth and highly excited by our presence.

We were standing there handcuffed, bags at our feet. We said nothing. Everyone else milled around or else was looking grimly for any sign of a rescue attempt. After a few minutes the soldiers mounted their vehicles and drove out the main gate. I was glad to see them depart. The hand-over was complete and this place was to be our new home until someone decided what to do with us. We had thought we would probably be deported for using passports in other people's names, which was not a very serious charge in Colombia. However, the excitement of the soldiers and prison guards was because we were also going to be charged with training FARC guerillas.

"Edward Joseph Campbell?"

It was the name on my passport, although the Brits had told the Colombian army that the fingerprints belonged to James Monaghan, whom they had held prisoner on IRA-related charges in the early 1970s. When I stepped forward, the INPEC officer gestured to me to go inside the building a few metres away. I started to pick up my luggage.

"John Joseph Kelly?"

That was the name on Martin McCauley's passport. The Brits had also recognised his fingerprints.

"David Bracken?"

Niall Connolly had no fingerprint record, and so neither the Brits nor the Irish Gárdaí could have named him. Eventually he gave his correct name, because otherwise he could not have received family visits.

The three of us went into the huge concrete building, mostly two or three storeys high, with parts that were up to four storeys. It was surrounded by a high wall which had watchtowers every 50 metres or so. Above all was a central watchtower, which was taller than everything else in the prison. The watchtower, of a more modern design than the prison buildings around it, was made of concrete with a large glass observation platform on top. There were several exercise yards and even a football field inside the prison walls. Armed guards patrolled the walls and sat in the watchtowers. The guards inside the buildings had batons but not guns, probably for fear of the prisoners grabbing them.

Armed guards handed us over to the guards in reception. My handcuffs were removed so that I could be fingerprinted, photographed, measured and stood in front of a wall-mounted video camera. Colombian officials have a mania for fingerprints and video films, which is probably necessary in a country where there is a lot of illiteracy and corruption. All signatures are thumbprinted by the person signing, and all proceedings of a legal nature are video recorded. They took palm prints as well. I was given the use of a rag to clean off the fingerprint ink. It was messy and impossible to wipe off completely and I was black up to the wrists. Each of us went through the same procedure, so we were there for quite some time.

We were taken upstairs to the office of the director, who is roughly equivalent to a governor in an Irish prison. We had to put all of our possessions on a big table. Each item was noted and most were put aside, some were given back to us as they were things which were allowed in the prison. Our money was separated into pesos, euros and dollars, and the serial number of every note was entered in a ledger. While this was going on, a video film was being made and photos taken. I think the photos appeared on the evening news, at least we saw one of those photos in papers and magazines later. It was very intimidating to be at the centre of attention and not easily understand the language. The guards were excited, questioning, talking, directing and ordering us about. Niall could only give the two of us an occasional update on what was being said.

When we were finished in the director's office we were taken downstairs again and through long grey corridors to the high security block. There was a large room with an airport style metal detector that appeared not to be working; at least the guards did not make us walk through it. The room served more as a sort of holding space where the outer set of doors had to be locked before the inner set was opened. The inner doors led to a short corridor, on one side of which were steel bars forming a sort of cage in which lawyers could talk to prisoners and still be in view of the guards. On the other side of the corridor was the guards' office, where they signed prisoners in and out, took fingerprints, checked visitors and drank coffee. In general the guards were not hostile to us, just very curious.

When we had gone through the whole fingerprinting routine again, we were given a rag to wipe off the ink and then led through another set of steel barred double gates and into a large floor space. Around the sides of this space there were cell doors set in the concrete walls. The doors were of sheet metal with a small window through which the guard could look in to see the prisoners.

The three of us were put into one cell about four metres by four, empty and bare, with a strange wallpaper border running around it about a metre from the floor. The border pictured a line of fish! There was a doorway with a curtain at the back that led to a toilet and shower. The shower had once had a spray head and a heating unit, but all that was gone now and only a horizontal steel pipe remained. When you turned on the shower a jet of cold water hit the far wall. A part of the main room's concrete floor was raised a little to form a sleeping space. There were no beds or furniture. This was to be our home for the foreseeable future. A guard slammed the door, locking us in.

Niall sat down on his bag. He was worried-looking, not his normal cheerful self. The weather in Bogotá is not tropical at all, because the city is about 2,500 metres above sea level and the sky is often cloudy. It was necessary to wear reasonably warm clothes there, so we were all wearing jeans, boots and jackets. Martin also sat on his bag. He was searching his pockets, hoping that a packet of cigarettes had somehow survived the search of our pockets and things. As usual, he was lucky!

I was worried, although I don't know if it showed on my face. The search had been much easier than what I had experienced in previous prisons in England and Ireland. I had been pleasantly surprised at being allowed to keep my bag, clothes and boots. Colombian prisons were obviously different, but perhaps not better. I looked around at our grim surroundings and decided that the only appropriate thing to do was to sit on my bag like the other two and jointly take stock of our situation.

After a while we started to explore our little world. The toilet worked and the shower was a source of water for washing and drinking. If the valve lever on the water pipe was moved just a little, the stream of water was controllable, so that you could catch it in a cup. There was a small window high up near the ceiling on the same wall as the cell door. It allowed air to circulate and had bars but no glass. There was also a small window in the cell door so that the guard could look in by opening a cover on it. Each of us had a look at the scene outside our cell. We could see four or five other cell doors across the way from us, and an area cut off from our floor space by a wall of metal bars and steel mesh. There were two very young-looking INPEC guards sitting on white plastic chairs outside our cell door.

Niall asked them, in Spanish, what kinds of prisoners were in the other cells. The guards answered that the other prisoners on this floor of *alta seguridad* (high security) were awaiting the outcome of extradition proceedings. They were mostly from Spain, Italy and the US and were in on drug-related charges. They told us that there were around 4,000 men in La Modelo, mostly 'social prisoners' (ordinary criminals) doing short sentences.

The guards told us that they were sitting there to protect us from attack by the paramilitaries. (The right-wing armed groups opposing the left were referred to as 'paramilitary' while the left-wing armed revolutionary groups were referred to as 'guerrilla'.) The paramilitaries were held on the floor above us and in the cells along the corridor that we had entered by. We had not seen them as they were outside on exercise at the time when we had come into the cellblock.

One of the guards told us that if the paramilitaries did come to attack us, they would come armed with guns, and because they, the guards, had only batons, we would have to fend for ourselves. That was not very comforting to hear, but at least they were telling the truth. We were left under no illusions about our situation. Being frightened is an emotional high that cannot be sustained for long periods. We were frightened but had, over the past week, accepted that as the normal state of our existence. Like hunger or a toothache, you just learned to live with it until better times.

These thoughts were going through my head as I sat in the cell in La Modelo. I wondered how the prison guards would treat us, and what would be the attitude of the various groups of prisoners held on other floors here in high security. There were paramilitaries and guerrillas as well as drugs prisoners and social criminals in on serious charges. It might be that we were better off in the high security wing than in the crowded and chaotic wings that held the ordinary prisoners on less serious charges.

There were about 1,000 prisoners in the north wing, guerrillas from the FARC or ELN (*Ejército de Liberación*–National Liberation Army) or other smaller groups and people charged with assisting them in various ways. People could find themselves held with the guerrillas if they were jailed in connection with a strike or protest against some government or big business policy.

All prisoners in a paramilitary wing of the prison are not paramilitaries. When a new prisoner arrives at the prison reception, they are asked whether they would rather be held with the paramilitaries or with the guerrillas. There is no other option. Life with the guerrillas is more orderly and safe from bullying but you could be killed in an attack on the guerrillas. Life with the paramilitaries is more violent and the prisoner may have to pay rent for a sleeping space on the floor, and perhaps be a servant to a paramilitary leader. The real deciding factor is that when released after the sentence, the prisoner would be classified as an enemy of the state if they spent their time with the guerrillas. Their lives and the lives of their families will be affected for ever afterwards. Not surprisingly, most social prisoners spend their time with the paramilitaries.

After a few hours a large group of heavily armed INPEC guards arrived at our cell and ordered us to accompany them. We were led back along the corridors and past the paramilitary area. The paramilitaries knew who we were by then, but did not seem to have any plan regarding what to do about us, so they glared at us and said nothing. We went on to the director's office. I wondered would our state-appointed lawyer, Carlos, be there.

The director was waiting for us along with several other people. Carlos was there too and he gave each of us a hearty handshake. There was also a FARC prisoner who was a representative of all the guerrilla prisoners. He shook hands too, in a comradely fashion. Niall spoke for the three of us. He said that we would be safer if we were held with the guerrilla prisoners in the north wing, as there we would have people who could watch our backs and the paramilitaries would find it harder to get near us. The director, a retired army officer, agreed with the logic of the request but he said that he could not allow us to be held in a less secure area, as we were designated high security.

The FARC representative accepted the situation given by the director and successfully negotiated to send food and coffee to us three times a day. This was to ensure that our food was not poisoned. He also got permission to send us foam rubber mattresses to lie on and a blanket each. He said that if any harm came to us the guerrilla prisoners would regard it as an attack on themselves and hit back. After the meeting we were escorted back to our cell by the large group of armed guards.

Three guerrilla prisoners accompanied by several guards brought the coffee, food, mattresses and blankets from the north wing later that evening. The prisoner who brought the coffee and food gave us greetings from the prisoners' leaders and news about our arrival that they had seen shown on the TV. There had been film shown of our arrival and of the recording of our possessions in the director's office.

He also told us a bit of the history of this prison. Four or five weeks ago there had been a gun battle between the guerrilla prisoners and paramilitaries. It had lasted twenty-four hours and resulted in ten deaths, mostly guerrillas. The paramilitaries had been much better armed and could have inflicted even more casualties except that they were afraid of the explosives used by the guerrillas in the narrow corridors and landings. The paramilitaries were armed with AK-47s, Galils and R-15s, while the guerrillas were mostly armed with pistols. On 2 July of the previous year, it had been worse, with twenty-six prisoners killed. It was claimed that another seventeen prisoners simply disappeared, their bodies never found.

He told us that the media in Colombia were using our case as a reason to break off the peace talks in the zone, saying that our presence there was proof that the FARC were not interested in reaching an agreement with the Pastrana government. That line was being pushed hard by the army and the United States. He also told us that Amnesty International had described life in Colombia's prisons as being violent, with chronic overcrowding and severe shortages of food, water and medical care.

A journalist had come here to La Modelo on 25 May to interview a paramilitary leader in the director's office. She had been abducted, taken away from the prison and raped by four men, beaten up and thrown on a rubbish dump. She was accused of being a guerrilla sympathiser. The paramilitaries had a large measure of control of the prison. What we had just learned put the threat by 'the man in black' to send us to such a prison, into deadly focus. The guards stood around us and listened to what we were saying, making no comment. After a few minutes our meeting was ended and the guerrilla prisoners were escorted back to the north wing. We settled down for our first night in our much-improved new home.

As the days passed, we settled into a routine. In the mornings we would stack the mattresses and blankets in the form of a seat. That gave us some space to walk four or five paces back and forth. We were never allowed out of the cell except to make a phone call. Niall and Martin sometimes did press-ups but I was content to walk. The cell was stuffy and unpleasant to be in. We tried washing socks and underpants but there was no circulation of air to dry them. The arrival of the food and the minute's talk with the man who brought it was the high point of the day. The visits were as welcome for the bits of news and information they brought as for the food. Sometimes Niall could talk to other prisoners who were passing if the guards outside the door were okay, and he got to talk with the guards. We talked among ourselves about all sorts of things, but were always conscious that the army might have the cell bugged and might use something we said as evidence against us. It was hard to avoid being paranoid in such conditions.

We were entitled to make phone calls to our lawyer and families. From the phone calls we became aware of the huge interest by the media in our story and also of the systematic distortions of the facts for political ends. Although the IRA was engaging in discussions about putting its arms 'beyond use', the Irish peace process was at an impasse because of the lack of progress on removing the British army forts and surveillance towers from nationalist areas and on fundamental changes to policing which would change the police from being a repressive force into a community service.

As a result the IRA was saying that it might withdraw its offer on its weapons. The British and Unionists were unwilling to move from their hard-line positions and so were making the most of the opportunity for hostile propaganda as a way of turning public opinion in their favour. The US administration was full of self-righteous indignation about us. That really got up my nose as they had framed us precisely to create that situation. Most of the newspapers were only too happy to be used for sensational speculation by 'security sources' printed as if it were factual.

The phone that prisoners on our floor used was at the base of the stairs leading up to where more of the paramilitaries were held. It was outside the gates to our area, beside the guards' office. Each day guards escorted us one at a time out to the phone for a five-minute call. One day, after the three of us had finished our calls and were in the cell drinking coffee, there was a loud explosion outside. The alarms went off, guards were running around and there was a lot of commotion and confusion. They would not tell us what had happened.

Later on, one of the extradition prisoners shouted over to us that the paramilitaries had thrown a bomb down the stairs to where the phone was. Luckily they had got the time wrong for when we would be making the calls. By good luck the guards had been a little early that day. From then on, we took our phone calls in the guards' office. There was no privacy there for calls to our lawyer, which Niall had to make in Spanish, but since we were of the opinion that the phone was tapped anyway, it did not matter a lot. We also had our doubts about whether Carlos, our lawyer, was on our side or theirs.

Soon after that day we heard hammering and scraping on the concrete ceiling of the cell. The guards outside heard it as well and speculated that the paramilitaries were trying to make a hole in the ceiling to drop in a hand grenade. A guard officer came to talk to us about it. He advised that if a grenade was dropped into the cell, we should take cover in the toilet. It had a concrete wall affording some protection. When asked why he did not send some of his guards to the floor above, to make sure that no one dropped a grenade through the ceiling, he said the guards could not do that because the paramilitaries would not allow them stay there. When he had gone Martin made a heroic speech: "If a grenade lands in here, I will grab it and fuck it into the toilet!"

It seemed that with Martin's imperfect Spanish he had misunderstood the advice about us taking cover in the toilet.

The next day INPEC guards arrived with a welding plant. They told us to move our things back from the ventilation window for fear of sparks causing damage to our bedding and clothes. They welded some steel mesh over the ventilation window so that a grenade could not be dropped in through it. Whatever they did about our upstairs neighbours, the hammering and scraping stopped. It seemed that we were reasonably safe for the time being. We could never have exercise in the open air because the exercise area in the high security block was in a large cage on the roof. To reach the roof it would be necessary to go up the stairs through three floors which held paramilitaries and narco (narcotics) prisoners who were allied with them. They took their exercise on the roof and were not prepared to allow a time slot for us. There was also a very real risk of being shot on the way up to the roof or on the way back down, as a prisoner from our floor had been recently. Because we were confined to a cell with no air circulation, we could not even dry our towels after a shower, and had no visitors to take away and wash and dry our towels and clothes for us.

The atmosphere in the cell was one of tension and boredom. The tension was due in part to the threat that hung over our lives, and in part due to the legal and family problems of our being in prison in a foreign and violent place. There was real danger to anyone who visited us, but even so we did get some visits.

The British Embassy sent two representatives to see us because my passport and Martin's were British. The visit was not a social success. At that stage we also had contact with the Irish Embassy in Mexico City. The Irish Embassy official was Síle Maguire, who came to La Modelo and visited us three times during that week. Niall and Síle had already met at a reception for Irish people living in Cuba which was attended by Irish Embassy officials and visiting members of the Irish Dáil (parliament). She was very efficient and pleasant to talk to, although there was not much she could do except keep an eye on our treatment and safety and also to help us contact lawyers. We asked one of these lawyers to represent us and he agreed.

On 1 September 2001 we had a visit from an Irish businessman arranged by our families. His name was David Hogan and he was accompanied by the prison chaplain, Father Andres Fernandez, and his assistant Freddy Cordana. On the way in, David had spoken to the prison director, who was concerned for our safety and because our presence might cause renewed fighting in the prison. David told us that he was here with the approval of the Irish diplomat Síle Maguire and that he would send her an account of the visit.

He asked about the conditions that we were held in. We told him that our new lawyer, Ernesto Amezquita Camacho, was working along with Carlos on our case. He had wanted us to go on TV to combat the propaganda against us, and we wanted guidance about whether we should do so. Ernesto was also talking very big money, about $300,000, with $100,000 up front, if he was to get us released. We knew that there was no hope of raising so much and warned that the money could easily disappear on 'expenses' if it could be raised. We were reluctant to press for a transfer to the north wing as we thought it would be better to get a transfer to La Picota prison in the south of the city. We thanked our visitors for taking the risk of coming.

On Sunday a guard handed me a note from someone outside at the prison gate, asking would I like a visit. It was from an Irish woman living in Colombia. I filled in the necessary form and put my thumbprint on it, as was required. After a long time had passed she appeared at the cell door and was let in. Her name was Anne Barr. Anne was tall, slim and had a nice friendly face framed by long brown hair. She was from Buncrana in County Donegal, which is within sight of Rathmullan, where I was born and lived until I was twelve. She was a member of Atlantis, two of whose members I had met in Dublin. Anne was on a visit to Bogotá.

Anne had assumed that what was said on the TV about us being IRA explosives experts over in Colombia to train the FARC was true, but thought that the right thing to do was to visit the Irish prisoners, as we were far from home. She said that she would be in Bogotá for a few weeks and would visit if we wanted her to. We were glad both of the contact and the news and things that she could bring in such as newspapers, writing paper and pens. We looked forward to those visits, which lasted a couple of hours, but we never discussed anything connected with our arrest or legal matters, as our lawyer had insisted.

Anne told us her story, and that of the Atlantis commune. The commune had been in Ireland for years before they decided to move to South America. Land was cheap in Colombia – especially in remote areas, so they settled here. The children grew up and became friends with local children. Atlantis became more of an ecological group and worked with the local *campesinos* (farmers) and indigenous people planting vegetable and fruit gardens. It seemed an almost perfect existence but the war was getting nearer year by year. The FARC guerrillas came and ordered them to leave their land and not return. Foreigners were not trusted. The commune sold up and bought another place a few days' walk away. Becky Murray's son wanted to go and visit Ireland, so he and his Colombian friend, both eighteen, went back to the old place to say goodbye to their friends and godparents. The local FARC militia killed them both.

The deaths of Tristan and Javier were a terrible shock to the whole commune. Anne and two of the teenage girls went to the Talks Zone to confront the leadership of the FARC. They set up camp and sat around the fire playing guitar and singing protest songs. Eventually, some of the leadership of the guerrillas came and sat with them and listened to their story. One of the senior FARC men came back with his guitar and

ANNE

Sé '03 LA MODELO

they played music and talked late into the night. There were no promises made but they felt relieved at having had a sympathetic ear.

Some time later, the local FARC militia sent word to Anne to go to a certain place where she would find the remains of the two boys. There was a sack of bones waiting. They had reported the murders and got the local district attorney (*fiscal*) to draw up a report. They brought the bones to the DAS which did forensic examinations. Anne was in Bogotá in December awaiting the results of DNA tests and answering questions about the boys. It turned out that there were bones belonging to five different people in the sack.

Our lawyers gave us updates on our case. No specific charges had yet been made, so they could not prepare a defence except in the most general way. They told us that a strong point in our favour was that the very extensive forensic tests conducted by the DAS in the army barracks had not shown any trace of either explosives or drugs. The US Embassy had conducted twenty-four tests on samples, of which ten were positive and fourteen negative. The paperwork on file for these tests was a brief two-page statement and was not accompanied by any explanation of methodology or any graphs. The DAS conducted fifteen different tests on each of seventeen samples – a total of 255 tests – and all of these were negative for explosives and drugs. They also submitted extensive paperwork to explain the methods used.

We got word that we should decide ourselves whether it was a good idea to give a TV interview. We decided to do it. The lawyers wanted us to and it seemed to be a good idea. We needed to counter the constant army, US and British propaganda against us, which would be damaging to our case unless contested. The propaganda was taking the line that the peace process in Colombia should be abandoned and the de-militarised zone invaded by the army. The FARC were accused of abusing the peace process by having us in the de-militarised zone where we were accused of training them.

Our case was also being used by the British in an attempt to get big concessions in the Irish peace process. It was all lies but unless we contested it on the TV, it would become accepted as the truth. Our lawyers described our case as being 80 per cent political and 20 per cent legal. We agreed to have the TV interview in our cell. The state had no problem with that because anything said by us on TV could be used in evidence in the trial. The state had a lot of political motivation, but no evidence, and they were desperate for a conviction. Just why they were so desperate was not apparent to us at the time.

The camera crew and the interviewer from Caracol TV arrived and set up their equipment and lights. Niall spoke for us as he had a good command of Spanish. We had gone over likely questions and the best way to answer beforehand. The interview was tough but Niall handled it well. I thought that the most important question was about the forensic evidence presented by the US Embassy. Niall pointed out that the US Embassy had fabricated the test results; and that their results were totally contradicted by the Colombian State Security (DAS) tests, which showed absolutely no such traces of drugs or explosives on our clothes or bags. The DAS tests were scientifically much more advanced than the tests carried out by the US Embassy, and the qualifications of the DAS expert were much higher than that of the US man, Molloy.

The prison director showed some consideration for our welfare and allowed us some things in the cell to make life a little easier. One of the things we had enough money in our prison accounts to buy was a small TV set. The extradition prisoners around us were allowed TVs, and the prison staff ran wires to connect them into the piped TV service. We passed the time watching soaps in Spanish and drinking our flask of coffee. That helped us to put in the days and it allowed us to see the news so that we were aware of what was happening both in Colombia and in the wider world.

The FARC man who came with the food told us that the paramilitaries had put up a reward of $40,000 apiece for killing us. Anyone could collect, including prisoners who wanted the money to go to their families outside.

One evening when we were watching the TV, the cell door suddenly burst open. A flood of heavily armed INPEC guards rushed in. They were kitted out for combat. They wore black flak jackets and ammunition pouches, gas grenades, radios and pistols in holsters over their dark blue uniforms. Each carried an Israeli Galil assault rifle or an Uzi sub-machine gun.

Listo!

Listo!
Listo!

I could not understand what they were shouting at us, or what was happening. They would not allow me time to tie my bootlaces; I had to run as I was. Martin and Niall were already ahead of me. Two guards pulled me out of the cell and through the gates. There was a general uproar all around. I ran as fast as I could. We ran past where the paramilitaries were held. They were all lined up, fingertips to the wall, legs spread and leaning forward, covered by the assault rifles of several INPEC guards. I kept running. Out of breath, I stumbled on as best I could. At every gate there were more armed guards, waving us through or pointing their guns down long empty corridors. What was happening? Was it to do with the paramilitaries? Was there an attack by the guerrillas on the prison? What?

We were run up the stairs to the director's office. We were handcuffed and told to sit on plastic chairs at the director's desk. I recalled that this was the same desk that the journalist had been sitting at when she was kidnapped and taken away earlier in the year. The office was full of guards and rifles were handed out to them. They were pointing their weapons towards nearby windows and the stairwell. We were in a defensive ring of steel, but no one would tell us what was going on. Eventually Niall picked up from the director's TV, which was still switched on, that there had been a shooting in La Picota prison in the south of Bogotá. FARC guerrillas had killed a leader of the paramilitaries. Retaliation could easily fall on our heads.

Several hours went by. The tension subsided and the guards relaxed a little. The handcuffs were removed and we were given coffee and then told to go downstairs with the guards. They put us into a tiny holding cell near the front entrance to the prison. The cell was just big enough for two men to lie down in but it had no bed or furniture of any sort. A few minutes later a group of guards arrived outside the cell carrying all our possessions. It was very unusual for a guard to carry anything; so we concluded that all of the prisoners must have been locked up. The door was opened and they piled in our foam rubber mattresses, our blankets, our bags, our clothes and towels, even our TV. There was no room to stand up or lie down.

We spent the night squatting on top of the pile of our belongings. The next morning we ate our breakfast in the cell on top of all our things. The worries about being poisoned were forgotten in the confusion. One at a time we were given a half-hour of exercise, surrounded by all that massed firepower, with armed guards on every roof and in every doorway.

The next day we were taken from our tiny cell, handcuffed and put into the back of a large, completely closed-in van. The back of the van was divided into two compartments, with a steel mesh wall between. We were made sit in the front compartment near the driver's cab and handcuffed to a steel handrail and chained by leg-irons to the spare wheel. Six heavily armed INPEC guards sat in the rear, guns at the ready. They were very excited and nervous, fingering their rifles constantly. Several other vehicles full of combat-ready INPEC guards drew up behind and in front of ours. The rear door of our van was slammed shut, and then padlocked, leaving us in almost total darkness. The convoy roared out of the gates and through the streets.

Were we being deported? Where were we going? Had the Irish Embassy made contact with the Colombians over the danger that we were in? Did anyone know that we were being moved out of La Modelo? Would our lawyers and families know where we were? I was feeling sick with the violent motion of the van, the smell of exhaust fumes and the claustrophobic darkness. After a while my eyes got used to the darkness and I could make out the shapes of my friends and those of the guards in the back. We talked among ourselves about whether the van had headed in the direction of the airport or not.

It was not totally dark as little chinks of light came through small holes in the sides of the van and from a small ventilation grill. One tiny beam of sunlight entered high up near the roof and slanted down to hit the far side of the van. It acted as a pinhole camera, projecting an inverted image on the flat surface. I could see the tops of trees and buildings as we passed them, all upside down but quite clear. If I had been in Dublin, I would have been able to recognise some of the buildings, but not here in Bogotá. I had no idea where we were going or how much time it was taking. The sick feeling made it difficult to think clearly, but the body language of the guards suggested that something big had happened and that our being moved out of La Modelo was the result of a decision taken at a very high level.

Chapter 4

Police Holding Centre DIJIN (Dirección Central de Policía Judicial y Inteligencia)

THE VAN SLOWED and stopped, then started again but moved at a slower pace. I judged that we had entered through a gate of some sort. After a few sharp turns right and left the van stopped again. We all waited but nothing happened. We could hear movement and raised voices giving orders in clipped Spanish, which I could not fully understand. An eternity passed before the rear door was unlocked and opened. Five of the guards got out and the sixth opened the padlock on the steel mesh door separating our compartment from theirs. He handed his rifle and pistol to a companion outside and then came in and unchained us. I was last out, blinking in the strong sunlight.

The van was stopped in front of a two-storeyed red-brick building. On the other side of the road I saw a couple of small, beautiful purple flowering trees and a high red-brick wall with two watchtowers. There were men in green uniforms everywhere and they were all heavily armed. The uniforms were not army, although they carried the same Israeli weapons as the army. I saw that they were police by their shoulder badges. Quite a few of their guns were pointed at us while others were in a more defensive attitude. Neither the army nor the INPEC prison guards were undisciplined enough to point a weapon at you unless they were threatening to fire. Their usual way was to carry the rifle or sub-machine gun pointing diagonally upward so that an accidental discharge would go harmlessly into the air. These men were nervous and not under strict control. It was a tense situation.

We were ushered into the red-brick building and then into a small office. This was the DIJIN, a police holding centre. It seemed that we had been removed from the custody of the prison service and placed in police custody. In Colombia the police and prison services are part of the armed forces just like the army, air force and navy. They are all very heavily armed and they treat each other as rivals. I imagined that the decision to move us was not taken lightly, as it implied a failure on the part of the prison service to hold us securely. Had any or all of us been killed or rescued, or had we escaped, that would have looked bad for the government in a case with such international interest.

We went through the signing-in process, which was similar to the one in La Modelo. Part of the process was a strip search. With the unwashed clothes and the half hour in the hot, sweaty van, there was a vile smell. After a shower, and a change into clothes from my bag that were not as sweaty as the ones I had been wearing for the last couple of days, I was taken to the cells at the front of the building on the ground floor. The cell was a tiny one, just long enough to hold a bed, and just wide enough to stand beside the bed. The bed was a narrow concrete shelf, with a foam-rubber strip for a mattress and one blanket and a small pillow. Above it there was another hinged iron bedspring, for a second prisoner.

The walls were covered in white tiles and were about the height of a standing man, open at the top so you could see out. The door was made of steel bars so you could see through it to the cells on the other side of the room. You could climb over the top of the tiled wall, but there was not much point in doing so because there was always a guard around, and there were closed circuit TV cameras on the wall so that guards in a control room, and in their headquarters, could see what was happening.

I was regarded by the police guards as a special prisoner, and so I did not have another prisoner in the cell with me. Since there were not enough cells for all the prisoners, several cells held a second, or even a third prisoner, who slept on the concrete floor under the bed. There was a small TV set on a shelf fixed to the front wall of the room. By standing on the bed, the prisoners could watch it. There were other cells behind where we were, in another room. Niall was put in one of those. Martin was put in a room of cells to our left at the end of a short corridor. We were told that we were not allowed talk to each other, or take exercise or food together. The idea seemed to be that we were not to be allowed get together to come up with an agreed defence, but we had already been before the *Fiscalía* and interrogated, unlike the other prisoners held here.

A week later the police major in charge made the comment to Niall that the security precautions had been ordered because they had been told of an escape that I had made from a court holding cell in Dublin's Special Criminal Court in 1976. We had used explosives to blow out the doors. Four of us had escaped, but I was recaptured shortly afterwards and served ten years for it.

Being kept separated made life more difficult for us in many ways. However, the other prisoners were very friendly to us – *Los Irlandeses* they called us. Because almost all the prisoners and guards believed we were guilty of training the FARC, we were treated with respect and even a special degree of friendship – almost as guests of the Colombian people. It was a paradox. If they had accepted that we were just curious and well-intentioned visitors paying a low-key visit to see what was happening in the Colombian peace process, they would not have been half as good to us.

Each of the rooms had about fifteen or sixteen cells in it. Women prisoners were held upstairs and also in a large communal cell between us and the room where Martin was held. Finally, there was a relatively large, well-furnished cell, for rich prisoners. All prisoners were held twenty-three hours a day in their cell and had one hour of exercise, although the prisoners did get out of the cell two at a time for a few minutes at 5.30 in the morning for a cold shower. They also got a few minutes out for meals. The exercise period was called the 'hour of sun', and we only got it if the weather was dry. Several days could go by without exercise in the roadway in front of the building. When there was an exercise period, the space on the road in front of the building was cordoned off with a line of crush barriers and guarded by armed police watching from the watch towers and on the road. It was surprisingly cold in the DIJIN and we needed warm clothes especially at night and in the early mornings.

Most of the prisoners were only held from the time of their arrest until a judge decided what to do with them. That was usually a few days, but some were held for long periods there. One of these was a 'Don' from the Cali drugs cartel, awaiting extradition and trying to do a deal with the US Drugs Enforcement Agency, the DEA. He told us that he had been part of the group who had worked with US and Colombian government agents to kill Pablo Escobar. Another prisoner was an informer, a guerrilla deserter, whose release depended on his giving the right evidence in a court case against his former comrades.

We got a visitor from the Irish Consulate in Colombia. Normally they deal with business matters, and our visitor, Karl Gardner, was plainly not used to visiting prisoners. He brought us clothes and soap, which were very welcome; we were feeling dirty after weeks of being unable to wash our clothes. The narco prisoner sent his clothes out with his visitors to be washed; the other prisoners were only there for two or three days. Soon afterwards the police major in charge arranged for a woman to collect and wash our laundry, which we paid her for doing. I think that Karl wanted to see for himself what our conditions were and report that back to the Embassy in Mexico City.

I spent my day watching the TV. The other prisoners constantly changed the programmes using the remote control that the guards gave them. It became annoying because halfway through any good film someone changed the channel. I learned some Spanish words by watching *Los Simsons* (The Simpsons), and I spent time learning more Spanish from other nearby prisoners. I even taught one of them some Irish sentences.

One morning while I was watching the TV news, Martin arrived at my cell door. There were no guards around and he took the opportunity to visit me, having been let out to the toilet. He said in his usual reassuring way: "Well, the good news is that things can't get any worse!"

A few minutes later the TV news showed New York and reported that an aeroplane had just crashed into one of the Twin Towers. I assumed that it was an accident until the next news reported that another plane had just hit the other tower. It dawned on me that suddenly, things had got a lot worse. It was 11 September 2001, four weeks since we had been arrested.

On Saturday 15 September, my brother Gerry came to visit me. Big and friendly, he smiled easily although he was worried about the safety of us and the visitors. He told me that the IRA had put out a statement saying that they had not sent anyone to Colombia nor interfered in its internal affairs. That was good as it took some pressure off us. Sinn Féin president Gerry Adams had initially said that Niall was not working for the party in Cuba but later found out that he was. In a later statement Gerry clarified the matter when he was told that a party member had asked Niall to represent Sinn Féin in Cuba without following procedure or informing the relevant party officials.

Martin's wife Cristin and Niall's brother Dan Connolly were visiting also. Our other visitors were a Belfast solicitor and the woman who was to direct the campaign to look after us and get us home. Peter Madden, of Madden & Finucane solicitors, was a lightly built, quietly spoken, thoughtful man with a wicked sense of humour. He had defended Martin years ago in a case about a 'Shoot To Kill' ambush by the police in Armagh. Caitríona Ruane was slim and of medium height, with brown hair and a ready smile which might have misled any guard that tried to intimidate her! Caitríona had excellent Spanish and had worked previously in Latin America, so she was familiar with the language and culture. She was head of a group which became known as the 'Bring Them Home' committee.

We got our visits with Caitríona, Dan and Peter at a little table out on the roadway, one at a time as we were still not allowed speak to each other. Caitríona filled us in on the news about our case and about what was happening at home. Our visits with our relatives were also kept apart from each other. They were able to give news about how our families and friends were getting on. The ordinary prisoners and their families were very friendly and good to our visitors, sending over their children with sweets and fruit.

Peter Madden had come to sort out our legal representation. He questioned us as to what our defence had done so far. When told that they had not made detailed notes about what happened when we were arrested, or when we were interrogated, or about the forensic tests, he asked us whether we wanted a new legal team. We left it up to them as we were in no position to meet alternative lawyers.

When the visit was over the visitors told us they would get another visit or two in the coming week. The police major was willing to stretch the 'one visit on Saturday only' rule.

Peter went with Caitríona and Niall's brother Dan to meet with Agustin Jiménez, president of the Foundation for Solidarity with Political Prisoners, and Pedro Maecha of the José Alvear Restrepo Lawyers' Collective. Both organisations are human-rights-oriented and funded by Trócaire and a network of human rights agencies throughout Europe. The lawyers' collective is affiliated to the International Federation for Human Rights (FIDH) and has consultative status at the Organisation of American States. The outcome was that the two organisations made a joint defence to pool experience and give some protection to the lawyers, who would be taking a considerable risk to their lives in defending us.

The new lawyers were able to find out that the investigation was only concerned with our travel documents and with training the FARC; they were confident that the US Embassy tests would not stand up in court, and the charge of 'rebellion' was no longer being pursued. Unlike in the Irish legal system, in Colombia charges are not formally made until the investigation by the judge is fairly advanced. We were not yet formally charged with anything.

Gerry had left me a small sketchpad and a 5B pencil for drawing, and it became very important to me over the weeks that followed. I started to do sketches of other prisoners who were nearby. It was a bridge to other people, a means of contact and a source of gifts to give.

This letter gives an idea of life in the holding centre as the weeks went slowly by. We had been about three weeks in the holding centre at this stage.

I am writing this in the hope that I will find a route to get it out of here. This is a police holding centre and very unpleasant to be in, because of a lot of petty restrictions and the tiny cells, the lack of exercise, and the poor light that makes reading difficult. We have temporarily lost contact with Anne who was our reliable way of getting letters in and out. She might be gone from Bogotá.

We changed our legal representatives last week and still have got no contact with our new ones, the José Alvear Restrepo Lawyers' Collective. They are well known as human rights defenders and they get little or no co-operation from the police. My lawyer is Pedro Maecha, Martin's is José Luis Velasco and Niall's is Eduardo Matyas. It is called after a human rights lawyer who was murdered by the paramilitaries.

A general from the army made a statement about us on TV last night. He said that FARC deserters saw us delivering a planeload of rockets to the FARC. So far this is only on the TV news and in the papers, we have not been charged with this new one. The previous evidence was getting discredited and new witnesses can easily be bought or threatened by the military to keep the case alive. What it does indicate is that as far as the army is concerned, they do not want any early release.

Today is a special 'family visiting day' and although we had no visitors we were let go outside too. (Some of the police are okay.) The Irish and Colombians are a bit alike in making friends. We were all on the road in front, which was fenced off with metal crowd control barriers, with armed guards all around. Plastic chairs were provided so that prisoners and their families could sit and talk. Children from other prisoners' families came over to shake hands. We were talking to the adults. After a while the plain-clothes guards (their Special Branch) intervened to tell us to stay on our own.

Niall is very popular with other prisoners and with some of the police as he speaks Spanish well enough to joke with them and he has a very outgoing personality. I am just myself, although the women who bring the food at mealtimes made enquiries about whether I was married, how many kids I had, how many women etc. Sometimes I wonder how faithfully Niall translates as the women were doubled over with laughter about my answers to their questions. The women are very friendly and always ask how we are getting on.

We want to be moved from the DIJIN to a prison with reasonable facilities for prisoners awaiting trial, which this place clearly does not have. We have asked to be moved and when nothing happened we wrote a tutela, *which is a request to a special judge to examine our situation to see whether our human rights are being abused. It was a remedy brought in by the 1991 Constitution to prevent the systematic abuse that had been common practice. The judge had to give a ruling within ten working days and the state had to act on it to end the abuse. In practice it often takes much more than the ten days but it is still a very valuable safeguard for prisoners and others who police and soldiers might want to harass.*

The judge found that we were held in conditions that were clearly in breach of our human rights and ordered that we be moved to a proper prison. So far it has not happened.

Slán, Jim

Anne Barr got in on a visit. She had been refused the right to visit us by the police and went to the judge who was in charge of our case looking for permission, as we were foreigners and only get rare visits from Ireland. He granted her permission. She had to have a half-hour visit with each of us as they would not allow us to be together. She brought in e-mails and took out letters from me. I tend to write much more than Martin or Niall.

Our lawyers had come in to see us and told us what the legal situation was. The video film taken of the forensic tests in the army barracks had gone missing. It was important because it carried the admission by Molloy that he had no proper qualifications and it showed that the tests were carried out in a room full of people, without any of the normal precautions.

We asked why the military had not simply ordered the DAS to support the US version. We were told that the DAS, and indeed all parts of the Colombian administration, had decent honest people in them who stuck to the laws, as well as a lot who were anything but decent or honest. There was a conflict going on between those who wanted Colombia to be a modern democracy and those who wanted to preserve the rule of the elite and the military at any cost. The DAS forensic expert had been able to resist whatever pressure might have been applied either directly or by the media coverage of senior military who were saying that we were guilty. The DAS as a professional organisation were probably annoyed at the US interference in what they considered their area of work.

The Embassy test results were the pivot of the whole case against us. As a result of the interview shown on Caracol TV, the US Embassy was left in no doubt that the evidence they had presented in court was being challenged by us as false. It is a serious crime to knowingly present false evidence to a court, and the Embassy was obliged to either brazen it out or to withdraw the false evidence. They refused to withdraw it, and that refusal was having serious effects on the Irish and the Colombian peace processes. We were aware that we were pawns in a much bigger game, but we were still not aware of the full extent of the game.

The papers for the case had not yet been made available to our lawyers. They did not have the written forensics reports or the interviews with the RUC (Royal Ulster Constabulary) who had come over to Colombia. The RUC was so unacceptable to the nationalist community that it was replaced by a police service called the PSNI shortly afterwards as part of the Irish peace process.

I was watching the TV news one day in October and as far as I could make out from the pictures and the odd bit of Spanish that I could manage, the police shot dead a medical student in one of the universities in Bogotá. The students were protesting about the American invasion of Afghanistan. I had read that the Afghans are a very proud and independent people and had historically made invaders pay dearly. The British lost an army of 20,000 in the Khyber Pass. Was it too much to hope that history might repeat itself?

There was nothing much happening – we had not been moved from the DIJIN. Our old home, La Modelo was in the news again. The paramilitaries had shot five prisoners dead, but I did not know who they were or why they were shot. In a follow-up search a half dozen pistols, ammunition and two or three grenades were found. The prison spokesman said that women visitors brought them in – but I doubted that.

None of our things from La Modelo had arrived yet, apart from what we had carried with us. Our lawyers were having trouble with the police in getting in on legal visits to us. The guards were harrassing them by insisting on humiliating searches that other lawyers never had to submit to. If they refused to undergo the search (as they sometimes did), the visit would be refused. Also, the guards would not let us meet them together. Martin and I did not have enough Spanish to prepare a legal defence, while our lawyers had no English. Niall was the only one who could speak both languages. He was also having trouble getting out of the cell to phone them about what was happening in the case. The lawyers were taking the matter up with the judge in charge of our case. However, the good news was that they had got the papers to the case.

There was a friendly bunch of six men at DIJIN for a few days. I got on well with them and practised my Spanish and learned a lot about playing dominoes. I eventually made out that they were arrested for supplying guns to the paramilitaries. It was too late and also useless to stop being friendly with them.

10 November 2001

I have got a black biro, as the blue one was not very good for sending e-mails via the scanner. Anne takes out my letters and scans them. It's great because I can get a reply within a few days. The ordinary post to Ireland is useless.

Yesterday I was reading a big book on Leonardo da Vinci that the visitors brought over. One of the guards asked me was it about Ireland. I found that he had some English so I was able to explain that, no: it was about an Italian artist. It turned out that he had a good knowledge of art, including a bit about Leonardo, but had never done any painting himself. We spent a lot of yesterday talking about art and he ended up saying that he would buy some brushes and acrylic paints and start painting himself. He was planning to leave the police and go back to his hometown to work with his family. I was trying to convince him that art was something he should do because he wanted to. The other things would follow if he did it well.

He lent me the book that he had brought to read during the night – a book in English on sixty great thinkers in history. I lent him Leonardo.

[....]

The guard went off this morning. Before he left we exchanged our books again and parted friends.

Anne is away for a few weeks or months. I am not sure how I will get this to you but something will turn up.

Slán go foill

Sé

Three ELN prisoners had arrived in, beaten by the police and in a state of shock after their arrest. We gave them blankets as, at that time, we each had two blankets that we had got in La Modelo.

On the TV news they showed a large-scale search of La Picota prison, which uncovered three tunnels and some escape equipment such as duplicate prison stamps in the FARC patio, which was probably the reason why we had not been moved from DIJIN to La Picota yet. I hoped that the escape attempt did not mean that we would remain in the DIJIN. It was impossible to prepare our defence and the psychological pressure increased all the time, making even routine things difficult, such as staying in good health and good humour.

We were told by our lawyers that the high security section in La Picota mainly caters for drug barons with some paramilitary and a few FARC activists on serious charges. The paramilitaries usually get on well with the narcos because of their increasing involvement in drug shipments to finance their activities. They also told us that some time before we were arrested, one of the Colectivo lawyers was killed by the paramilitaries, and because they took up our case, the Colectivo has received bomb threats that have forced them to change their office to a more secure location. In the strange world of Colombia, a bank offered them office space.

It was about this time that we first heard from our families about the Delahunt Enquiry. This was a congressional investigation in the US into our case, headed by a Democratic Party Congressman called Delahunt. From what we heard, the enquiry was hostile but we did not know much about it or why they were holding it. I was told that in *The Irish Times* on 7 November 2001 the same William Delahunt was pressing Sinn Féin to join the PSNI board (Police Service of Northern Ireland) and saying that the US Congress ban on the FBI training the police should be lifted.

On Saturday 17 November 2001, I was waiting for a visit from Andy Higgenbottom, who was a friend of Anne's, but he was late. I had been worried that perhaps no one would come to visit that day but things worked out very well. A group of DIJIN officers stopped at my cell with two women and a man. One of the women introduced herself as a human rights activist from Europe – the other two people were from the Defensoría del Pueblo, a Colombian state human rights body that was okay if ineffective. With their high profile, the three of us were allowed for once to sit together around a table out on the roadway.

The European woman impressed me as being in touch, well aware of human rights abuses and prepared to do something about it. She had come to Colombia to attend a human rights conference and took the unpopular decision to visit us against the advice of the US and Colombian officials – but supported by the Defensoría del Pueblo woman and her assistant. She promised to use her contacts in the conference to try and get the South African delegate to get in touch, and possibly to visit. One of the things said by the human rights people was that the US representative was very anxious that Colombia be regarded as off limits to the press in regard to what was happening here, especially about human rights abuses by the Colombian forces.

Shortly after the human rights people sat down with us, Andy arrived. We made the circle wider to include him. At that stage the conversation had moved on from our situation to the wider situation in the DIJIN.

Andy had not been able to get the sketchpad I had asked for but he gave me a wad of typing paper. I gave him the letters I had written and sent out the books that I was afraid of losing in the promised move to La Picota, including the one on Leonardo. I gave him some pencil drawings for Anne in gratitude for the efforts she had made in visiting us, bringing phone cards and fruit, etc., and for the work she did in keeping communications open.

One of the drawings was the Mona Lisa; another drawing was of Ché Guevara – taken from the cover of a book that was left in for Niall. As I was drawing the image of Ché, one of the prisoners saw it and asked me to hold it up for the rest to see. Some made admiring comments but some sounded not at all pleased by my choice of subject! Were they paramilitaries? Or right-wing hoods? I didn't know, but one young prisoner made great efforts to get a copy of the drawing and for me to sign it. I said I would draw it again – after the visits.

After the visits I spent a few hours reading letters and the e-mails left in from Anne and the others in the commune. The e-mails were about the things going on there and about the wars and preparations for wars in the world. The Atlantis commune were very much into the peace movement. I was thinking about what to do next when I noticed movement. A lot of blue-uniformed INPEC guards in bullet-proof jackets

By, Jim Monaghan
Dijin Holding Centre
Bogota, Colombia

M.McCauley
BOGOTÁ
CHRISTMASS 2001

N Connelly

FOR ROSE
FROM JIM

came in. There were also heavily armed DIJIN guards in green uniforms, with weapons and ammunition hanging all over them.

The wee lad who wanted the Ché picture and a few others were taken out of their cells with all their belongings, mattresses, clothes, etc. He dived through them all to my cell to plead for the drawing. I tried to explain in my awful Spanish that it had gone out on the visit. He was taken away. Ten minutes later, he managed to get back through them all again and tried desperately to get the drawing, which I no longer had. I saw him looking very disappointed as he was led off for the last time. He was not FARC or belonging to any rebel group that I know about.

Niall told me that on the TV news, the army said that the guerrillas were using 'IRA techniques' and Semtex (a plastic explosive used by the IRA), but on the other hand the news described a new witness against us as 'mad'. This witness was to be cross-examined by our legal team in the following weeks.

The lawyers thought that we would be in prison over Christmas. In that case I wondered could a demonstration be organised outside the US Embassy in Dublin, demanding the withdrawal of their fabricated forensic evidence.

In La Picota prison a new 'North-American-style wing' was just about ready and we would probably be sent there. I suspected that the US was forcing prison changes on Turkey and Colombia as part of a counter-insurgent policy based on British experience with fighting the IRA.

One day we were told to pack our things and be ready to move out. No one said where we were going. We were handcuffed and chained to the vehicle floor and driven in a convoy to the south of Bogotá. Our new home was to be La Picota.

Chapter 5

La Picota Prison

THE CONVOY DREW up on a dusty dirt track in bare fields, beside a huge wire mesh fence five or six metres high. There must have been thirty heavily armed guards around us. In the distance the earth was covered with makeshift houses and roads cut into the red clay of the hills. La Picota was in the middle of the poorest part of the city, a huge area of poverty and unemployment.

I was told to get down from the van and go to a hut where I was given the possessions that I had on entering the DIJIN. Most of my things were promptly taken away again and put in my property here at La Picota. I was told I could hold on to three pairs of socks, three underpants, three vests, two trousers, a pair of shoes and a pair of runners from the clothes left in on visits over the time that we were held in the DIJIN. It took a long time, but when the three of us were processed, we went through a big double-gate 'airlock' into the prison.

We had to put our bags through a huge conveyor belt type metal detector and then each of us were put through the kind of metal detector that you walk through in airports. Finally we were sent, one at a time, into an office where we were signed in, fingerprinted and photographed and measured as usual. We entered the main prison building and were brought along corridors to an office where we went through the same routine all over again. Finally we were taken into a newly built patio with twenty-four cells, twelve on the ground floor and twelve upstairs.

This was Patio A, *alta seguridad* (A Wing, high security). Most of the cells were not yet occupied. Each cell was for two men, but each of us was given a cell since there were only about twenty prisoners in the patio at that time. Each had two concrete beds, built one above the other, a concrete table, a toilet and shower, and, of all things – a TV set!

Outside the cells was an open patio about the size of a tennis court to take exercise in. At one end there was a covered-in area for use on rainy days. The US Federal Bureau of Prisons had recently taken over the running of the high security prisons in Colombia, and the two new patios here were built and run to their specifications.

The routine was that the cells were unlocked at 7am and breakfast was in the canteen at 8am. The canteen was a large dining area with seats and tables firmly fixed to the floor, so that nothing could be moved in a riot. Behind the canteen was a kitchen.

Prisoners from our patio worked at preparing the meals, which were quite good. Richer prisoners gave extra money to buy a better selection of food than could be bought from the INPEC food allowance for the patio. That extra food was for everyone. It was a source of prestige to those rich enough and generous enough to enable the others to have better food. The really rich prisoners also ordered special food for themselves. In Colombian culture, food is very important as a status symbol. It is also important to be seen as a powerful but caring figure of authority.

The US had a policy that there was to be no recognition of political prisoners, such as left-wing guerrillas and right-wing paramilitaries. They were insisting that all prisoners be put together in the same place. They did not call it criminalisation, but of course that is what it was. Criminalisation is the deliberate treatment of political prisoners as criminals, refusing to recognise their political motivation because that challenges the legitimacy of the state, while 'ordinary' crime does not. The Colombians traditionally had the more sensible approach of separating hostile groups, which saved a lot of lives and suffering. The Colombian elite would not survive the anger of their own population without North American firepower, so they did as they were told.

Most of the prisoners who worked in the kitchen were paramilitaries, because it was considered a good job, and also carried some remission of sentence. Outside the canteen door there was a telephone, which could be used by prisoners during the day. It was a matter of queuing for the phone, and using a phone card to pay for the call. It was a big improvement on the phone situation in the DIJIN. Access to a phone was very important to all prisoners facing a trial, and especially to us.

I got friendly with a big indigenous man from the Amazonas (the region where the Amazon River is). They resent being called Indians as they are not from India, and they have their own identity, which does not depend on Europeans, or on what white people think of them. I pointed out that my people also had a foreign language and culture forced on them at gunpoint. One of the first moves of conquerors is to attack and destroy the culture of the colonised, because without a sense of their own separate identity the colonised people are unable to unite to resist the occupation. He told me about the herbal cures that his people had, including a cure for rheumatism. I tried hard to communicate with him in my broken Spanish and felt that I was making some progress.

There was a meal at midday and another at 5pm. Lock-up was at 7pm. Most of the day was spent walking around the open space in the patio, talking to other prisoners. When that got monotonous we could go to the shade of the cell and read a book or write a letter, or have a cup of black Colombian coffee, which they call *tinto*. Most of the men seemed to be in prison for drugs-related offences, but some were in for robberies and some for paramilitary-related matters. The paramilitaries were not openly hostile to us. Things were relaxed and much better than in the DIJIN. Five days later all that came to an abrupt end.

One morning, before the rest of the prisoners were unlocked, the guards came for the three of us. We were told to pack our things and accompany the INPEC officer to the entrance. When asked where we were going he said it was to the airport. I tried not to get excited, as it could be a little joke by him. We were handcuffed and put in a jeep instead of the prison van. That seemed to be a good omen. He said very little as the convoy of vehicles made its way north through the city in the direction of the airport. Would they just deport us or would they make us sit around for days awaiting deportation? Would we have to pay some sort of fine before being allowed to leave the country?

Each of us was careful about allowing our hopes to rise too strongly. The convoy veered on to side roads and even dirt tracks. I thought that they were making sure not to travel a known route so as to avoid any possible rescue or assassination attempt. Eventually the convoy pulled up at a red-brick wall that I recognised. I could see the branches of the lovely purple flowering trees over the wall. It was the outside of the DIJIN holding centre: we were back in hell!

Chapter 6

The DIJIN Once Again

A S WE CAME through the door into the building, we got a big cheer of welcome from the prisoners who knew us from before, especially from the three ELN men. They repaid our giving those blankets some weeks ago with a great welcome back. In the meantime they had got blankets from their families and they gave their spare blankets to us, along with some food they had.

After our shift back to the DIJIN we were still unsure about why they had moveded us back here. There were so many agencies in Colombia – INPEC, DIJIN, DAS, *Fiscalía* – that speculation was not very useful. We did not think it was because of anything that we had done, but even that was uncertain.

We were later told by a guard that the reason we were moved back to the DIJIN was that a loaded pistol had been hidden behind a light fitting on the outside wall of a cell where we were in Patio A in La Picota. An assassin, probably one already charged with multiple killings, would have removed the pistol from its hiding place, killed us and surrendered. His family would then have been given the money on our heads.

Caitríona Ruane and Peter Madden were to come and visit us before going with our lawyers to visit the places where we had been in the zone. They hoped to find witnesses useful to the defence. She explained that in the Colombian system, the prosecutor is supposed to collect evidence both for and against the accused before taking the decision whether or not to press formal charges. The prosecutor was unwilling or unable to go into the FARC-controlled zone to collect evidence, and so the defence would have to do it for them. However, a new law was passed following our arrests that anyone, Colombian or otherwise, needed military permission to enter the zone. The military refused the permission for our defence to go there.

Caitríona did tell us that they were putting a full-page advertisement in *El Tiempo* and in the *Sunday Business Post* consisting of a thousand names of people calling for our release. Both newspapers have wide circulation in their respective countries. There was also a 'Bring Them Home' concert on 11 November featuring very well known artists such as Christy Moore and Frances Black.

On Saturday, 29 November, we got the first visit from the international observers. The lawyers had advised the 'Bring Them Home' campaign that the most effective thing that could be done for us was to have highly qualified observers from different countries observe and report back to their peers on what was taking place at our trial. This measure would break through the paper wall of media manipulation of news from Colombia. Three observers, all lawyers, were due in, two from Ireland and one from Australia. We did not know what to expect from them, and tried to figure out what sort of questions they might ask, and the best way to answer.

The lawyers were not trying to put us on the spot, but rather each had a specific brief. One was sent by Madden & Finucane and was there to report on the conditions under which we had to prepare the defence. The Australian lawyer was examining the legal aspects of the trial for a report to an international group. I could not remember what the brief of the other Irish lawyer was.

Two lawyers from the US visited the following Tuesday. They were from a 300-strong group called the Brehon Law Society, who took an interest in legal matters with an Irish connection. On Wednesday Síle Maguire from the Irish Embassy also came on a visit to see that we were okay.

I got a letter from Anne Barr saying that she would not be back in Bogotá for some months and she thought that our trial would be over and us away home before then. I hoped that she would reappear, as I liked her a lot. She sent in some literature that would keep me reading, including an article about the coalmines. Colombia has the biggest open-cast coalmines in Latin America and they are under North American control.

There was conflicting news about the family visitors expected over from Ireland. We had been told to expect them the following week –

and that arrangements had been made for visits on the Monday and Thursday. Then Martin was told on the phone that there was still a problem with visas to enter Colombia.

I was getting ready to make a phone call when a police major came into the cell block and thought things were too lax. He gave the police guards a right dressing down and ordered a total search, of everyone and every cell, toilets, etc. Because the DIJIN was full when we had arrived, with seven or eight women prisoners in the room where they had previously held Martin, he was put in the same room as me but in the opposite corner cell. An officer doing the search tried to look at some legal papers and Martin tackled him, telling him in no uncertain voice that he was not entitled to read his case documents. There was a stand-off in broken and colourful Spanish before the police backed off. When it came to my turn to be searched, I was all tensed up to resist any attempt to read documents related to our trial, but the police just made a passing comment on an agricultural booklet that I had.

I had done about twenty-five drawings so far of prisoners' wives and children and also some for friendly police of their wives or children. I did not charge anything for them as I wanted the practice, but I got gifts of fruit, fruit juice, water, sweets and biscuits. I was doing okay out of it.

We had a visit from one of the most senior officials of the Defensoría del Pueblo, whom we had met before, and her assistant about our conditions and security, and our wanting to move from here. She was very helpful and in parting asked if I had got the art material. It went up that far!

A prisoner had got two pages from my notebook. That frequently happened. Prisoners very often had nothing, except for the few millionaires involved in cocaine 'exports'. The ordinary prisoners needed paper to write home or to write about legal matters. Colombians seemed to have much more of a spoken than a written culture and tended to write as little as possible – except for the legal and other bureaucrats who loved filling forms and pages of details.

Martin talked to some of the other prisoners about the 'Americans' in Afghanistan. He was firmly told, 'We are the Americans; the Gringos are only a small part of the people of the Americas.' He told

me about what they said and their world view made an impression on me. He also told me a little story about that morning.

Martin had pulled back the shower curtain and emerged in a cloud of cigarette smoke. He has perfected the art of smoking while having a shower. As bad luck would have it, a guard happened to be walking by. Martin gave him a broad wink and before the guard could gather his wits, a packet of biscuits settled the matter to mutual satisfaction.

By December, the general atmosphere of the country at the time was affecting us directly. For example, it was on the news that the Oil Workers Union was on strike and the paramilitaries had kidnapped their president. The paramilitaries demanded that the government's chief negotiator with the FARC and ELN go to meet them in one of their bases. He refused, as he knew they considered him as being too friendly to the guerrillas, and they shot the union president. The ELN alleged that the Minister for Defence organised the whole thing. President Pastrana had tried to distance himself from the paramilitaries by publicly telling the top military that any soldier who helped the paramilitaries was a traitor.

There was large-scale fighting going on between the FARC and paramilitaries in the north of the country. All the TV film was shot from the paramilitary side of the lines. President Pastrana's protests that his government was hostile to the paramilitaries was in conflict with the ready access they had to the TV cameras, and also with their openly existing bases, such as the one they wanted the negotiators to go to.

One day, Niall shouted to me that the visit was on – according to his telephone call the visitors had got their visas to enter Colombia.

We had a family visit on Thursday and Friday 13 and 14 December. My brother Gerry came to visit me, while Martin and Niall also had members of their families in. Caitríona came to give us a run-down on the legal situation and also what was happening in the peace process at home. She asked me to write an account of a day in the DIJIN that they could use in the campaign.

We did not have a visit on Saturday. So that we could get some sun, the guards let us out into the yard where visitors were meeting with other prisoners. Immediately, we were sent over food and fruit juice from various prisoners' families and in general got very friendly treatment. It was a real morale boost. The Colombians were really good people and treated strangers very well; I wondered would three Colombians in an Irish jail get such a friendly reception.

I had been trying for the previous few days to draw a portrait of a wee girl from a photo. I judged her age to be nine or ten but the picture kept turning out looking as if she was much older. Her father introduced us during the visiting – she was only six or seven. I decided to try again – some photos and faces are much harder to draw than others. Age is conveyed by slight changes in shape, contour and shading and it was often quite hard to spot what was wrong. I made a new sketch immediately I got into the cell, and it did look a lot younger, but still not six or seven.

A prisoner gave me some literature to learn Spanish, which had a good lot of sentences translated from Spanish to English, which suited me. I couldn't make any progress on grammar and I didn't learn as much as I should have because every shift and development in the case caused a distraction that took a few days to settle down.

A woman called Angela from the Political Prisoners Solidarity started to come on visits to the three of us every two weeks. She left us Internet printouts of the Colombian, Irish, UK and US newspapers that mentioned our case or political developments in Ireland. She brought news and e-mails and took our replies out to scan and e-mail to Ireland. She was of medium build, dark-haired, dark-eyed and about thirty-five; she had two children who really liked chocolate. There was a real element of risk in her work and she was brave to continue to do it.

We had a different attitude to the guards here than would be normal in Ireland. They were generally okay, with some quite genuinely friendly. Most didn't have that arrogant and vindictive attitude that I was so used to in Portlaoise prison and in prisons in England. Colombian society was divided – the higher up you went the worse they got.

Niall was telling me that there were about 200 dead in the fighting between the FARC and paramilitaries and that the paramilitaries were saying that by this time next year they will be in control of all areas now held by the FARC.

ANGELA. LA MODELO

We expected developments in our case with the return of our legal team from their trip to Ireland where they held consultations with Peter Madden. We were anxious to hear what had been decided.

Síle from the Irish Embassy came in on a visit to us. She was very good. It seemed that the plan by the Colombian government was to leave us here in the DIJIN as the most secure place – but we did not want to stay because of the twenty-three hour lock-up and the general claustrophobia of the place.

A high-ranking police officer came in and spoke to us. One of the things he said was that the National Police should be neutral in the war. That was so unexpected and was such a different point of view that I had to reassess my own understanding of what was happening in Colombia. In the North of Ireland, we had always looked on the police as the eyes and ears of a repressive government, the main interface of repression between the state and the people. The idea of a neutral police service in Colombia was new and almost unbelievable. There were local, unarmed police in San Vicente, in the FARC controlled peace talks zone, who were neutral and got on with keeping the peace among the local people. I should have asked more about their role and powers.

By now we had been in El DIJIN for about twelve weeks. I wrote an account of my 83rd day there.

Sounds of voices intruded on my dreams. I tried to hold on to the dream, because it was a pleasant one, but it slipped away and I became aware of the world around me. It was dark but I could hear the splashing of a shower, and voices talking in Spanish. I was awake. The lights went on. A voice shouted 'Libertad!' from the cell across the passage from mine. It was a cry for freedom, but with absolutely no hope of getting it. I pulled the blanket tighter around my shoulders against the cold. It was a thin pink blanket, more an over-blanket because it had a fluffy edging that was still intact in places, and a big biro ink stain at one end. I was glad to have it. An ELN prisoner had given it to me.

Padre Andres, the prison chaplain, had got us foam rubber mattresses so we were as well off as most of the other prisoners here.

The guard came to my cell and then, seeing me looking comfortable, he passed on to the next man to make him get up. The special treatment was appreciated. Yesterday, when the change of police guards had taken place, he had been shown drawings I had made of some of the old shift's children and wives. He had come to me with a photo of his eight-year-old daughter and asked me if I would do a drawing of his daughter, and sign it.

I got up, folded the blanket and put away my two pullovers. One was a large heavy black one sent over by Ann in Coiste, the Dublin office of the ex-prisoners' group that I had worked for. It provided extra warmth draped over the blanket. The good grey one served as a pillow. They were kept in bin liner bags under the bed.

The guard came back. "Buenos días, puedo ir al baño?" *(Good morning, can I go to the bathroom?) I said.*

"Baño del gato?" *he replied.*

The cat's lick – he must have noticed that yesterday I skipped the cold shower and had just given my face a quick wash.

I picked up my spare T-shirt and headed for the lockers. Each prisoner had a small 10-inch square locker with a locked door in which to keep his personal washing gear and objects considered too dangerous to leave overnight in the cell, such as boot laces, a pencil or a biro. I took out my shampoo, soap, razor and toothpaste. A woman police guard sitting behind the desk gave me a big smile and a cheery 'Buenos días' as I headed to the shower. It was empty but a big black prisoner was standing near it. He looked disoriented and he was entitled to be. He and five or six others had been arrested the previous day, suspected FARC militias involved in kidnapping ten or fifteen occupants of a block of luxury flats a few months ago. Secuestros (kidnappings) are the equivalent of bank robberies back home. I spoke to him in Spanish, which left him even more disoriented.

I went into the shower and stripped off. The shower was wonderfully simple in design — a bit of pipe coming out of the wall and a tap to turn on the water. The trick was to keep moving under the cold water so it did not get to chill any particular bit. The temperature in Bogotá was very like that in Dublin on an average day — around ten to fifteen degrees. I dried myself off with the T-shirt, because I did not have a towel. I then left the stuff back in the locker and sneaked into the block of cells where Niall was. Martin was already talking to him through the bars. We had a quick chat. The video camera in his block was out of focus but even so it was only a couple of minutes before a guard appeared to separate us and lock us up again.

Back in the cell I took out the hardback book of paintings by Monet that Rose from Tar Isteach had sent me. It sat nicely over the six-inch square mesh of flat steel strips that are the fold-down bedsprings, providing a firm surface to draw on. My technique for drawing from a photo was to make a quick, light pencil drawing, and then come back to it the next morning with fresh eyes to compare it with the photo and make necessary changes before finishing it. I might have to leave it and return to it several times to get a good likeness. The pencil needed sharpening often and I had to do this on the rough concrete on the underside of the bed slab.

The news programme came on the TV. There had been a bomb in central Bogotá — which was not good news for us as the military have accused us of training the FARC guerrillas, especially on how to wage urban guerrilla warfare. Most of the war is in the jungles and in the countryside or mountains, but not in the cities.

One of the prisoners, who is a trustee, came over to me with a small plastic cup of tinto *with sugar. It tastes very nice. They never use milk, and by now, after five months in Colombia, I would never think of putting milk in coffee. About 8.30am we got breakfast – a cup of drinking chocolate and a bun or biscuits. The next meal was the dinner at 1pm and by then I could eat a horse.*

For mental stimulation, we have the TV. There is a 14-inch TV fixed to the wall in each block of cells. The cell that I'm in is right next to the TV, which at news time is a blessing but at other times can be a curse. It may be that my years are having an effect on me, but idiotic cartoons at full volume do not appeal to me. Some of the lads get great enjoyment from them and especially from that bunch of idiot North Americans – 'the A Team' – who make a lot of noise at full volume.

The trustee came around shouting to find out did anyone want a spare cup of drinking chocolate. I stuck out my hand and got it. For five months an internal war has been raging between my Irish tummy bugs and Colombian invaders – every time I eat or take a drink the attackers get reinforcements – it makes sense to drink the chocolate as it ought to be reasonably bug free. So far I am doing okay compared to my comrades who have spent considerable time sitting on the DIJIN toilets – although in Martin's case it could be more to do with having an illegal, and therefore more enjoyable, cigarette. He is only allowed to smoke during the one hour of exercise outside each day. To cover up the telltale smell of cigarette smoke, he has used up a month's supply of bleach so the toilets reek of chlorine, so much that the guards can hardly breathe in there, let alone smell cigarette smoke!

Our boot laces have been taken from us and it is difficult to walk in boots without laces. We tried using strips of plastic bag but a better solution was found. I got a new mop to clean out the cell and removed enough strands of cotton to make laces by plaiting the strands together.

The laundry woman comes every few days. I had T-shirts, socks and underpants to send out. The three of us pooled our dirty clothes and paid her the equivalent of about €2 for each wash. There were around twenty-five men and five women prisoners at any time, so she had a nice little job going.

I worked on a drawing of a prisoner's child who was aged four or five, from an over-exposed photo. That kept me busy for an hour.

I asked myself whether I would read more of Ché, watch the TV or learn some Spanish, read Monet or even write a letter. The Spanish was logically the most important thing to do, but at that moment the book on Monet was more interesting. I should have read the two-inch-thick file about our case – fifteen to twenty years for illegal training and two to eight years for false passports, which should have given me enough motivation. At least they dropped the charges of rebellion!

One profound thought surfaced – I was almost out of toilet paper. This was no joke because, besides its obvious use, it was essential for cleaning the lenses of my glasses and wiping a runny nose when I had a cold, which is often, and also for wiping up spilled tinto and fruit juice. There was no cloth here for cleaning up.

The T-shirt that I had used as a towel is hanging from the top bunk and it is almost dry. It looks a bit grubby but if I sent it out to be washed, I would have nothing to dry myself with. My other clothes are not cotton and do not make good towels. Our towels, blankets and other property have not arrived from La Picota. Our property left in La Modelo had never arrived. We were moved to the DIJIN carrying what we could tie up in a blanket. My watch was left in La Picota. I could tell the time roughly by how hungry I felt. The hour of sun was late. We did not get exercise at all because there were not enough guards available. If it was raining, we would not get exercise either, but fortunately that does not happen very often because if there is any break in the rain, they let us out. The guards had by this stage got to know us and were much more relaxed.

When the door of the cell was opened I thought, food! I made for the corridor that we ate in. Niall and Martin were not there so I went to Martin's block. They were both there. The three of us went to the corridor together. The guards often did not enforce the rule about keeping us separated. We waited until we could get a table that we could sit at. The only prospect was a table with one tough-looking prisoner sitting at it, and making no move to go. The three of us sat down beside him. As we ate, he started to talk.

"The government and the paramilitaries are the one," he said.

As he got up to go, he said in Spanish, "I pray for you every day." He was very genuine.

We all said, "Muchas gracias". You should never judge a person by their looks.

Back in the cell I started studying my Spanish, using the examples of adjectives, verbs and nouns from the Spanish/English dictionary. I could not make any headway with grammar as such, but I could learn how to say a sentence in Spanish and its English equivalent. When stuck for a Spanish word, the Irish word always sprung to mind. There are quite a few Irish words that are very similar to the equivalent Spanish word, such as oibrí and obrero *(a worker)* or coinín and conejo *(a rabbit)*. It must be that the brain holds the words of a language learned later in life in a location separate from that of the childhood language. Words of similar meaning in languages learned later in life seem to be stored near each other, in my case Irish and Spanish.

The day was well on and there was no sign of getting out for an hour in the sun – although the sun really was shining. I can see a bit of a brick wall and a small tree outside a window, which is in line with the open door of my cellblock. The tree has beautiful purple flowers and it has been flowering for the eighty-three days that I have been here. The rules are posted on the wall at the door for all to read. The third one is that a prisoner cannot be held for longer than thirty-six hours in the cells of the DIJIN. It was a case of the authorities neglecting to do what they were legally obliged to do, probably not out of bad intent or cruelty, but rather because the rights of prisoners were a low priority for them. Although the sun was shining, we were not out in it, and prisoners could not be held for more than three days in the DIJIN, and we were still here after eighty-three days.

My friend with the mop came back. We talked in English to give him some practice. He has done AutoCAD, a computer drawing programme widely used for drawing plans of buildings or mechanical parts. It occurred to me that maybe he was pumping me for information for the military but he moved on to another subject and I have seen him doing design work on harnesses for use in workshops. I did a sketch from a photo of him and his girlfriend mountain climbing somewhere in the Andes. He told me that the glaciers are melting on the high mountains due to global warming. He said that carbon dioxide levels in the air are the highest for 50,000 years, when alligators lived north of the Arctic Circle. My friend went to mop the clean floor for the second or third time just to be out of the cell a bit longer.

I am running low on A5 drawing paper. I had asked for some things to be brought in for me by another prisoner's visitor and got two 6B pencils and a rubber, but the paper was not as heavy as what I wanted. I should have ordered sketchpad paper. The guards let in things like these for me now, which some weeks ago they would have refused to allow. Anne, who lives here, told me that in Colombia they have all sorts of rules, but that being an easygoing people they soon revert to what is practical and sensible.

When the prisoners started moving from the cells in Niall's room, I knew that it was food time again. The guards seem to time the evening meal to hit the TV news. A new prisoner came over to shake hands. He said that he had seen us on TV. I said that we would be happy not to be on TV at all – and just to be on a plane home. He asked when would we be going home and I told him about the year 2020.

I wondered what was keeping the guards. I was anxious to talk to Martin and Niall and my best chance to do so was just after the meal. I would go to my locker, collect my toothbrush and then go into Martin's room to brush my teeth and hopefully get a chat for a few minutes. The food was very late. There were a lot of new prisoners arriving in and there seemed to be a shortage of police guards to cope. Later in the TV news there was film of our new arrivals being captured. I did not catch what the charges against them were. There were a lot of heavily armed soldiers and DAS involved.

The grub came at last – it was the same as that served at dinner: some rice, meat, vegetables and a spud – not bad. Afterwards I got my toothbrush and headed in to where Martin was. I had only just started chatting to him when a friendly guard rushed in, pointing at his shoulder rank markings – brass on the way! Go to the cells now, and he will turn a blind eye later. It was a choice of drawing or reading or TV until lights out at 8:30. What to do? I had not put my pencil in the locker. I could do that later by going out to el baño (the toilet). I could read the rest of the Ché Guevara book. His time in the Congo was a complete fuck-up. I expected him to get things in order and counter-attack the mercenaries, right up to their evacuation across Lake Tanganyika. It's reassuring to find a hero who does not always win out, who makes mistakes, has bad luck and is unable to overcome some situations. That's my kind of hero.

I put all my bits and pieces on the top bunk and made my bed on the concrete slab. The lights went out. I got into bed, pulling my blanket up and draping my pullover over my arse. That was the end of the 83rd day in La DIJIN.

By Christmas we had been held for four months. The guards allowed those of us who had been there for a long time to have a Christmas dinner around a big table, made by putting all the small tables together. A bottle of rum had mysteriously appeared, paid for by the narco prisoner in the big cell, I suspected. Each of us got a tiny drop in a cup to flavour the fiesta. We each got a Chinese takeaway meal and had a bit of laughter and some songs. Even the FARC informer cheered up!

The three of us held a meeting to discuss our situation. We could stay in the DIJIN in relative safety and bad conditions, or we could put in another *tutela* demanding a move to a prison with facilities for prisoners who must wait months or years. We decided to put in the *tutela* and take our chances with the paramilitaries and other prison dangers. We discussed the possibility that the government might take advantage of our request and order us split up or to be moved to a very remote and rough prison – "at our own request" – but we decided to meet that situation if it arose.

Early in the New Year of 2002, the *tutela* was answered with an order by the judge that we be moved to a proper prison where our legal and human rights would be respected. Two days afterwards we were handcuffed and put on board a van with the familiar escort of armed guards. The van joined a convoy of vehicles and we arrived at La Picota for a second time. I was a bit surprised that we were sent to La Picota and not to a remote and nasty prison in the cold mountains, or to a hot and humid one in some river valley. La Picota suited us for visits from our families and from our lawyers because it was in Bogotá. The price on our heads could just as easily be collected in any prison in Colombia, so it was best that we were here in spite of the apparent attempt to kill us in Patio A.

Chapter 7

La Picota Again

WE WERE PUT into Patio B, right next door to where we had been before. Patio B, *alta seguridad*, was just like Patio A in layout. When we walked in carrying our belongings, the twenty or so prisoners held there greeted us warmly.

The INPEC guards directed each of us to separate cells, to share with a prisoner already there. That can be a dodgy time if the other prisoner decides that he does not want your company. There can be threats or an actual attack by a man whose nerves are in tatters and who has nothing to lose. Anyway, none of the three objected to sharing a cell with the Irish.

We also had our own special concerns. Our cellmate could decide that his family needed the paramilitary money to tide them over while he was in prison, and he might cut your throat while you slept at night. A lot of prisoners in high security are there because they are accused of serious offences carrying long sentences. That was another thing we could do nothing about, so we tried not to worry about it.

After putting our things on the allotted beds, we went out to the patio to meet the others. Niall translated for Martin and me as men introduced themselves. Two of the prisoners had a special interest in us. One was El Comandante Alfredo, a FARC guerrilla leader. The other was a less senior FARC man called 'Robinson'. Many Colombians use an alias or nickname. I have no idea what his real name was because no one ever seemed to call him anything else, except the guards for visits. Robinson had already influenced our lives. The story he told was that when the new wing was opened, he and five paramilitaries were put into it, as part of the new 'criminalisation' policy of the US Federal Bureau of Prisons. He was known as a tough middle level FARC leader, and one of the paramilitaries was a top assassin of theirs.

Confronted with a new situation, neither side had weapons or any plan of what to do, but Robinson knew that they were going to kill him. He managed to survive until he got an automatic pistol smuggled in, then he went to the cell where the paramilitaries were and shot four of them. The real bad one was killed and three others wounded. Robinson put the pistol on the ground and walked to the exercise area with his hands in the air. The uninjured paramilitary had asked for special protection from INPEC and was locked up twenty-three hours a day in a cell on the balcony. Robinson refused special protection and was walking around the patio exercise yard.

Originally I had an Italian narco sharing the cell with me for a month or so, but he was extradited back to his home country and then I shared the cell with a Lebanese. He was good-mannered and well-educated, about fifty-five years of age. His hair was going grey and his body looked as if he had never done physical work or suffered hardship. He was in for money laundering and was not at all comfortable with prison life. We got on well, except for him wanting to play parquets all the time while I lacked the patience for it. Parquets is the most popular board game in Colombia. It is very like ludo but much more complicated and requires a lot of concentration. My friend was also fond of playing chess. I beat him in our first game because he got over-confident, but after that he won every time. I was happy enough with his company because he was easy to get on with and did not take drugs.

Martin's cellmate was called 'Cuba' because that was where he was from. He was a useful man to know because he worked in the kitchen and knew all the gossip. Niall's cellmate was the problem. He took cocaine and there was always the danger that on a cell search some of it might be found. We were worried that Niall could find himself accused of owning it. We were very aware of the delight that some Irish and British newspapers would take in using such a situation as anti-republican propaganda, even when they were quite aware of the facts. To head off this possibility Niall formally requested INPEC not to put any of us in a position where such an accusation could be made; our lawyers also put that case to the prison authorities.

Martin's wife, Cristin, regularly downloaded newspaper articles from the Internet and e-mailed them to Angela in the Political

Prisoner's Solidarity group, who delivered them to us. In that way, we were fairly up to date on developments about our case, the 'Bring Them Home' campaign and the peace process.

We had a routine for dealing with the mosquitoes in the cell. They mostly entered the cell in the early part of the morning, so my cellmate made sure that the cell door and the glass window were closed each morning until the day got hot. When it came to a half hour before lights–out at night we would start a hunt with rolled–up newspapers. The mosquitoes hid in shadow or on the ceiling and waited a half hour or more in the darkness before biting you. There were usually six or seven of them hiding. After lights–out we would lie in the darkness, me in the upper bed, waiting. If one had survived, it would emerge and fly around making a high–pitched sound, until it decided to feed. In the darkness, I pulled my blanket right up so that there was no exposed flesh, and shooed it away if it approached. After a long time it would settle on my Lebanese friend, and he used to show me the big bites in the morning. Eventually he moved to the cell of a friend of his and a Colombian drugs runner called Frank replaced him.

After a week or so one of the senior INPEC guards on the patio said to the three of us that he knew none of us were taking drugs. We asked how he was so sure. He claimed that he only had to watch a person for a few days and he could tell not only whether they were on drugs, but which drugs they were taking. I did not doubt him.

I spent my time walking in the patio, talking to Martin and Niall, or to El Comandante Alfredo or Robinson or some of the other prisoners. There was some work that would give time off a sentence, and sometimes there were education talks by INPEC-employed teachers, which also earned time off. The work that we three undertook to do was to sweep and mop the concrete patio before breakfast every morning. Each of us had an area to do and it took about a half hour. It was also useful in getting a chance to think about things. Doing routine work seemed to encourage thought that would not happen while idle in the patio or while lying in bed at night. The breakfast was in a canteen that had rows of massive concrete tables. Prisoners cooked the food, and it was okay to eat. There was still the threat of being poisoned, so I made sure that I did not eat any special food or have a special place in the queue. It worked for me, but Martin had a bad experience.

One of the prisoners, a drug baron, complained of pains in his stomach and chest, and he was not satisfied with the prison doctor's diagnosis. He got an outside doctor to examine him and traces of strychnine were found. At the same time Martin and another prisoner were unwell. The prison doctor examined them and he sent samples to be tested by an outside laboratory. The paramilitaries working in the kitchen were removed from their posts, as it seemed that they were suspected of the poisoning. Everyone recovered.

In February, we had two visits from David Andrews, a Fianna Fáil TD (Teachta Dála, a member of the Irish parliament), who was asked to visit us by Niall's mother. He was chairman of the Irish Red Cross and a former minister for foreign affairs. He came to observe our conditions in prison and our difficulties in getting a fair trial. He also met our lawyers and senior members of the Colombian administration, including the Minister for Justice. Caitríona and an official from the Irish Department of Foreign Affairs accompanied him to Colombia.

On the first visit he was a bit sharp and wary, although he later relaxed as our answers to his questions were satisfactory to him. He was very experienced, and his report back would carry a lot of weight with the Dublin government.

Over the weeks I got to know both El Comandante Alfredo and Robinson well. El Comandante Alfredo was a man of considerable natural authority, forty, tall, medium build, clean-shaven and going a little grey. He was a leading figure in any activity concerning the running of Patio B. The other side of his character was that he enjoyed practical jokes, playing football, and was very sociable. Robinson was good-humoured and very fond of the women visitors who came into the patio on Sundays. He was maybe thirty, solidly built, medium height with close-cropped black hair and full of energy. He did not appear to be down about the forty-year sentence he was going to get for the shooting, or that the paramilitaries had him marked, or that INPEC were going to make life hard for the next forty years. Both of them were 100 per cent committed FARC guerrillas, who lived cheerfully for their cause without any hint of being fanatical about life or death or the fine detail of politics.

There were five guerrilla prisoners now in this patio. The two most senior of them had the same story of how they came to be here. Julio Serpa was twenty years fighting in the jungle but eventually needed an operation on his eyes and had to go to a hospital, where he was arrested. El Comandante Alfredo needed an urgent operation for an appendix and he was arrested while in hospital too. They were both colourful characters. Julio was always full of enthusiasm and was very much into politics. There was also a jolly fat FARC militiaman from Bogotá called Marine, and an ELN man called El Chino (the Chinese; he was not Chinese but like many indigenous people looked Asian) who spent a lot of time studying for examinations through a correspondence course.

Martin had a big woolly head for a couple of hours in the morning and always told Julio to 'stop wrecking my head with politics early in the morning!' El Comandante was always at practical jokes or cheating at football, but he certainly knew his politics as well. I could imagine guerrillas following Julio because he had a rank, while they would follow El Comandante because he was a natural leader. Robinson was the kind of man that you would like by your side in a tough spot, but I am not sure how good a leader he would be. The more Spanish we learned, the more we could take part in discussing things with them.

The guards came for Robinson, El Chino and some other prisoners before we were unlocked one morning and moved them far away from Bogotá.

We had a visit from David Andrews, Caitríona, Síle Maguire and three officials from the Defensoría del Pueblo. The meeting took place in a corridor that was noisy and open and lasted about ninety minutes. David asked us about our conditions for preparing our defence and our living conditions. They told us that earlier in the day they had met our defence lawyers and Colombia's ombudsman, Eduardo Cifuentes, who expressed "serious concern" at the news that the state prosecutor's office, *Fiscalía*, had closed the case against the three of us. We had been formally charged with training the FARC and travelling on false documents.

Caitríona Ruane had submitted a list of twelve witnesses to the prosecuting authorities, but none were called to give evidence, raising fears that only witnesses sympathetic to the prosecution would be heard when the trial took place.

The visit occurred in an atmosphere of considerable tension as the prosecutors claimed that the FARC were about to launch an attack on the prison. State prosecutor Guillermo Mendoza Diago of *Fiscalía* had requested permission the previous week to move the three of us to a more secure prison in Valledupar, sixteen hours drive away. INPEC refused to transfer us as it was for convicted prisoners only. A political analyst observed: "This bizarre attempt to move the men to Valledupar shows the three have been convicted before the trial even begins."

Caitríona Ruane wrote this next piece about their visit for a Republican magazine called *Spark*, in the spring 2002 edition, and it is valuable for the account of what it was like for a visitor from Ireland to come and see us.

A Visit to La Picota

It was a beautiful sunny Sunday morning in Bogotá. I was walking up a long avenue to La Picota Prison, watching women and children fly past me, excited at the thought of visiting their loved ones in jail. We had just passed the first security gate. I was dressed in a skirt, because women are not allowed wear trousers, and I felt alone and apprehensive. This was the first time I had visited Niall, Martin and Jim in La Picota. During my two other visits to Colombia they were in a different jail. I consoled myself by telling myself I could be sixteen hours away from Bogotá, in the heart of right-wing paramilitary country. If the prosecutor had his way, the three Irishmen would have been moved there three days prior to our visit. Fortunately, following a strong lobby by the lawyers, Ombudsman's Office, Minister for Justice and director of the Prison Services, they were not moved. I also reminded myself of the courage of people like Nelson Mandela, Rigoberta Menchu, Bobby Sands, Martin Luther King and others, began humming 'something inside so strong' and held my head high.

On the left hand side I saw the houses for the 'privileged prisoners' – nice little houses, with their gardens and families sitting around talking to them. These are the prisoners that get special treatment. I can only guess why. I thought to myself – 'some chance our three being treated like this'.

I went through a few more checks. My passport was taken off me a few times and 'los Irlandeses' were mentioned all the time. Everyone knew who they were. Why wouldn't they, given the trial by media that the three men had received to date. I was then brought to the High Security Wing, Pavilion B, and the entire mood changed. I had my photograph taken by a tiny camera and was given a sticker to wear with my fingerprints, barcode, and a very unflattering photo of myself. I had to leave my watch, jewellery, money, passport, and papers, anything I had. I left in Nelson Mandela's autobiography and thought that this will be a good read for them. I got my fingerprints taken twice, got an indelible ink stamp on my arm.

The last time I got an indelible ink stamp on my arm was when we were in holidays in Spain with the children visiting a fun park. I would be telling you lies if I did not tell you that I wished, with all my heart, that I was beside my two excited children, fighting over which ride they wanted to go on first. I bizarrely thought that my little daughter would have been fascinated at this stamp on my arm. She would have loved getting her photograph taken. Such is life.

I had to take my shoes off and they were X-rayed. Had another body search or two, passed into a dark, dreary room with grey steel doors that clanged, got an infrared stamp on my arm and another body search. There was a concrete chair that looked like an electric chair and, fortunately, they did not ask me to sit in it. Apparently, it is an X-ray chair.

I was brought into the basketball court and there we had our visit. It was lovely to see Niall's big blue smiling eyes, Martin's cheeky grin and Jim's quiet smile. Three such different characters, 'Los Tres Amigos' as they have dubbed themselves. They filled me in on their new conditions – who was on the wings with them, what it was like. I spoke to them about David Andrews' visit and the legal case. We all spoke about the political crisis in the peace process and I noticed the tight lines around their eyes when they spoke about this. The headlines in all the papers and the TV showed the Colombian Army ready to invade the zone, the hawk jetfighters provided by the US Government, and the guerrillas in the zones packing up all their belongings and moving into more mountainous areas. The three men were acutely aware that their fate is very dependent on the peace process and how an intensification of the war would affect them.

I have often marvelled at the Irish sense of humour in the bleakest of circumstances and these men are no exception. We had great craic on the visit. Their humour was incisive and funny. They told me all about the people on the wing with them. Each of them are in separate cells and sharing with alleged top drugs dealers or 'narcos' as they are known in Colombia. I shivered as they told me this. I did not like to think what could happen when the door is closed for the night.

They knew we were coming in on a visit tomorrow and were looking forward to the visit. They also encouraged me to try and get extra visits during the week to make the most of our being here. They all asked about their families, and I could see their eyes following the children of other prisoners as they played around the visiting area. All were very proud of their families and friends and the work they are doing at home to bring them home. They had heard about the wall mural in the Free Derry Corner and asked if I had a picture of it for them. Then, of course, they naturally went into slagging each other off about how they might look in the wall mural.

I left the visit, went through all the security checks again, it took an hour to get out of the jail. I took a taxi to my hotel and felt very low – possibly the lowest I have felt in a long time. I met with David Andrews and Síle Maguire (Irish Embassy in Mexico) and briefed them on the visit. I had to stop myself from getting upset.

Caitríona told us about the meetings that they had during the week with the Attorney General, the Solicitor General, the Vice Minister for Foreign Affairs, the Minister for Justice, the captain of the jail, the editor of *El Tiempo*, the Ombudsman, the United Nations, the International Red Cross, media interviews with people from Ireland and Colombia and meetings with our lawyers. It was a busy few days and very worthwhile. At all the meetings, David Andrews raised issues of security, our place of detention and access to lawyers. David Andrews was a member of the European Parliament and of the Fianna Fáil party which was in government in Dublin.

Caitríona went on to say that the profession of defence lawyer was a very dangerous one in Colombia. In 1998 alone, twenty-five were killed by right-wing paramilitaries, and collusion between state forces and paramilitaries was a recurring theme in any of the human rights reports. Their offices had high security measures to protect them, and the pictures of their assassinated lawyer friends and colleagues hanging on the walls were a testament to how dangerous it was. Many more lawyers had to flee the country and were living in exile.

The security getting into the United Nations or International Red Cross offices reminded them, all the time – if they needed to be reminded – how dangerous Colombia was. The discussions with both these organisations were confidential, but what Caitríona would say was that the United Nations were playing a very important role in the peace process, in the protection of human rights and in the case of the three Irishmen. And, while she was sitting there, she saw the picture of Mary Robinson and heard the affection and respect for her in the voices of her courageous staff in Colombia – and she was very proud of that wonderful Mayo woman.

In the article for *Spark*, she also wrote:

I went in for one more visit with them on my own the day before I left – it was a good visit though each of us was very conscious that this was the last visit for a while. Their courage and morale is very strong and I marvelled at it because they have been through hell on earth and know the next few months are not going to be easy. I left them with a heavy heart but buoyed up by their strength and determination.

The only evidence against the men is false passports and for this the normal course of action is deportation. The forensic tests contradict each other and the false witnesses against them have been discredited in cross-examination by the men's lawyers. Given the flimsy evidence and the violations of the Colombian legal processes, the men's lawyers have submitted a 24-page document calling on the Colombian courts to release the men immediately. We are awaiting the verdict of this court.

Meanwhile the prosecutor is deciding, based on the evidence available, to free or charge the men. It is worth noting that she has closed the case early without interviewing the witnesses put forward by the defence. This is obviously very worrying for us. It is also of no comfort to know that the current Attorney General has been criticised by international agencies for interfering in cases to protect high-ranking military officers from prosecution. We are now awaiting the verdict, though one is left with a very strong feeling that three Irishmen in Colombia are, to put it crudely, stitched up.

Chapter 8

Collapse of the Peace Talks

IN JANUARY 2002 the army and air force had completed their build-up and the generals were saying that they were ready to take on the guerrillas. The pressure in the media began to mount for an end to the negotiations. The talks collapsed on 20 February when the FARC hijacked a plane carrying a very important Colombian senator and landed the plane in the zone. The FARC wanted to exchange prisoners with the government, and they were building up a collection of political and military prisoners to exchange for their people who were captives of the state.

President Pastrana ordered the military to invade the zone. The TV news carried film of planes being loaded up with bombs and ammunition. Thousands of soldiers took part in the invasion. The army had been trained by hundreds of US military instructors and were supremely confident that they had the forces and the equipment to win easily. They were over-confident and took a hammering from the FARC. General Muro, head of the army, diverted criticism of his strategy by claiming that the heavy casualties were due to the FARC having the benefit of IRA technology and training.

In one fairly typical incident of over-confidence during the invasion, soldiers came on a farmhouse with a full drinks cabinet. They radioed other soldiers about their find, and when the FARC detonated a half-ton of explosives around it, thirty soldiers were killed.

As the weeks passed from March into April of 2002, the patio was filling up. Among the new arrivals were several paramilitaries. We kept our distance as the numbers of paramilitaries grew. Their leader was an evangelist preacher, a big, rough-looking man of about fifty, with a loud voice. Several minders always accompanied him. They would hold prayer meetings every Sunday morning with loud and long hymn-singing in a cell on the balcony. The preacher got in a children's plastic swimming pool and held baptisms in it. Being baptised seemed to be a necessary part of being one of the 'in' crowd. They tried to get us to join them. Martin was quite definite that it was not on, and I found myself arguing theology with the preacher as to why we would not go. They believed the British propaganda about the war in Ireland being between religious fanatics with the British acting as peacekeepers, and appeared to think that we were Catholic fanatics. Niall was the interpreter and seemed to enjoy the weird situation.

The preacher was in prison accused of murdering thirty-four *campesinos*, FARC supporters, and my impression from looking at him and his friends was that he probably did it. The human rights groups were insisting that he be put on trial for other massacres as well. Paramilitaries would be arrested when they became an embarrassment to the state or when police or army units who were not sympathetic to the paramilitaries caught them. In Colombia there were pro- and anti-paramilitary elements in all the state institutions as far as I could judge. The FARC men said that the *gringos* had a policy of funding fundamentalist Christian sects all over Central and South America as a counter to communist influence among the people.

Football matches were played on the concrete patio. The teams tended to be composed of guerrilla against paramilitary, which led to some rough football. Martin thought it was similar to a tough match between Armagh and Tyrone and he revelled in it. Eventually it was decided that teams would be mixed to minimise injuries among the players. That led to Niall and Martin always being put on opposite teams. Being Gaelic footballers they could take the rough play that soccer players just could not handle.

I used to play in goal to keep out of the rough stuff, but I hurt my knee anyway. The injury was an old one from even before the war in Ireland began. Thirty years before, while doing tactical weapons training, I caught my foot in a rabbit hole and damaged the cartilage in my knee. The surgeon said that I might get fifteen years out of his work before I needed an artificial joint. The knee became very sore and that ended my football playing in prison. Getting up and down stairs, or attempting to run, were difficult and painful for about a year after that. The guards wanted to believe that I had at some stage been injured in combat, so I did not argue differently.

On a visit from Anne we heard that it was dangerous to be Irish in Colombia because of us. The Irish human rights activist and writer Gearóid Ó Loinsigh was stopped at a roadblock by the army at Santa Rosa del Sur airport and told that he would require a special pass to visit the peasant community that he was going to. (He later learned that this was untrue). The army gave him a lift to the town of Santa Rosa del Sur and advised him to stay in a certain hotel. When the soldiers left, he also left the hotel and booked into another one as he was suspicious of their friendliness. Later that night the first hotel was raided by the paramilitaries looking for *'el mono'* (the fair-skinned one). Gearóid had to go into hiding from the army and paramilitaries and took a week to get out of the area.

We were getting word that a lot of pressure was being put on Gerry Adams to testify in the Delahunt Enquiry due in April.

On 11 April 2002, Major General Gary S. Speer, acting commander-in-chief of the United States Southern Command said, "As I am sure you know….there are three IRA members that were arrested in Colombia who had been training the FARC. And the indications are that the recent terrorist campaign throughout Colombia, certainly since 20 January, demonstrates some different techniques that were not previously used by the FARC, and the implication is that maybe these are techniques that the IRA actually provided in the training in the *despeje* (the demilitarised zone)."

The pressure on the Irish peace process was increased again by the British intelligence services using a 'leaked assessment' that we had been using Colombia as a training ground and for weapons testing. The BBC Northern Ireland ran the story on 13 June, saying that the training and weapons testing was sanctioned by the IRA Army Council. This provoked unionists to demand that Sinn Féin be expelled from the Northern Assembly. Sinn Féin spokesperson Gerry Kelly said: "They all come from the same anonymous British source who has been briefing journalists for almost a year now."

The big play on our frame-up by the US Embassy was made on 24

April 2002. The Delahunt Congressional Enquiry sat in the United States.

Committee on International Relations
US House of Representatives
Summary of Investigation of IRA Links to FARC Narco-Terrorists in Colombia.
April 24, 2002
Investigative findings on the activities of the Irish Republican Army (IRA) in Colombia
Prepared by the majority Staff of the House International Relations Committee.

Before the hearing began, Mr Bill Delahunt (Democrat), who had originally called for the hearing, said that the evidence before it largely consisted of innuendo, and the hearing had been called to suit another "pre-determined agenda" related to controversial US aid to the Colombian armed forces. He was joined in that criticism by Mr Peter King and Mr Ben Gilman, New York Republicans.

A number of expert witnesses were called, including General Fernando Tapias, commander-in-chief of the Colombian army and chairman of the Joint Chiefs-of-Staff, Armed Forces of Colombia.

He claimed that we had trained the FARC in the use of mortars, explosives, intelligence and combat techniques. He also asserted that they believed that there had been at least seven Irishmen involved in visits to Colombia since 1998.

"I can say we have facts linking them to training activities. They entered zones under FARC control where they actively buttressed its activities. The effect has been noticeable in changes in FARC techniques, particularly mortars and explosives."

He also said specifically in relation to me: "He is the boss of engineering of the Provisional IRA and according to the British press he is in charge of the design and production of bombs, mortars and pitchers of projectiles inside the IRA. He is expert in explosives and considered by the leading Democratic Unionist, Peter Robinson, as the most important man in the IRA."

Congressman Peter King:
On the issue of Mr Monaghan, you had stated that you had received information on him from overseas or European intelligence. In the document that was presented to us you say that the information on Mr Monaghan was provided by Mr Peter Robinson.

General Tapias:
Our intelligence units were in touch with British intelligence units, because we do not know these people in our area.

Congressman King:
But here it says that the information was received from Democratic Unionist Deputy Leader, Peter Robinson. Are you aware of three things: One, Mr Robinson is a political enemy of Gerry Adams? Two, Mr Robinson opposed the Good Friday Agreement and the peace process in Ireland? And number three, Mr Robinson has himself been arrested in Ireland?

General Tapias:
There is no mention of this person Robinson in the information that we have to present to you. We contacted the UK Embassy in Colombia, and our contacts have been therefore with intelligence agencies, not with a designated individual.

Congressman King:
So you are saying then that it was British intelligence that gave you information provided to them by Peter Robinson? This is on page 5 from the end. It says, "Information provided by Democratic Unionist Leader, Peter Robinson".
This is the information that was given to us by you today.

General Tapias was unable to explain the reference to Peter Robinson as a source. And while in the hearing record there are many entries of information subsequently provided in response to questions raised during the hearing, no further information or clarification was ever entered into the record on this matter.

The involvement of British intelligence with the Democratic Unionists opposed to the peace process in Ireland was exposed. This came about as a result of good cross-examination of the over-confident witnesses. The game plan of the conspiracy was revealed in the recommendation of the investigation:

As the forces of global terrorism, illicit drugs, and organised crime converge upon Colombia to produce new challenges to the international system, the United States must reassess its current policy permitting military assistance provided under Plan Colombia to be used exclusively for counter-narcotics programs. The threat of drug-financed terrorism and organised crime is of a global reach, illustrated by developments in Colombia, and must be addressed by changes in U.S. law that will permit American assistance for counter-terrorism programs.

The US policy that their military training presence in Colombia and military aid were to fight 'the war against drugs' was to be changed to one of fighting the civil war on behalf of the ruling elite. They were trying to use the charges against us to justify such a policy change. Both the Colombian generals and the US arms suppliers had big stakes in the frame-up.

I had received a cutting from the *Sunday Business Post* of 24 March saying that defence contractors with interests in supplying weapons to Colombia had donated $12,000 to Henry Hyde, the chair of the Congressional Committee, over the previous fourteen months. The article went on to list the helicopter and electronics companies that had made donations to him.

The conspiracy was certainly damaging to us three, and to the Irish and Colombian peace processes, but it was clear from the recommendations of the House International Relations Committee that its main victims would have been the people and government of the United States. It was aimed at US involvement in the Colombian civil war on the basis of false intelligence, as the US Embassy in Bogotá had fabricated the core evidence on which the entire 'global reach of terrorism' rested. It was seemingly a case of a non-elected arm of government trying to overthrow the policy decided on by the elected representatives.

On 19 May 2002, we were told by our families on the phone that our case was being used to influence the general election in the Republic in a way damaging to Sinn Féin. The US Department of

State annual report *Global Patterns in Terrorism*, due to be released by Colin Powell, was being leaked to fuel speculation about what might be in it regarding the IRA in Colombia. Hostile journalists were having a field-day of anti-Sinn Féin propaganda. To fuel the speculation further, Department of State spokeswoman Joanne Procobitz said the report would be "about twice the size of last year's and will look at events and developments in much greater depth". The speculation centred on whether a named senior IRA figure had also visited the FARC sometime before 2001.

The presidential elections in Colombia took place on 26 May. It mattered quite a lot to us who won. Pastrana was bad enough but Álvaro Uribe would be an out-and-out enemy of ours, because he was fanatically right-wing. Uribe wanted to escalate the war and bring in stricter repression, which we would be on the receiving end of, because they blamed us for training the FARC in urban guerilla warfare.

May and June passed slowly, and July arrived. Angela from the Political Prisoners Solidarity group was due to visit, so I was writing letters to family and friends for her to e-mail to Ireland.

We were getting reports that a leading paramilitary had been shot dead in La Modelo. The only detail that we had so far was that a weapon fitted with a silencer was used. We did not know whether it was his own men or the guerrillas or others that did it. In Colombia there were always plenty of suspects. The reason that we were concerned was that if he was shot by the FARC then we might be considered as good targets for retaliation.

I had got more X-rays on my knee. The prison nurse here was sceptical that INPEC would pay for medicine or treatment or an operation.

The atmosphere in the prison was affected by what was happening on the outside, especially when it had a bearing on the possibility of El Comandante Alfredo being part of a prisoner exchange. It came on the TV news that the FARC had released a video of greetings and appeals from two governors and several soldiers that they were holding prisoner. Some of the soldiers had been held for four years.

The FARC were also trying to get all the mayors and the civil administration to resign. The government was trying to get the civil war status of the conflict changed to one of 'a terrorist threat' so that the FARC and ELN could not have offices and recognition in countries abroad. They claimed that the guerrillas did not hold territory and so did not qualify as being engaged in a civil war. However, the guerrillas did hold about 40 per cent of the country. Up until now local government had stayed neutral and carried on as best they could whether the area was under the FARC or the Bogotá government. This development made the war worse as Bogotá was forcing the civil administration into taking sides. The army was appointing military officers as mayors to replace those who resigned.

We had cause to worry about what was in the news. Pastrana was to be replaced as president by Uribe. Uribe's proposed minister for justice had launched a strong attack on the Constitutional Court, which he wanted to abolish. Our trial – and indeed every legal process in Colombia – was under a threat because the laws were based on the authority of the constitution.

There had been an assassination attempt on President Pastrana. His convoy was ambushed. One TV station said that the ambush was by a FARC unit trained by the IRA. The public were constantly being conditioned to believe that the IRA was active in Colombia and that we were part of that.

We came in for a lot of hostile propaganda both in Colombia and Ireland following a FARC mortar attack in which 119 people were killed. Two army generals and a police general were under investigation about the incident. The FARC had attacked a town defended by paramilitaries, and the local people were sheltering in a church from the fighting. A heavy mortar bomb fired by the FARC hit the church. The senior UN representative who was in the area at the time had made a report that the military and police allowed the paramilitaries a free hand against the FARC, who then attacked the town that was the paramilitary base. The UN position was that if the army and police had acted against the paramilitary occupation of the town, the attack and its results would not have happened.

I was starting to paint again. I planned to keep painting pictures until the visit that was expected in August, and Gerry could take them home for people who helped out in the 'Bring Them Home' campaign,

or for use as fundraising prizes in raffles for the observers' visits and the cost of phone calls etc.

Twenty-three people had been arrested on a protest at the 'School of the Americas'. I had heard a lot about it from other prisoners, visitors and even when I had visited Nicaragua. It was the US Army Spanish language military school in Fort Benning, Georgia. About half of the really serious human rights abusers and death squad leaders in Latin American countries had been trained by the US army in it over the last forty years.

The protests were about its connection with torture and oppressive regimes, but I thought its major purpose was intelligence gathering on promising soldiers who might someday be senior officers in their own countries. I thought that the US wanted to build a profile on soldiers from Latin American countries and to find those who could be subverted from loyalty to their own country. They might be useful in organising a coup, should that suit US foreign policy in the future.

In the light of the forty years existence of the School of the Americas, and of its continuous involvement with dictatorships, repressive regimes and death squads, and its obvious close ties with the State Department, there was little room for doubt that a culture of criminality thrived within the State Department. False evidence was only a minor crime to them.

One night the police guards came and demanded the keys to the kitchen from the prisoner in charge of cooking, and when they did not get them they changed the lock. Up until then no one could enter the kitchen without the presence of a prisoner's representative. That gave some measure of security that the food would not be poisoned. Guards, not visitors, brought in guns, drugs and mobile phones, so the main danger was from a guard being alone in the kitchen.

The prisoners proposed two locks, one to be held by them and the other by the guards. The kitchen was not in use until the matter was resolved; it was not a hunger strike, although a press statement put out by the prisoners used those words. We expected the situation to be resolved on Tuesday, but by Thursday night we had not had a meal since the previous Friday evening. There was a promise of talks on Saturday. We had not been able to buy food, only water and non-food items. One of the prisoners gave me a small cup of instant coffee granules on Wednesday morning, which lasted the three of us until night. The coffee machine was still working although there had been no coffee to put in the water since the previous Monday, but we could make a drink with sugar from it. My cell-mate Manuel managed to get some soup, which he shared with me. It was very thin and very welcome.

La Picota was on the news that night. A tunnel was discovered in another patio that had got to within three metres of the outer wall.

Finally, on Friday, there was a settlement to the problem of access to the kitchen. The two locks formula proposed the very first day had been accepted. We kept out of the negotiations, as our job was just to get through prison life and home safe without heroics. I did enjoy the bananas we were given at 11am and scrambled egg with a rasher at 1.30. You have to be careful when eating after a long fast. After I was on a five-day hunger strike in Portlaoise prison in solidarity with the men on a full hunger strike, I ate a normal dinner and was extremely sick after it. Gandhi used to eat an orange first, and then wait and gradually ease back on to solid food.

There were a lot of rich, spoiled bastards, who were paying the guards a fortune so that they never went hungry. They had no problem taking their 'first' meal. At the same time, these men kept the worst of the paramilitaries out of the patio because that suited them – it also happened to suit us.

It was on the news that President Pastrana had been in Europe trying to get the EU to classify the FARC as terrorists. He would probably succeed because the EU was taking its line from the USA, not from the UN or NGOs on the ground. I thought that Bush's ultimatum that 'If you are not with us, you are against us' had the EU in a panic. Of course, EU states with imperial pasts would see the 'War on Terror' as a golden opportunity to bully the third world and get their hands on any natural resources worth stealing.

Friday was the last day for new evidence in our case. In the next three weeks or so there should be a meeting between the judge, the *Fiscalía* and our lawyers to lay out a timeframe for interviewing witnesses. There was a problem. The trial was to be in the town of Florencia, near the old peace zone. The judge there did not want to hold the trial, and no alternative had yet been arranged, such as holding it in Bogotá. The state had largely lost control of the south of Colombia and their hold on Florencia was not very secure. It seemed to be a battleground between paramilitaries and army against the guerrillas.

Around the beginning of August, I got the results of the X-rays on my knees. One leg had the bones touching according to the doctor. I was to see a specialist to confirm his diagnosis and we would be giving the X-rays and doctors' reports to Caitríona on the visit next Sunday. She would get a specialist opinion on the X-rays in Ireland. The United Nations rep said that if there had to be an operation, the UN would contribute half the cost; the prison should pay the other half.

The previous week, the doctor was sure that an operation was needed; this week he was saying that the artificial joints only lasted five years and so on – I believe that someone had pointed out to him that it cost money, which they didn't want to pay out. Anyway, the Irish Ambassador, Art Agnew, was here on a visit so we got him to talk to the doctor, who now said he was arranging a visit by a specialist. They had a specialist, but did not pay him, so he left the prison.

The three of us were taken to the judge's offices in the affluent north of the city, about the first week in August. This was by permission of the judge so that we could read the legal papers in the case against us, and get photocopies of important papers.

There was a man in the prison called Frank who was waiting to be extradited to the US. He was living on his nerves and was involved in a couple of fights about football and the phone queue. After he got out of fifteen days solitary confinement, they decided to put him in with me. I apparently had a reputation for being easy going, or else they thought I needed a challenge. Frank could not sit easy. My routine was to wash the cell once a week, my clothes once a week and myself most days. In between, I got art paint on the towels, pencil parings on the floor, banana skins in a box in the corner. I liked plenty of light in the cell and the TV was always turned down, except for the news.

Frank started the day by washing the cell; he told me to wipe my boots before entering and he offered me detergent most days of the week (which I thanked him for, said I had some and ignored the hint). He stayed in the cell on wet days with the TV on full volume, with himself doing exercises. I retreated to a shelter at the end of the patio to read, paint or write letters. Recently he had the TV turned down – but instead of madly exercising he was praying! Underneath all the nerves, he was a fairly nice person. He shared things and helped me with bits of Spanish. I did some drawings of his family and even met some of them on a visit. His wife brought me a pair of jeans because I did a painting of the family.

I had not been doing so much painting lately – between the problems with my knee and Frank. I was doing a bit of maths with Martin and three classes a week with teachers who come in. One class was origami – paper folding, which I could not make head nor tail of. Another was psychology and the third was relaxing exercises. All of them were good for learning Spanish and offered a break in the routine. I read Irish language articles from the newspaper *Lá* to Niall and Martin.

On Wednesday, 7 August, the new president, Álvaro Uribe, was having his inauguration ceremony in the Narino Palace in the centre of Bogotá. The news was full of detail about the ceremony. In the elections he had won because he was the hard man who would deal severely with the guerrillas and impose neo-liberal measures on the economy. The oligarchy and the foreign diplomatic corps, including Art Agnew, were in attendance at the presidential palace. Martin, Niall and I were walking in the patio of La Picota, talking about it all.

There was an ear-splitting noise as three delta-wing jet fighters flew just above the rooftops over the prison. Because they flew so low we did not hear them approach, and the noise was all the more shattering because of that. I caught another glimpse of the jets as they rose over the mountains that surrounded the city. Shortly afterwards we heard the news that the presidential palace and the army officer training school had been hit by large-calibre mortar bombs.

TV coverage in the days leading up to the inauguration had shown the army doing sweeps of the mountains and setting up look-out positions on every vantage point to prevent just such an attack. We talked as we continued to walk around about how it could have happened and the likely military response. Later news bulletins said that some mortar bombs had overshot the presidential palace and caused heavy civilian casualties in a poor neighbourhood close by. The news said that the mortar bombs had been fired by radio control from a house in the city, and that a man on a motorcycle had been arrested in possession of a radio control device.

Very soon after, the TV and newspaper coverage of the attack were saying that it was based on IRA technology. There was media speculation that we were to be charged with involvement in the attack, but that was all propaganda. We were once again being blamed for the failures of the military and intelligence services, which made us even more vulnerable to attack while we were in prison.

On Sunday President Uribe declared a state of emergency, and part of his justification for it was that the FARC had received training from outsiders. He also put La Picota prison under the control of an army officer and ordered the police to leave. From the Friday following the attack, La Picota was run by INPEC guards.

The mortar attack took place on Wednesday and Caitríona arrived to visit us on the following Sunday. The fact that the country was in uproar, that a state of emergency was declared that very day, that we were being accused of involvement, did not intimidate her at all. She saw the lawyers and gave us a good briefing about the state of the case against us.

When Caitríona met Patricia Ramos from the Defensoría del Pueblo, she was told of their great concern that we would be moved on some pretext to the prison of Valledupar at the earliest opportunity. Only sentenced prisoners were supposed to be held there. Their other and even greater worry was for the safety of Caitríona herself.

A side issue in the new repressive laws was that, alone among European Union states, Irish people would in future require a visa to enter Colombia.

In September I wrote a letter that was more a story than a normal letter, but it was descriptive of life in La Picota.

Do you believe that old rubbish about Friday 13th? This morning was Friday 13th. I was half awake at the usual time for getting up, about 6.00 in the morning. I was dimly aware that there were more footsteps than normal and thought – another bloody search! The man that I share the cell with, Frank – he was more awake, but he was speechless – they were coming to take him away for extradition to the United States on drugs charges. He had been living on his nerves for the last month dreading this morning – but every other morning had passed without anything happening – until Friday the 13th!

The door slammed open, and sure enough the blue uniformed INPEC screw shouted to get dressed, addressing the unfortunate Frank. Over Frank's shoulder I saw Niall at the door – he had a bunch of family photographs and about forty postcards that he had painted for the family visit on Saturday. He told me that they were taking him away too! He did not know where or even why they were taking him, but he did know that he could take nothing with him and wanted me to look after his things. I said that I would ring Caitríona in Ireland and tell her what was happening so that she could get on to the Irish Embassy in Mexico and also tell the families and lawyers.

I tried to get to the phone, although it is not usually switched on until around 7am, still there was a chance that it might have been left on since yesterday. The guards stopped me and were shouting orders in Spanish at me that I did not understand – but I thought that they were saying that I was going to be moved out as well. I went back and told Niall that I would ring if I got the chance, and that I thought they were going to move me out as well. I went to Martin's cell but he did not have a clue either about what was happening or what we could do about it, apart from getting in contact with the lawyers and Ireland as soon as one of us could get to a phone.

Art Agnew, the Irish Ambassador, had told us that we would not be separated or moved out of Bogotá because he had got assurances at a high level that we would be kept together in Bogotá until our trial was over.

I got back to my cell just in time to see Frank being led away and several other prisoners with him. Niall was gone as well. I went into my cell to see what had happened there, when a senior INPEC guard shouted something at me. He shouted it again and slammed the door, locking me in.

One of the FARC prisoners was still outside, and he told me that he would ring our lawyers' colectivo as soon as he could get to the phone. The FARC and ourselves have the same lawyers – it's enough to get you convicted before anyone says a word in court!

I settled down to sign all Niall's postcards which Martin and Niall had already put their names on. Dan would be very upset after travelling half way around the world to find his brother gone.

I rooted about half-heartedly in the things that Frank had left behind him. Everything of his was now mine. I also had got a big box of Niall's things that I would keep for him, if we ever saw him again. I had never been so rich since I had arrived with empty hands and empty pockets in La Picota. But I could not enjoy my riches; I was troubled by Niall's removal – both for what would happen to him and by how Martin and I would cope with our limited Spanish. The family visitors would be arriving by plane in Bogotá this afternoon and be coming in for a visit tomorrow morning. Everything was now in total confusion and Niall was the only one with enough Spanish to make the necessary arrangements.

The time was passing well beyond when I should have been out of the cell and able to phone, so I started banging on the door and shouting.

"Qué pasa? Qué pasa?" (What's happening? What's happening?)

I could see a prisoner through the cell door, and he told me that the guards were doing a cell-by-cell audit of our possessions. Anything in excess of what the United States Federal Bureau of Prisons allowed would be taken from us.

For the second time on the morning of Friday 13th my cell door burst open. I vaguely knew the guards as they had often come over to watch me painting in the patio, and I had done some drawings for guards, perhaps even for these two.

How many socks? How many vests? How many shirts? Trousers? Runners? Sheets? Blankets?

They put the allowed number in a heap and the excess clothes in another heap. Then they went on to everything else in the cell; the not-allowed heap grew and grew.

While that was going on, another guard entered and took down the curtains, which were made from black bin liner bags. A companion pulled all the masonry nails from the walls that were used for hanging things on. The cardboard box that I used to keep my clothes in was taken and so was the unravelled pot scrubber used as a TV aerial. (The original aerial had been lost long ago.) One of the guards gestured with his head for me to move over to the corner of the cell. He pointed to a painting and gave me the thumbs-up sign, telling me to go outside to the patio. Later on, when we were put back into the cells, I found that the two guards did not take my 'excess' belongings, but in fact left me my art materials and clothes sitting on my bed!

Later we were allowed to use the phone, and I called Caitríona to tell her about the latest developments but Martin had already got a call through to her. I phoned home and let them know what was happening. The FARC lad had phoned our lawyers, so everyone was buzzing and getting on to other people – the Red Cross, the United Nations, human rights in Bogotá, the Irish Embassy in Mexico. Sinn Féin had got Gerry Kelly to put out a statement about what was happening. Síle in the Embassy in Mexico City was on to the Colombian authorities.

Martin and I discussed whether it was a local decision by the INPEC prison authorities to move Niall, or was it taken at a higher level, and if so, what was the motive. It certainly messed up the visitors, and there was a very important meeting with our lawyers set for next Wednesday and Thursday in the judge's offices. The meeting would be useless if Niall was not there to translate for us.

We were assembled in the patio and told the new prison rules. In future, we were told, we would be locked out in the patio from 8.00 am until 6.00 pm every day – regardless of the weather. There was a shelter at one end of the patio for wet days. Phone calls would be limited to from 9.00 am to 11.00 am and 2.00 pm to 4.00 pm and not at all on Saturday or Sunday. The visits would continue as they were, except for the special visits during the week in the legal cubicles. These had been around a table in an informal and relaxed atmosphere; from now on they would be from behind a glass panel, and conversation would be by telephone to the visitor on the other side.

The Colombians were usually not as nasty as their US bosses and we would just have to wait and see how much of the orders they would actually carry out. The rumour going round was that the men were moved out because of an escape plan that was about to be carried out.

I had taken a newspaper, a sketchpad and a pencil out to the patio, but the situation was too unsettled to draw or to read – we were trying to rearrange the visits. Officially we only got a visit every fourteen days, the bottom and top level of cells taking turns each week. The way that the Colombians worked it was that one week you could get a visit in your own name and the next you got one in the name of someone on the other level, if you could arrange that with someone. We let them have a visit in our name in return. The guards would know that the Colombian family that turned up to visit the Irishmen would spend the time with their own relatives instead. They were practical and usually humane, and in that respect Colombian culture was a lot better than the petty and vindictive treatment of prisoners in Irish, British and North American prisons.

It just happened that on the week of the family visitors arriving in Colombia, we were not officially entitled to have any visits. Most of the men from the top level cells – including the ones whose names we were to use, were now gone. We were trying to get new names, and at the same time trying to get the Irish Embassy to intervene directly to get us the visits in our own names – and what about Niall's family? If his visitor could not visit him, then we wanted that he could visit us, so that at least they would have seen someone during their trip to Colombia. Arranging all this in Spanish was complex.

We heard a big cheer from the guerrilla prisoners. Something was happening at the entrance.

Niall was back! Bald!

He told his story. The guards had taken him to the line of men waiting to be moved out. The guards then called out each man's name. "David Bracken!" He had not answered. They came to him and asked his name – Niall Connolly. They radioed someone asking why Niall Connolly was sent as his name was not on the list, and were told that he used both names. Along with the other prisoners he was taken to a military airfield near the prison and put on board a giant Russian helicopter. Another Russian transport helicopter was carrying more prisoners and two US Blackhawk helicopters, which were flying escort, accompanied their helicopter on a long flight to Cómbita prison in the mountains away to the north.

Inside Cómbita prison, he was lined up with the other prisoners, showered, and had all his hair cut off. He was standing in line waiting to be given a prison uniform and was wondering would he refuse to wear it, because he was a political prisoner, not a criminal. An INPEC official called him out of the line. He was put in a vehicle and driven back to the helicopter, which was refuelled and flown back to Bogotá. He thought that it was because of pressure put on the Colombians by the Irish Embassy. For whatever reason they returned him to La Picota, we were much relieved.

I rang Caitríona and she already knew, but never said how, except that it was a great victory for us all. Things relaxed a good bit after that and Niall was able to clarify the position about the visits, getting an assurance from one of the majors in charge of the patio that there would be no problems. It was hard to get to sleep that night without the curtains to keep out the glare of the floodlights, but at least Friday 13th was over!

I had a visit from my brother Gerry. He left me in a set of acrylic art paints and art paper to paint on. After that I would often pass the time painting. I did pictures from postcards, which people in Ireland liked to get, as well as our own 'Colombia' postcards for Christmas and Easter. I also painted imaginary scenes and did portraits of other prisoners. I was not allowed paint any scene from the patio that could be useful to an escape plan. I painted several versions of the famous Ché picture. One day the guards came and confiscated not only the Ché pictures but also the entire stock of red card that I had. They were popular with the Colombian prisoners as well as for fund-raising at home. I was warned that any more subversive paintings would lead to their

COLOMBIA

SAOIRSE !

taking all my art materials. I had been resisting with a biro, a pencil and a paintbrush, and now they had started to counter-attack.

We had other visitors over from Ireland. Among them was Barry McElduff, a Sinn Féin representative in the Northern government from Tyrone, who gave us a good run-down on political developments at home. The peace process was long and difficult but Barry had a great sense of humour and we enjoyed his company.

Our first appearance in court was due. The Colombian justice system resembles the French advocacy system rather than the Irish and British adversarial system. Rather than having two sides argue opposite sides of the case, one agency, *Fiscalía*, is charged with presenting all the facts to the judge when deciding whether to proceed with the case. Once the trial is under way the defense lawyers also question each witness and call their own witnesses to be questioned by the defense, the *Fiscalía* and the judge. The *Procuradora* is a second state agency which oversees the trial to ensure that it is fair and in line with best practice. Of course that rarely happened; the evidence usually consisted only of the things damaging to the defense. It was our belief that the *Procuradora* in our trial would watch for opportunities to convict us that the *Fiscalía* had missed, and then act in effect as a second prosecutor. The court would sit several times. A sitting might be to hear a particular witness or the like. The trial consisted of all these sittings and final sessions for the defense and the prosecutor to sum up their cases and for the judge to present his findings.

We decided that it was better not to attend the preliminary appearances at the trial. Both the *Fiscalía* and the *Procuradora* were hostile and would use our presence in the most damaging way that they could think of. We were legally entitled not to attend and decided to avail of that right.

We told the guards and told the judge in writing that we did not want to attend the trial that day, so we were surprised when the guards informed us that we were to leave for the court in a half-hour. The three of us went to the bottom of the patio to discuss our options. We decided to resist any attempt to force us to attend the court. When the guards came for us, we said we were not going. This was taken as direct defiance of an INPEC order and they tried to grab each of us but we

held our ground. Immediately the other prisoners saw trouble they gathered around. The guards withdrew.

Ten minutes later the riot squad appeared. The FARC prisoners asked whether we needed their help but Niall explained what was happening and that we would be better to handle it alone. When the riot squad attacked, Niall put up a fierce resistance, while Martin and I did the best we could. In my case that was token resistance because of my knee. We were held by the riot squad and put in the reception cell waiting to be brought forcibly to the court. In the meantime the judge was told of our resistance. He ordered that we be left in the prison, which was our legal right. I suppose that he only did so because he could imagine the bad publicity for his court if we were dragged in against our will and against our right not to attend. I am convinced that had we not been prepared to make a stand on it, we would have been forced to do what suited the state. Our lawyers told us that Judge Acosta was about the best judge for respecting human and legal rights, but that he was under immense pressure from both the President and the generals to find us guilty.

Caitríona told us that the prosecution had opened its case against us by saying that we had entered Colombia on false passports and spent about four weeks in the demilitarised zone with the FARC. Strangely, we were not being charged with training them during that time but instead they would bring witnesses to accuse us of training them at earlier dates. Captain Pulido, the army officer who was in charge of the squad that arrested us, was to give evidence.

The three of us were returned to the patio but later the guards came for Niall and put him in solitary for a week. It was supposed to be solitary but the only cell available was the reception cell at the entrance to our patio. The next day four or five men arrived into Patio B because of a riot in their own patio, so he shared the cell with them for most of the week. While having the company was better than being in solitary, there was a downside – most were paramilitaries. But there was also an M19 guerrilla, whom Niall became friendly with.

The M19 movement had once been a very important part of the war. They had captured the Palace of Justice in Bogotá, with most of the Supreme Court judges and their staff inside. They tried to negotiate but the military stormed the building and killed a lot of the occupants, including the judges. Some years later most of the movement not only had a ceasefire but went over to join the state. A small number of them continued to fight against it.

At this time I started to write fairly regularly and send the material home when there were family visits. In Irish and English prisons I had had first-hand experience of the obsession with censorship and was relieved that the Colombians were different. Their culture was a lot less repressive intellectually, if more so in physical terms. I often thought about the possible origins of that.

On Thursday, 3 October 2002, we had a visit by Barry McElduff and other international observers. Barry mentioned that the prison administration was being very difficult and petty with the observers on the way in. There was another visit by Barry on Saturday 5 October. On this visit he told us about a hostile and aggressive demonstration outside the court by government supporters.

On 6 October I got word that a spokesman for the US Embassy in Bogotá had indicated that the forensic tests carried out by an American expert from the US Embassy were unlikely to play any central role in the case. Jim Foster said that, due to the risk that the tests might have been contaminated, it was likely that the case would be decided on the basis of the eye witness testimony and our failure to explain our presence in the region or the use of false passports. I thought it interesting that the embassy was getting cold feet about facing cross-examination in front of the international observers and a sceptical press corps.

We got the news that Caitríona was coming on a visit with some of the international observers. She would bring Seán Crowe, a Sinn Féin TD; Finian McGrath, an Independent TD; Senator Mary White (Fianna Fáil) and Paul Hill, who had been wrongly imprisoned for fifteen years in a British prison with the Guildford Four.

Chapter 9

Three Days in October

O<small>N</small> W<small>EDNESDAY</small> 16 October the electric door locks opened in a series of bangs right along the landing. The sound woke me and I got up, intending to get to the phone quickly before anyone else got to it. I often phoned Anne Barr, who lived in Huila, fifteen hours away by bus, just for a short chat using up the tail ends of phone cards used to call Ireland. Three thousand pesos would hardly get sixty seconds to Ireland but would get me six minutes talking to Anne.

Before I could leave the cell, a guard was at the door handing me a large black bin liner. "*Traslado*," he said. I could not understand the rest, but I got the message that I was being transferred to another prison. This was unexpected. Our court case was on, but we had sent a letter to the judge explaining that we would not be attending and that our legal representatives would look after our interests there. This had all been agreed. Had there been a misunderstanding? Obviously the guard could not answer. He slammed the cell door shut.

I turned to the other man in the cell – Pedro, an ELN guerrilla. He repeated "*traslado*" and indicated by gesture and words in Spanish that I should pack my things. I could hear Niall and Martin in cells either side of me shouting through the little barred windows in the cell doors. We confirmed that each of us had got the black bags and were to be transferred to some unknown destination.

Could it be a trick by the guards to bring us to the court? But that did not make sense as the judge had already agreed that we had the right not to attend if that was our wish. Niall asked for a senior ranking guard to explain to us what was happening.

"Everyone is being moved to Cómbita."

Cómbitas was a hard-regime, top-security prison for prisoners serving long sentences, far from Bogotá. It was not unexpected that at some stage we would be sent to one of the top-security jails. We expected that to happen after the trial was over, as we would be convicted for our passports even if all the rest of the charges fell. We were a bit reassured that we Irish were not being picked out for special treatment, but that everyone was going. This was plausible in the atmosphere of the new Colombian state of emergency.

There was a bit of a commotion outside our cells and I went to the door hatch. It was Robinson, being brought out with his belongings. He had recently arrived back in La Picota for a hearing in relation to his shooting of the paramilitaries here. He said he was going to Valledupar, another high security prison with a very bad reputation. I wondered whether we all were going there and not to Cómbita.

I looked at the shower: no time to wash or shave, better get packed. The question was, what to take and what to leave? Cómbita was a cold place, high in the mountains, so I should take warm clothes. We were only allowed a limited amount of clothes anyway: three trousers, three vests, six pairs of socks and so on. I selected the best I had. I knew I would not get any extra clothes through the search when entering the new prison, and I might not even get clothes through at all because they might insist on me wearing a uniform.

I gave the excess things that I had to my cellmate. He was one of the twenty-two prisoners sent to our patio after a riot in Patio A, next door to us. We had heard the shouting and smelled the tear gas but had not been involved in the rioting. My cellmate had only the clothes he stood in. On his first day with us he was shivering with the early morning cold and I gave him a pullover. Since then, he had got a toothbrush, soap and a few other possessions. It must have been like Christmas for him as I gave him everything that I could not bring with me.

Niall shouted something about phone numbers. While I could not hear clearly everything he said, I got the message to take anything connected with being able to phone our lawyers and families if we got a chance. I had a big bag of letters and postcards from friends in Ireland and from my family. I was only allowed two photographs. I tore up the rest and kept the two best photos. Books? The US regime allowed five books. In Cómbita we might be locked up there for long periods, so I took *Stupid White Men* by Michael Moore and *Leaving Cert Maths*.

Should I take a book about the properties of light? Yes. And how about a book on deep-sea exploration? Yes. Spanish Grammar? Yes. *The Art of Drawing?* Yes! I took it. I had another decision to make – to take a writing pad or a sketchpad. I took the sketchpad and a 2B pencil and a graphite rod for artwork. They would probably not allow it or the black biro, but it was worth trying.

I pulled the shaving mirror from the wall; it had been glued on with toothpaste. There was no point in worrying about shaving anymore. I was leaving this cell and I needed to see what was going on. I pushed the mirror out the cell door and could see all the guards gathered at one end of the landing in a huddle of indecision. Word came along the cells that some men who had been taken out were now being sent back. Not everyone was going.

A guard came to our door. *"Pedro! Traslado."*

Poor Pedro – all his newly acquired riches were suddenly gone. Well, not all. He put the soap and his clothes in his plastic shopping bag. He did not need to ask for a bin liner. Everything he owned fitted in the bag. I gave him one of my sturdier Roches Stores plastic shopping bags. Gerry used to bring me lots of ten or more of the Roches Stores bags on each visit because they were strong and in great demand by the Colombian prisoners. The door opened and with a last *"Suerte!"* (Good luck!) my guerrilla friend was gone out of my life.

After a while, the noise and commotion died away and there was only the sound of the TV in the cell. In a peculiar turn of the North American mind, they had put a TV set in each cell in the high security patios. I thought that it was probably because statistics show that TV is like a powerful addictive drug. Even outside prison, people will spend several hours a day watching it, and the dumber the content the more they watch it. If they administered a chemical tranquilliser that had a similar affect in stupefying people, the human rights organisations would raise hell. We assumed that the TVs were bugged.

I turned the TV off and got the graphite stick and a sketchpad out. I put the mirror up on some books so that I could see myself comfortably and started to sketch a self-portrait. All sense of time passing soon disappeared. When I finished the drawing, I became conscious of my back muscles, stiff from the concentration, and distant banging on a

IN THE MIRROR

Sé
22/1/02

door with someone shouting, "*Comida! Comida!*" It was about 2pm and I immediately felt hungry. We had not eaten since yesterday.

The doors opened. I grabbed my mug and headed for the coffee urn – mistake! The guards slammed the doors shut again as soon as we were outside the cells. I had some cold coffee to drink and I did not have my warm pullover. Luckily the weather was not too cold and we walked around the patio talking about the morning's events and speculating about what was in store for us. There were seventeen of us left out of forty-seven that morning. After a while, we were let in to the canteen area to have breakfast, or at least to have a meal to cover both morning and midday. It was very tasty – hunger is a great sauce. We had rice, potatoes, meat and onions with a drink of *panilla* (a dark sweet liquid made from raw sugar cane and boiling water).

Back in the almost empty patio the sun was shining warmly. I got a book from the newly installed patio library, a schoolbook about history and culture covering the ancient civilisations of the world and with a special part on the native cultures of the Americas – the Incas, the Mayas and the Aztecs. I find that reading Spanish is a good help in speaking it. Just as I was getting really absorbed into the part on Inca culture, a senior guard came and announced, "*Traslado – todos!*"

Everyone was going! I did not catch the rest, but I saw Martin and Niall heading for the library and grabbing the two guitars. Our visitors had sent in one guitar for Martin and the other had belonged to 'El Chino', an ELN prisoner who had been sent to Cómbita. I asked Niall what was happening and he said we were going to the next patio, not down the country. I grabbed my paints and brushes from the library shelf, but what about the six finished paintings? I could not take them because they were large and I was carrying all that I could manage.

Two of the paintings were really hard to leave behind, one of a guerrilla girl with her AK-47 and the other a Celtic warrior picture for my son, full of Celtic designs and mythological details. Anyway, I was delighted to be able to bring the paints. I went back to the cell and under the mattress of my bed there were two small unused books of painting paper that I stuffed into my black bin liner along with the paints. The plastic was not able for the added weight. The guards were saying to bring our sheets and blankets, mops and brushes. I went after the guard with the black bags and eventually found him and got another bin liner bag to reinforce the first.

Niall had been told that the move was just to the patio next door, Patio A. We set out, handcuffed in pairs, carrying bags, brushes, mops, buckets and blankets. Martin and I were trying to carry our possessions and at the same time not get separated from Niall who was handcuffed to another prisoner.

When we got into Patio A, there were about twenty prisoners sitting around in the patio. We put down our bundles and the three of us got together for a discussion about our new home. We knew that there were paramilitaries here.

Niall and another man were allocated cell to number one. I was allocated to cell number four. Then the captain called out the name of my cellmate – it was Martin! We carried our bundles inside.

"It must be bugged. Why else would they put us together?"

I slung my bag on to the bottom bunk before Martin could reach it. Martin smoked, and it was better not to be above him. It was 6.50 – ten minutes to news time on the TV. We were anxious to find out what had happened in the court and whether it had made the news. We expected the lawyer from *Fiscalía* who was prosecuting us to name his witnesses and we were very interested to hear which were in and which ones had been dropped.

I switched on the TV. Snow! Not a picture on any channel or any sounds other than an electronic hiss. There was no aerial on the set. The US Bureau of Prisons instruction to the Colombian guards did not work very well. They were told to confiscate any wire or other non-regulation material. They confiscated the TV aerials made from pot scrubbers taped to the wall, which were better for reception than the original supplied aerials. Those had long since disappeared. What to do? Martin saved the day. He had three packets of cigarettes. Each had an aluminium foil lining which could act as an aerial when they were joined together. A staple from a notebook provided us with a contact into the aerial socket. Soon we had both picture and sound.

The news on Caracol TV reported a fierce battle being waged in Medellín by the army and police, backed up by Blackhawk helicopters. They were trying to drive FARC and ELN urban guerrillas out of a *barrio* (district) in the poor suburbs of the second city of Colombia. The paramilitaries had been trying for months without success to establish their control of the area and now Uribe, the President – a near paramilitary himself – was sending in the big guns. There were fourteen dead so far, ten civilians and four soldiers. Our case was totally overshadowed – not a mention.

I could hear Niall shouting. He said that Channel 7 had carried news of our trial. The prosecution had called two informers and the *Procuradora* had called another two. The case would resume in six weeks on 2 December. We said we would watch the news at ten o'clock and settled down in bed to wait. Both of us fell asleep. I woke up about midnight and switched off the TV, then went back to sleep.

I woke up before 6am and waited for the doors to open before getting up; then I got dressed and went out to see the sights. There was already a queue at the phone, all trying to let people know that they had been moved.

Later in the day we had a half-hour legal visit. Martin, Niall and I had a meeting with Caitríona and we wanted to know about what had happened in the court. Half an hour just flew, and before we could get talking about the situation in Ireland, following the suspension of the Assembly at Stormont, the time was up. Niall asked for five more minutes and the guard said okay. But, of course, that was gone in a flash and we were saying goodbye to Caitríona. Another visitor, Francie Molloy from Sinn Féin, did not even get in to see us. The Colombian authorities decided not to let him into the country.

After the visit, we went over all the questions and the answers and were fairly happy with the result – our court case and the political coverage in the news media seemed to be going all right.

It was a good sunny day so I spent most of it sitting in the sun reading my drawing book and drawing exactly what I could see of my other hand, while turned away from the paper. The purpose was to separate out what you know from what you see while drawing. Knowing the shape of a hand, fingers etc. interferes with drawing them because of the way the brain handles information. I got absorbed in the drawing without looking at it, until I saw the crowd of curious prisoners gathering round me.

"Jim!" It was my turn on the phone. I did not know when I would get another chance and I decided to phone my brother Gerry in *Tar Isteach*. I would get him to pass on the news of our move to everyone else. I got through but only had enough credit on my phone card for two minutes out of my allotted ten.

The prison 'shop' arrived. The shop was really just a guard who took a list of what you wanted, discounted the cost from your account and came the next day with some or all of what was ordered. We got what had been ordered in the other patio. There was a phone card, a bar of chocolate and a roll of toilet paper for each of us. Using the phone card, we were able to make another phone call out to our chaplain friend in Bogotá. We asked him to send us in by phone some 30,000 peso phone card numbers. Each card would give seventeen minutes talk time to Ireland, which we usually divided into three calls. Luckily the numbers were available straight away.

At 5pm we had to line up against the end wall of the patio in twos. The two prisoners in each cell stood together. We had done that in the morning as well. The door from the patio to the cells was opened and so were the cell doors. The day outside had been long and noisy and it was a relief to get in. After a while we had supper – an *arepa* with a fried egg on it. The *arepa* is a flat disc of maize flour dough cooked like bread with the egg fused on the top – it's delicious.

The TV news at 7pm was all about the *barrio*, Comuna 13, which was still holding out against the combined army, helicopters and police.

We had a new aerial for the TV. Martin managed to get a metal pot scrubber from the kitchen, which we unravelled and taped to the wall with paper and toothpaste. Caracol TV had a good picture and sound in the area of La Picota, but it was very much a government propaganda channel. Channel 7 was less subject to their influence.

I awoke early on Friday and waited for the door lock to operate. As there was no water, the toilet was smelly and there would be no wash or shower. When the electric door locks opened I went out on to the landing looking out on the patio. A man was carrying a big pot of water from the kitchen to the coffee machine in the shelter at one end of the patio so at least we would be able to drink something.

I saw Martin with a cup of water. He said that there was a bucket of water in Niall's cell. I went and got a cupful and drank it.

It was time to go out to the patio where the first thing we did was to get on the phone list. We were told that the phone would be available to the prisoners for two hours in the morning and two hours in the afternoon on Mondays, Wednesdays and Fridays. More crazy rules from crazy Uncle Sam! The phones would lie unused all the rest of the time because the *gringos* from the north said so. This would cause us a great deal of trouble keeping in contact with our lawyers and families, not to mention friends. It was a great hindrance in preparing a defence, because everyone in the patio wanted to speak at length with their lawyers, all of them facing very long prison sentences if the defence was not good. Because of the numbers wanting to make calls, each man would get only five minutes. At first I had thought that the *gringos* had contempt for the rights of Latin Americans, but later came to realise that they have contempt for the human rights of all prisoners, even those in their own country.

The midday news was still dominated by the fighting in Medellín where the military and police had hooded informers with their patrols as they went through the little streets making arrests. About twenty people were reported dead and forty or so wounded. The military did not discuss their own casualties.

After the news a patio meeting was called by the representatives of the various groups of prisoners. These were men from both patios who had been in administrative and other roles. A paramilitary from the AUC (*Autodefensas Unidas de Colombia*–United Self-Defence Forces of Colombia) introduced the representatives of the AUC, the FARC and ELN guerrillas, the social prisoners and the drugs prisoners. He asked the assembled prisoners whether they agreed with the rules that their representatives had drawn up. These were:

1. The telephones would be regulated by a list and each man would get five minutes; then if he wanted another call, his name would go on the end of the list. There would be no more than three calls in a day for any man.
2. The prisoners who could contribute to the cost of extra food to supplement the INPEC ration would not have

to do cleaning duties. The other prisoners were no-one's servants and their cleaning duties were their contributions to the general good.

3. A man would be appointed to work the washing machine and dryer so as to prevent damage to them. All washing would be given to this man who would be in complete charge of the machines.

He asked again did everyone agree. No one had any objections but there were questions about the arrangements for visitors – men on Saturday and women on Sunday. Who would make the list? The same person who made the list for the conjugal visits would make it. Conjugal visits were in future to be only once a month.

He said that the captain of the guards had indicated that it was possible to have more telephone time if the prisoners made life a bit easier for his men at lock-up times and so on. Perhaps the *gringos* were not as crazy as it first seemed or perhaps Colombian common sense was coming into play. He finished by calling for mutual attitudes of respect between right and left, social prisoners, drug prisoners, gays and straight; even the guards needed respect.

Comandante Alfredo, the FARC leader from Patio B then spoke, again saying that prisoners of all kinds in the patio had to make an effort to get along. Each representative then spoke briefly and someone mentioned the religious tensions and that Catholic and Protestant had to get along with each other and with non-believers. These were real tensions because Colombia was a Catholic country with a growing number of Protestants in it. Of course, when Catholic and Protestant were mentioned, the Irish were asked if they wanted to contribute! Niall asked us and then said that our position was to cooperate with everyone in the smooth running of the patio. The whole meeting then formed a ring, everyone holding hands – although one or two FARC left quietly at that point.

Niall was talking to the leader of the AUC paramilitaries. They discussed the politics of the AUC and about how Ireland and the IRA were perceived by the AUC. He was told that the bomb that was set off near us in La Modelo was just to give us a fright. The AUC were waiting to see what the outcome of our trial would be; if we were found guilty then we would be targeted. I did not believe him; they had not withdrawn the reward for killing us. They would hit us as soon as they received instructions from outside to do so. He said that if we were found guilty, then the AUC would consider the entire IRA to be targets. The AUC already considered everyone who was in any way opposed to their politics or to their methods to be targets.

A football match was being arranged. One man asked would I lend him my boots. I said no, as they were hiking boots and not football boots. Refusing someone caused a bit of tension, but at times it had to be done regardless of how it was taken. It was quite a good game – with very hard playing.

Chapter 10

La Modelo Again

W<small>E WERE NOT</small> long in Patio A. After a week or so we were all told to pack our things in the bin liner bags again. The atmosphere was not tense, which indicated that the move was not to some distant prison. I was handcuffed to a man of about twenty-five, tall and dark, whom I did not know but thought that he must be a social or drugs prisoner. He must have been one of the original Patio A men. We were loaded into vans and driven in convoy through the city. Our destination turned out to be our old home, La Modelo. We were back in the same spot where we had got down from the army truck around fifteen months ago. This time we were only three among many prisoners, our novelty value obviously gone.

I went through the fingerprinting and video filming with the others and walked the long corridor that we had run down when leaving the last time. At the top of the corridor there was an office at a junction with other corridors. Outside the office we were assembled in a line of handcuffed pairs. The cuffs were removed from each pair and they carried their belongings to either the left or the right hand side of the corridor, forming two lines of men. When it came to my turn and the cuffs were removed, my companion was asked did he want to go with the paramilitaries or with the guerrillas. He chose the paramilitaries, I chose the guerrillas. We smiled at each other and parted company for ever.

Martin, Niall and I were near each other in the line. We were happy at being moved into the North Patio where the guerrillas were. It would give us relief from the constant tension of being in daily close contact with men who would kill us when they got the order. We were in for another surprise: the corridor we were told to go down was the one leading to Piso 1, *alta seguridad*. That was where we had been held

NIALL
LA MODELO OCT 02

the time before: we were still high security prisoners and would not be held with the ordinary security prisoners in the North Patio.

Sure enough, the twenty-five of us were led into the same floor space where we had been held the previous time. The barred gate was locked behind us, leaving us inside the barred-off floor area that contained the cells. Two or three prisoners occupied our old cell and the cell door was permanently unlocked. The other eight cells were the same, occupied but not locked. There were already twenty or so prisoners when we arrived. The whole floor was a big cell. The guards stayed outside the barred area and watched us through armoured one-way mirrored glass

MARTIN
LA MODELO '02

windows and using CCTV cameras. The resident prisoners made coffee for the newcomers. We got a warm welcome from them, with much hand shaking, as was the Colombian way. A meeting was called and we assembled to hear the arrangements that had been agreed between El Comandante Alfredo and the resident Comandante Luis of the FARC and Comandante Tito of the ELN and various others.

The cells were the prime locations to sleep and live in, but there were only nine of them altogether. Although they were one-man cells, three would live in each. The rest of us would sleep and leave our belongings in a draught-free space. It was an area with a wall of blankets to provide privacy. Each man would be allocated to one of five food groups and take turns at cooking the meals for that group. Each group would also be allocated a shower and toilet to use, and they would take turns at cleaning it. Finally each man would be part of a guard group who would do two-hour shifts during twenty-four hours, before being replaced by another group. If anything suspicious happened, we were told who to wake.

I wondered if we had access to guns in that situation, but of course you didn't ask. The guard group would also brush and mop the common floor space and the telephone booth. It was agreed with the INPEC guards that the prisoners would be responsible for cleaning our side of the one-way glass. This suited us as otherwise prisoners from other parts of the prison would have been used, and they could potentially have given useful information to aid a paramilitary attack on us all.

The three of us settled down in adjoining spaces on the floor of the sheltered area. Blankets and foam rubber mattresses were sent in by the Political Prisoners Solidarity, who worked closely with our lawyers' collective. That made life a lot more bearable. The prisoners divided up the space with cloth or blankets so that each two had a

FRONT ROOM LAMODELO OCT 02

space. The whole place came to resemble a shantytown of makeshift homes. We were much better off than in a normal prison in spite of the apparent chaos, because everyone had a choice of immediate neighbours, a good deal of personal privacy and a feeling of security about their personal belongings.

Stealing and fights were very rare and quickly sorted out. For stealing, a man would be told to leave the political prisoners group; INPEC would have to put him somewhere else. No one wanted that. For fighting, the punishment was the exact same as it had been when I was in Portlaoise prison in Ireland. Both parties to the fight would have to mop the floors, for how many days depended on how serious the fight had been.

The other punishment I saw among the guerrillas in La Modelo was more interesting. The comandante and other members of the staff there were ordered to call a full meeting of the forty-three of us and make a self-criticism of themselves. They not only had allowed gambling at cards and parquets, they had also taken part in it. The gambling was stopped.

They also had to rotate sleeping in the cells with men who were sleeping on the floors and passageways. Having a cell was a luxury,

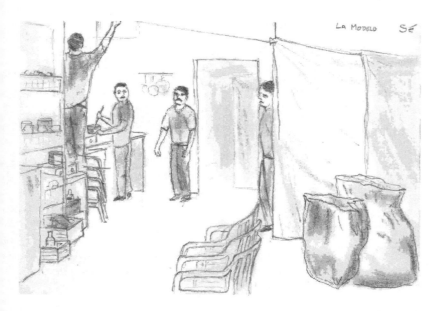

especially because there was a raised concrete area that served as a bed, and there was basic furniture in the cells. It was not good enough for leaders to talk about equality; they also had to practice it. At the same meeting they had to deal with another incident.

Two men had been involved in a fight over a burned-out light bulb. One of them had apparently switched his burned out bulb for a good one that was in their group's toilet. When challenged by another man, he denied it, and they got into a fight. Both were invited to make a self-criticism to the assembled prisoners. One did and the other declined. Everyone was invited to criticise the one who declined to criticise himself. The other prisoners told him that he was arrogant, that he did switch the bulb and that he was generally useless as a comrade and several old instances of his poor behaviour were mentioned. If I had been in that situation I would have given a bit of self-criticism, giving myself the benefit of any possible doubt, rather than have to listen to the rest saying what they really thought of me.

The prisoners were a mixed bunch. There were the three of us, the FARC prisoners, the ELN prisoners and a trade union leader from

MAKING A HAMM
LA MODELO OCT

USO, the Oil Workers Union. There was also a man in on serious drugs charges who was in danger from the paramilitaries, and several others who were probably militia men loosely attached to either the FARC or the ELN guerrillas.

The trade union man was not too worried because his union was on strike and he was confident that once the strike was over, the charges of rebellion would be dropped. He was there for several months, and, as he predicted, the charges were withdrawn a month or two after the strike was over. Art Agnew, the Irish Ambassador, had hotly argued that there were no people in prison in Colombia for trade union activities, and of course he was correct. Trade union people were always charged with something else. Now and again the army just shot them, justifying it by claiming that they were 'guerrilla collaborators'.

Soon after he got out, the trade union man sent me a photo of a poster I had designed and painted for the oil workers, which they had put up outside the oil company offices. I was delighted that he had asked me to paint it, as I had been a union man myself in Ireland when I was a metalworker.

After three weeks the Political Prisoners Solidarity group sent in six bunk beds, mattresses and blankets, pots and other cooking gear, so that life got a little easier. We three Irish got space in the bunk beds. It was a huge relief to be up off the hard floor and into a bed. Blankets were hung between the bunk beds to provide some privacy and living space. I ended up on the bottom bunk, because of the difficulty of climbing the metal steps with my injured knee. Julio Serpa, a FARC political officer, was in the bunk above me.

Anne asked could some of the girls from the commune who were visiting Bogotá come in to see me. I was delighted and the three of them came in one Sunday. The visit ended up almost a concert with lots of the prisoners and their visitors joining in the singing. The girls composed their own songs as well as playing a wide range of Colombian guitar music. The prisoners who played guitar also played their own favourites.

We had family visits in November and also a visit on 28 November from a team of international observers. The group included lawyers from the USA, Ireland and Australia. It also included political and trade union people and personalities who would have credibility in their own circles. Among these were Seán Crowe, a Sinn Féin TD, and independent TD Finian McGrath.

PARQUETS GAME
LA MODELO '02
SÉ

The observers were assured by a senior Colombian official on 29 November that the three of us would be kept in Bogotá and would not be separated.

The following are extracts from a report on his visit to Bogotá written by Finian McGrath.

My aims:

a)   To ensure a fair trial

b)   Safety of the three Irish citizens

c)   Report back to our Parliament, The EU, ICTU [Irish Congress of Trade Unions] and DCTU [Dublin Congress of Trade Unions].

Friday 29 November

After being searched and fingerprinted, we passed through the security checks to the inner prison, a dull grey, gloomy place, where we could feel the tension. Prisoners convicted of or on remand for criminal offences stared out at us with blank faces from behind bars. When we reached the compound, or cage, where the Irish men were detained we were met by three faces, familiar from the posters of the 'Bring Them Home' campaign. They were absolutely elated that we had come. We joked with Martin McCauley who

VISITORS
LA MODELO '02

WEAVING AT THE BARS
LA MODELO '02

had put on a shirt to greet us. All of them seemed more concerned about our safety than their own personal situation.

It was at that moment that I knew I had made the right decision to travel. I thought about those in the media and in the Dáil who had tried to discourage me from going to Colombia to act as an observer, using all sorts of spurious arguments and attempting to score political points. The succour we offered these three men was the support to which they were entitled, the concern of fellow human beings, fellow Irish citizens, anxious for their safety and that they would get a fair trial...

We sat in white plastic chairs (up until a few months ago the men had little furniture and had to sleep on the floor) and chatted for about half an hour. A radio played in the background. The other prisoners nodded to the strangers from Ireland and gave us warm smiles. We were handed a cup of coffee. Some men sat weaving or chatting in groups. Others began preparing lunch, cooked beans and potatoes that they had made especially for us. The prisoners have nothing to do but wait. I met one man who had been on remand for ten years, never having faced trial...

As we stood talking one of the prisoners pointed to a manhole cover on which we were standing and it was explained that this was where the *paramilitaries had dumped the bodies of some of their victims, having cut them up first. In that incident thirty-two prisoners were killed. In a later incident another ten were to die, most of them at the hands of the 3,000-strong right-wing paramilitary prisoners...*

The FARC jail commander, Julio Serpa, told us that when his movement had attempted to enter democratic politics four thousand of their candidates were assassinated by government forces or those right-wing paramilitaries acting as their surrogates. Despite that, and the war that followed, they still want inclusive dialogue and to develop a peace process. He was an impressive figure whom in any other circumstances, I thought, would be a senior civil servant, a bank manager or even a backbench TD! However, this is Colombia and anyone left of centre is an 'extremist' or a 'legitimate target' for the death squads.

The time passed quickly and we soon had to leave. We said our goodbyes and it was sad to leave them behind, amidst such danger. It occurred to me that their smiles were now struck for our benefit. We were leaving. They were staying. We walked nervously through the corridors of the right-wing paramilitaries, and to tell the truth it was nerve-wracking and I could not wait to get to the main prison gate... It was a relief to get away from the hell of La Modelo.

Sunday 1 December
2pm: Meeting with the International Committee of the Red Cross. We saw at first hand the great non-political work of the Red Cross...

Monday 2 December
9am: Spent the whole day at the trial. We met the judge and the prosecution. It was fairly obvious that both were under extreme pressure. Difficult to see how the judge could make a balanced objective decision.

7pm: We then had a meeting with the Ombudsperson's Office. A very open and positive meeting – they gave us a detailed briefing on the whole prison system. They too wanted to ensure human rights for prisoners. They could make recommendations but did not have statutory powers. They confirmed the many deaths in the prisons. They would come back to us with detailed information. The prison situation was worse than I thought. I now have major concerns about safety.

At *Tar Isteach*: Ray Lakes, Jim Monaghan, Eddie O'Neill, Martin Coughlin, Brian McNally.

Caitríona Ruane.

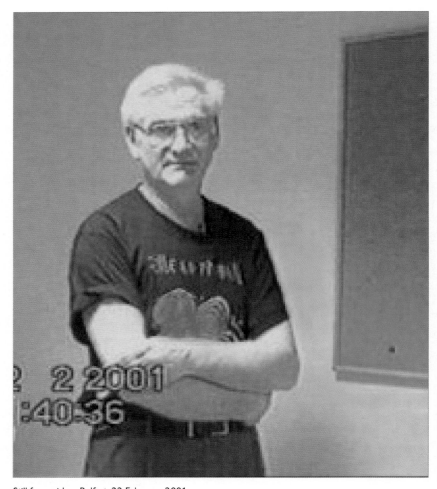

Still from video, Belfast, 22 February 2001.

Members of FARC (*Fuerzas Armadas Revolucionarias Colombianas* – Revolutionary Armed Forces of Colombia).

Eileen Sheils, Maureen Fanning, Cristin McCauley, Gerry Monaghan, Nessan Quinlivan.

Sunday Visitor to La Picota.

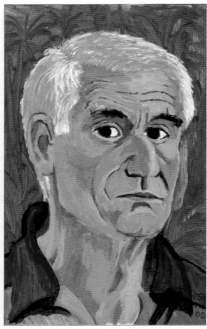

Jim Monaghan self-portrait in La Picota.

Niall Connolly, Martin McAuley and Jim Monaghan in DIJIN.

The banner and poster for the USO strike.

Niall Connolly, Jim Monaghan and Martin McAuley in La Modelo.

Jim Monaghan, Martin McAuley and Niall Connolly with fellow prisoners in La Modelo.

Army Sweep, painting by Jim Monaghan.

Guerrillas bathing, painting by Jim Monaghan.

Four cards painted in prison by Jim Monaghan.

Tuesday 3 December
9am: Court all day again. Military intelligence officer gave evidence. Not impressed with his quality and made a lot of silly statements. In fact I was shocked at his lack of professionalism.

5pm: Met the United Nations Commissioner for Human Rights. He gave us a detailed account of human rights abuses in Colombia. Constant breaches of international humanitarian law committed by members of the Armed and Security Forces. Human Rights defenders on death lists. Major displacement of people over the last six years. Two million displaced. We gave a commitment that we would bring this message home to Ireland. Military guilty of war crimes.

Wednesday 4 December
Met Minister for Foreign Affairs (Junior). Explained our visit and our terms of reference... Our legal observers gave their concerns about the build up. The Minister responded by saying that they would do their best to ensure fairness and justice. She also pointed out that Colombia was in the middle of a civil war and that the situation was complex. We explained that we, too, had come through thirty years of conflict and the only way forward was inclusive dialogue.

Meeting with Trade Unions: Very sad and difficult meeting – particularly with the slaughter of trade unionists. Three thousand eight hundred killed since 1986. One hundred seventy-eight in the last year alone. They told us about the deaths in Coca Cola factories. They urged us to contact the American Government, the Colombian Government, the Irish Government and the Irish Congress of Trade Unions. I gave a commitment to do this when I returned home. They thanked us for coming and expressed their deepest appreciation for our efforts...

Thursday 5 December
8am: Visit to jail again. Following major publicity, I felt under major threat. Tension in prison. Right-wing paramilitaries knew who we were. The three men were in reasonable form despite being disappointed. There was a bad air around the prison. I spotted men following us. I was very concerned about our safety. I could not wait to get away.

3pm: We went to the airport. The incident with Paul Hill and the tearing up of his passport was a disgrace. [Paul Hill, one of the Guildford Four, had his passport torn up by a member of DAS at immigration.] I lodged a formal complaint with the airport authorities. I also made a complaint to our own Minister for Foreign Affairs when I returned home.

CONCLUSIONS OF THE VISIT:
1. The men could not receive a fair trial.
2. Major human rights violations in Colombia.
3. Breaches of international humanitarian law.
4. Men seriously at risk in the prison.
5. Major internal conflict.
6. Trade Unionists, lawyers and human rights groups need our support.
7. Colombia needs a peace broker.
8. The ordinary people are demanding a peace process.
9. The U.N. and E.U. have got to assist the Colombian people.
10. Seventy-five percent (75%) of outside aid is military. This is not what is needed. They need economic aid and inclusive negotiations.

Caitríona came in on a visit and explained what had happened in court. When the court met, the prosecution wanted the defence to present its case first, saying that the prosecution case was not ready yet. The defence strongly maintained its right to hear the prosecution evidence before starting on the case for the defence. No legal system requires the defence to put its case without first hearing the prosecution's case; it was only possible to defend when the case being put by the prosecution was known. Yet, here in Colombia, that was happening to us. The judge seemed to have lost his nerve in face of the hostility of the army. The *Fiscalía* and the army were stalling and trying to force the defence to go first.

The only evidence that had any credibility in Colombia was the forensic evidence supplied by the Embassy of the United States. (The US official who made the tests seemed to have changed his name from Molloy to Anthony Hall, perhaps because Molloy was not qualified.) They said that a forensic test had shown traces of explosives and drugs on our luggage. The defence had engaged Dr Keith Borer, an English forensic and explosives expert, who had a very high international reputation, and he had stated that the US forensic evidence had no credibility.

In my opinion, the US decided to back off as soon as they realised that they were up against such an expert. The US Embassy was trying to distance itself from the trial by not defending its forensic evidence in court, while at the same time not withdrawing it. By playing for time the Colombian government, the British and the US could continue to milk the political benefits of the 'international terrorist' link.

Two witnesses for the prosecution, deserters from the FARC, failed to turn up for the trial. Judge Jairo Acosta read out a deposition from one of them, who said that he was afraid to travel to Bogotá by road as his life had been threatened.

Edwin Giovanny Rodriguez was described as a former FARC guerrilla, currently in detention for unspecified reasons in the town of Villavicencio, about an hour's drive from the capital.

When defence lawyers asked why he could not have been brought by plane, the judge, who was deciding the case on his own, said he would make a request to this effect for the resumed hearing and he would also ask for adequate security to be provided.

The two witnesses shared the same name of Rodriguez although they were not related. The court was told that although the second man, John Alexander Rodriguez Caviedes, was in a state witness protection programme he could not be found in time for the hearing.

The court was also told that two police witnesses for the prosecution could not be present as no budgetary provision was made for their travel expenses or airline fares. They were understood to be members of the Garda Special Branch from Dublin. When our lawyers took a firm stand against the judge's decision to make the defence present their case before they had heard the prosecution case, the judge backed down and made the prosecution call Major Carlos Eduardo Matize of Colombian Military Intelligence. His testimony was nothing short of astounding. He identified two manuals – one in Spanish and the other in English – which were sent to him from "somebody" in his superior's office and which were allegedly found among the captured possessions of FARC guerrillas. He did not know what the circumstances were but he stated that they described military mechanisms for bombs similar to those used by the IRA.

The international observers and the Irish Ambassador, Art Agnew, attended. Although the prosecutor had had fifty-four days notice to prepare, nothing was achieved at the hearing and a new date was set for 5 February 2003.

On 13 December 2002 the media reported that on a visit to Bogotá the US Secretary of State, Mr Colin Powell, said, "But after 9/11, as we looked at terrorist activities around the world – and maybe the [Colombian groups] do not have global reach – but when you start to see members of the IRA in Colombia sharing experiences, sharing knowledge, doing heaven only knows what, it suggests that these kinds of organisations are committed to destroying democracy in our hemisphere. Should that not be a concern of ours?"

Caitríona put out a press release condemning him for making comments that were prejudicial to the legal case against us. The US was adding to the tremendous pressure already on Judge Acosta. Diplomats such as Colin Powell carefully weighed up the effects of what they said to the media.

Chapter 11

Into the Mountains: Cómbita

O N THE NIGHT of Sunday 15 December 2002, a flashlight shone in my face. Behind it there was a commotion: dark figures moving in the dim light.

"*Traslado!*"

Someone was being moved out – I wondered who. A short, fat man in the dark blue uniform of INPEC spoke rapidly to Niall, who translated: "The three Irish are being moved to another prison. Pack your stuff." Fatty had full riot gear on, including ear protectors and a dark visor.

In the semi-darkness, we packed our clothes and possessions into our bags. It was about 5am.

"*Listo, Listo!*"

The guards were trying to hurry us up, but we delayed in order to pack properly and to give the guerrilla prisoners a chance to get up to say goodbye. I packed all the art material our visitors had brought from Ireland. Niall and Martin packed in a lot of good books. Then it was time to shake hands and say goodbye to our many friends among the prisoners. I shook hands with Commandante Alfredo and with Luis, the OC, and with Julio who had the bunk bed above me. My bag weighed a ton. We staggered out of the wing to the guards' office.

"Where are we going?" Niall asked. No answer.

Our fingerprints were taken and checked against the originals. We had to really hurry along a long corridor going through the paramilitary wing. There was a short speech by Fatty into the video camera about our rights and their duty to deliver us to the destination.

"What destination?"

No answer. We went down another long corridor and through more gates out into the open air.

A prison van was waiting, and I climbed in with my bag, which was no easy matter as I was handcuffed. There was a man already sitting in the van with his bag and he was also handcuffed. Martin and Niall climbed in as well. The guards put leg irons on each of us and slammed the van door shut.

Why were we being moved out of La Modelo? Were the paramilitaries about to make an attempt to kill us? It was quite likely after President Uribe had hinted strongly that we were involved when a book bomb blew off part of an ultra-right-wing politician's hand.

Still, if that was the reason, then why was this other man in the van with us? He said he was a FARC guerrilla prisoner being transferred from La Picota and that his name was Marine. He could be what he said and he could be a military intelligence man. We just had to wait and see, but be careful of what we said in front of him. There had been reports that the paramilitaries were hammering at the wall separating them from the guerrilla wing. It could be as a result of that. It could also be because our defence team had complained about two weeks ago that we were not safe in La Modelo. So, where were they taking us? Paul Hill, one of the observers at our trial, had told us confidently that if the guards come for us at 5am some morning, it would be to bring us to the El Dorado Airport to put us on a plane for home. So, were we heading for the airport and home?

We drove through the city before dawn. No breakfast, no idea of where we were going or why. We thought that we were going in the direction of the airport. A little bit of hope was rising in our hearts as we realised that we were definitely heading for the airport, but it turned out to be the military part of it. We could see the commercial planes, the passenger aircraft for France and Spain, a few hundred metres away. We stopped at the military air terminal car park.

"Are we getting a plane somewhere? Where?"

The guards gave all sorts of contradictory answers, obviously not telling us what was to happen.

It started to rain. We were all sitting hunched up in the small van with our luggage for hours.

Niall asked, "Can we have coffee?" The answer was "no". "Can Martin smoke?" The answer was "no". "We will buy the coffee,"

Niall said, "And coffee for all of the guards." The answer was still "no".

The guards were wearing caps that said 'Rapid Reaction Force'. Had they been called out especially to move us? They agreed that they had. Two of them wore caps that said 'Explosives'. They said that they had done a course on explosives and that we were mentioned on it as the real experts.

We asked to go to the toilet in the terminal building. Fatty ordered the back door opened and we set out across the 50 metres of grass and across the road. It was very difficult and painful walking in leg irons, in tiny steps and handcuffed at the same time. My knee was very stiff after the hours in the van with no room to straighten it. Leg irons were another import of North American culture. They had never really got out of being a slave-owning society. The chain gangs in the Southern states are one of the most repulsive and symbolic aspects of North American culture.

Martin went into the toilet and was out again quickly. He shuffled over to a group of military people smoking on the steps of the building. Somehow he got his lighter out of his pocket and lit a cigarette, no easy task when in handcuffs and leg irons. The military men were surprised but did nothing about the cheeky prisoner, who after all was white. An indigenous or black man would probably have fared very badly if he had attempted the same. Our guards were not a bit pleased but let him smoke the fag as we hobbled painfully back to the van.

The van had been changed for a bigger one, which was a relief to me. Our bags were already in it and the small van was gone. I sat down and started to think about the events of the morning. Anne was to visit me. I had confirmed that the paperwork was all done and phoned her on Saturday night. Everything was in order. She would be standing in a queue for two hours before they would tell her that I had been moved. They might even tell her that the paperwork was not correct as a reason not to let her in – rather than saying I was moved a couple of hours ago as part of their security measures. I had no way to contact her or anyone else.

The rain kept falling steadily. Eventually the guards agreed that we could get coffee if we paid for it. We all hobbled painfully back into the terminal building. We got coffee and a ham sandwich for each of the four of us. Our companion, Marine, was smallish, white, of medium build and a bundle of energy. The guards did not accept Niall's offer of coffee for them too. Martin managed another smoke. We returned to the van to sit and wait and watch the rain.

We found out that the military people included helicopter pilots. So, our destination was not Valledupar as it was too far to the north for helicopters; it must be Cómbita, which was about thirty or forty minutes flying time from Bogotá. This seemed the most likely as that was where they had taken Niall two months ago, and then returned him saying that the move was a mistake. I thought that they were testing the reaction of the Irish Embassy and the human rights groups to such a move.

Valledupar would be almost impossible for our visitors. It was very far away, nearer to the Caribbean coast than to Bogotá, and in country completely controlled by the paramilitaries, far too dangerous for any visitors to chance. Valledupar was nasty and hot. Cómbita was nasty and cold at 3,000 metres above sea level. Both were run under the direction of the Federal Bureau of Prisons in the US as part of the counter-insurgency war in Colombia. They were building five more of these new prisons.

We had told Síle Maguire from the Irish Embassy and Art Agnew, the Ambassador, that we might be put into a prison like Cómbita, where there was forced mixing of guerrillas and paramilitaries. We felt that we would be set up there to be killed by the paramilitaries. The Irish ambassador had told us that he had been given assurances from a very high official of the Colombian government that we would continue to be held in Bogotá and also that the three of us would be kept together for access to our lawyers, so that we could prepare our defence. Now it seemed that the high official had been overruled. But overruled by whom?

The rain continued to fall. The guards took turns to go and get something to eat. The pilots went off for a meal. Niall offered the guards money to bring us a takeaway meal, which they did. Afterwards, we asked to go to the toilet again and made our painful way there and back. If anyone were to lose his balance and fall he could not protect his head from injury because his hands were handcuffed.

At about 4pm a convoy of big cars and military vehicles drove up to the terminal building and fanned out, taking up positions in a defensive ring. The plain-clothes men were just like the Special Branch in Dublin; I wondered was there an original Branch man that they were all cloned from. One of them came over to the van and told Fatty and the Rapid Reaction Force to "fuck off". They quickly got the van moving and we left the airport wondering who was arriving at the terminal building.

The van drove through the rain and gathering darkness into the city and on through it. At last we arrived at La Picota in the south of the city. There were hundreds of lightly clothed women visitors leaving the prison. They were drenched to the skin in the rain as they made their way down the long drive. Prison rules were that women visitors could only wear a short skirt and no coat. We arrived at the gates looking for a cell for the night. There was a lot of discussion and false information for our ears but at last we were let in.

The four of us were brought into the reception area. Our leg irons and handcuffs were removed. Our bags were searched and our money and watches confiscated for the night. We were strip searched and got a metal detector test on the chair and were then put in the reception cell. We repacked our bags after the hurried packing of the morning to sort out any unnecessary weight or items that we did not want to be read by the authorities. I found that I had taken Julio's trousers by mistake during the hurried packing when the guards had come for us. After a shower, we had a light meal and then we settled down to sleep on thin foam rubber mattresses on the concrete floor.

Some time later I woke up and started to write down the events of the day. A stout man walked past the cell accompanied by a guard. It was clear from the way he looked that he was a *Jefe* – a big shot – and he was being treated as such. After a few minutes, he and the guard returned to the patio where the cells were. I had noticed on the wallboard on the way in that there were twenty-four prisoners in each of the two patios, which had twenty-four cells on each. When we were last held in La Picota, we were two to a cell.

We had been moved out of La Picota to make room for 'Los Corruptos' – rich people caught in corruption crimes. At the time, the propaganda on the television news was that 'Los Corruptos' were being moved from their luxury semi-detached houses outside the prison proper to the high security wing of La Picota, and that they would be treated as ordinary high security prisoners. Here was one of them wandering about the wing at night, long after lock-up, with a guard as his companion. So each of 'Los Corruptos' had his own cell and I expected that they had all their old privileges back.

I finished my writing and went back to sleep.

The Rapid Reaction team, led by Fatty, arrived for us at around 5am. We had a quick wash and no breakfast. In the reception area our money and watches were returned. We were handcuffed in pairs – me to Marine, Niall to Martin. We were searched and led out to the front of the building. After a few minutes we were fingerprinted and signed out. The van arrived and was loaded up with our bags and ourselves. They put on the leg irons as well as the handcuffs. At this point, Martin realised that the guards had taken his cigarette lighter from his pocket during the routine body search. No amount of cursing could get it back. Fatty and friends had found a vulnerable spot and exploited it.

We drove through the pre-dawn city looking at the early morning travellers boarding buses or walking to work. The poorer parts of the city, which was most of it, consisted of two-storey buildings. Eight million people lived there. At the entrance to the military section of El Dorado Airport there was a collection of vintage military aircraft. Both Martin and I would have loved to spend some time having a good look at them; Niall was less impressed.

We drove to the terminal building car park and waited. This time we expected to have to wait a long time so we took out our blankets and tried to sleep the time away. Every now and again a general would speak on the hand set, asking the Rapid Reaction Force for a report on what was happening; he would then give them their orders. After a few hours, Fatty asked us did we want to buy more coffee. We all got out and hobbled across to the terminal building. It was even more difficult to walk in pairs with the leg-irons, as you had to keep in step with the other man.

"It gets you out of the house," Martin told us. "If you weren't doing this, you would probably be fucking around on a bar stool in Dublin."

We got our coffee and ham sandwiches and for good measure ate a doughnut as well. Then we hobbled back to the van. None of the guards would give Martin a light for his cigarette.

I got my book about light out of my bag to read. It was called *Light Years* and was about the history of the science of light. Although I had read it in La Picota when we were there, it was worth a second read. I was getting absorbed in it when a commotion started. The Rapid Reaction Force had received new orders, and the van was moving towards the airstrip. I hurriedly repacked the book and blanket. Everyone else was getting his own things ready as well.

The van went through a gate on to the runway taxi area. I could see three Blackhawk helicopters, a blue and white Colombian Air Force helicopter and a small black helicopter. We stopped near the first of the Blackhawks. They were surprisingly big from close up. The passenger/cargo area was about the size of the inside of a minibus. Sticking out in front of the pilot's seat was a big nose containing things like radar and infrared cameras that could pick out targets in darkness. They had rocket pods on stubby wings and had two M60 machine-guns mounted, one on either side. We were thrown up into the helicopter and made to sit facing towards the tail. The guards chained us to the floor using extra handcuffs, joining our leg irons to cargo fixing rings in the floor.

The guards made themselves comfortable sitting on our bags. There was a pilot and co-pilot, two machine-gunners, six guards and the four of us in the helicopter, which was a total of fourteen people. After about ten minutes the engines of the furthest away helicopter started up, its four wide propeller blades picking up speed. Then the next one started its engine and finally ours did. The noise was like that of a badly oiled machine about to seize up.

The three helicopters taxied along the runway for about 200 metres and then stopped and waited for the order to take off. There were no passengers on the other two helicopters; they were escorts for us. The order from the control tower came and each machine lifted off. An escort went first, then us, then the other escort. We watched the city and countryside slip by beneath us. The airfield was near the outskirts of the city. There were very large green/brown fields, with isolated built-up areas where there was not a square metre of vegetation visible, just a vast mass of small buildings packed densely together. It looked like a huge area of broken bricks, but each brick was a house. The farms had huge sheds closely packed together and large open fields with sparse pine trees at the boundaries.

Mountains and clouds soon replaced the big farms. Between the clouds we could see the hilltops with small irregular shaped fields surrounded by broken ground and rough vegetation. I could not see any animals at all, neither cows nor sheep. On the other side of the mountain, the fields were bigger. There were farmhouses and there were small herds of cattle. Quite a lot of erosion was visible where the rivers had swept the soil away, leaving bare rock. The protective trees must have been cut down for firewood and to clear land for farming. The helicopters were flying quite low. Apparently they were not worried about ground fire from the guerrillas, although several helicopters had been shot down in the past year. I was thinking that it would be a bit ironic if the guerrillas shot down the three Irish – *Los Irlandeses* – who had become some sort of heroes to many Colombian people since being accused of training the FARC.

I would have liked to give a little speech to the Teamsters Union in the US who had lobbied for these killer machines to be sold to the Colombian tyranny so that their members would have a bit more overtime. One hundred and forty-four trade unionists had been killed so far in 2002 by the Colombian paramilitaries who worked closely with the Colombian army. The overtime cost a lot in Colombian workers' blood. On the other hand, I was told that some of the labour unions in the States had helped the Colombian unions bring legal cases against US companies who abused workers here.

The three Blackhawks banked sharply over the Cómbita prison complex. I could see that inside the walls were about ten or so large three-storey buildings along two sides of a football field. A bit away from the new prison buildings there was an old prison, which also had a football field in it. On one side of the prison there was a wooded area leading down to a big swamp. On the other side was a road and beyond was gently rising ground, broken by gullies and isolated trees. In the distance were the mountains where the guerrilla forces of the ELN were said to be in control.

Chapter 12

Prison Reception

OUR HELICOPTER LANDED and we were unloaded along with our bags. There was plenty of standing room under the spinning blades but the guards insisted that I keep my head well down and run clear of the rotors. We were put into a big prison van and driven into the prison complex through two big roller shutter doors arranged like an airlock. Inside we were again unloaded and brought into a single-storey building. My three companions were put in a central square cage of wire mesh.

I was about to enter the cage too when I was grabbed and pushed to a big chair beside the wall of the building. One of the guards was video filming all this and I thought it might be for propaganda on the television news: *Los Irlandeses* getting their heads shaved! What was I to say or do? I could not think of anything so I just tried to smile defiantly at the camera. When they had finished shaving my head, I was put into the cage. The others were taken out one at a time and also had their heads shaved. I was left standing there picking hair out of my pullover while we discussed what was likely to happen next.

We decided that they were going to try to make us wear the prison uniform. As we were political prisoners and not sentenced, we felt that we were entitled to wear our own clothes. However, they could use a refusal to wear the uniform as a pretext to disrupt our defence by making visits by our lawyers impossible while we were on punishment. They could also cut off telephone and letter communication. It might be better to make a verbal protest while getting legal advice on the matter, and wear the uniform for now. We were unsure as to the best strategy.

We were given some food and we stood there talking after we had eaten it. When we finished, Martin tried hard to get a light from one

of the guards. Eventually, with Niall's help with the Spanish, he succeeded. Niall was called out for processing, then Marine, then me.
Martin stood smoking in the cage. I was led, handcuffed, to a desk
where an official sat. There followed a very confused exchange with
him in Spanish before he changed to speaking English.

He asked if I had any valuables. I replied that my glasses were valuable to me. He then asked for money and jewellery. I handed over my
money and the watch I had won in a raffle in La Modelo.

I moved on to another table for the search of my bag. The guard
removed each item and the plastic bags of clothes, art material etc, very
carefully. When I had packed my bag, I had put similar items in plastic bags to make it easier to find things in a hurry and also to protect
them from getting wet. He put his hand into the bag containing the
tubes of acrylic paints and found that several had burst. The weight of
the men from the Rapid Reaction Force had been too much for the
tubes. When everything was out of the bag, I had to put it all back in.
Meanwhile, one of the guards was breaking up my graphite pencil into
short bits – fascinated at his ability for senseless destruction.

When everything was replaced, I had to strip off and sit in a special chair made to detect metal inside me. Then I had to put each ear
in turn against a special detector and my mouth as well. After that, I
was able to get half dressed and I was sent to the fingerprint section.
After the fingerprints were taken, I joined Niall at the clothes hatch.
He was being given a uniform. There was a woman behind a little
hatch in the storeroom wall and she issued the stores to each prisoner.
When Marine had finished, I stepped forward to the hatch.

"Name?"

"James Monaghan."

"Pass everything in your bag through the hatch."

I passed everything one item at a time and she noted each down.

"Pass me the bag. Now give me your clothes." I had to take off each
item and hand it to her.

She handed me a folded uniform. I put it on the ground and stood
on it while giving my speech of protest about wearing prison clothes,
which Niall translated into Spanish. I was putting on the uniform
when a more senior guard arrived and said that we did have the right

to wear our own clothes while we were non-sentenced prisoners. Niall and I took off the uniforms and returned them. Martin had arrived behind us. He tapped out his cigarette and started to sing.

"I'll wear no convict's uniform
Nor meekly serve my time.
That Britain might brand Ireland's fight
Eight hundred years of crime."

We glared at him and Martin started to laugh, saying we would never live this one down.

I was given a bin liner and the woman returned some of my clothes. Two pairs of trousers, three pairs of socks and so on. I was given two blankets and some washing items from the prison store as well as a blanket from my own bag. The next stop was the showers. There were three very cold showers in a single open-air unit, which everyone used together. I remembered the jokes about not dropping the soap in the shower, but with the temperature just about zero there was very little danger of a sexual assault. I took the shower as quickly as possible and tried to get dry and stop shivering. I wrapped the towel around myself and followed the guard to the reception cells. There were about twenty cells arranged in a square around a small concrete yard behind the reception area.

The cell was a bleak concrete cube about three metres to a side. It was grey all over, with a concrete sink unit and concrete bunk. The guard gave me a thin foam rubber mattress and went to great lengths explaining to me that it was not to be damaged. There was also a stainless steel toilet in the cell and a built-in 15-watt light in the wall that was controlled from outside.

I made the bed up quickly and got into it until I had warmed up a bit and stopped shivering. When I felt warm enough, I got out of bed again and went through my remaining possessions. I had lost all my telephone numbers and addresses, but I would eventually get letters replacing these. My money would be in an account from which I could buy telephone cards, pens, paper and so on, once I was transferred to one of the *pabellones* (prison wings). More importantly, the three of us were still together. I had no pen or pencil, but I did have three books that they allowed me hold on to. This was important as I might be in the reception cells for a week or more and then be put into an allocation block for weeks more. The books were *Leaving Cert Maths*, very useful for filling in time; *The Art of War* by Sun Tzu, a famous book written 2,500 years ago in China; and *Stupid White Men*, the bestseller about George Bush and his fanatical neo-conservative friends in the White House.

I settled into reading *Stupid White Men*. I was reading the introduction about the attempt to stop it being published at all after the attacks on 11 September on the World Trade Centre and the Pentagon. A guard came to the cell door and demanded all the books. I had to hand them over. No explanation was given, or anything said to indicate why the books were being confiscated. I had no pen to write with and no books to read. I settled down for a long wait.

After a long time I was taken from the cell to see the psychologist. Niall was there as the translator. The psychologist was a young woman and she asked a number of standard questions to which I gave standard answers. She was not hostile but to me it seemed that her task was to find out what sort of person you were and what trouble you might cause for them and whether you had a weakness that they could exploit.

Back in the cold concrete cell, I settled down to think about the situation. Each *pabellón*, of three levels, connected by steel stairways, was said to hold about two hundred prisoners in two-man cells and was built as a hollow rectangle with a roof like that of a barn. The roof only covered about one quarter of the central patio so the rest was open to the sky. The gable wall did not go up to the roof so a gale could blow through the open space. Each walkway connecting the cells provided some shelter to the level below it. There were eight of these *pabellones* or blocks and a separate block for visits.

Warmth was a big priority here. The Federal Bureau of Prisons apparently thought that because Cómbita was near the Equator, light uniforms and unheated buildings with no glass in the windows were good enough shelter from the weather. The place was high in the mountains, cold and often wet from the frequent rain. A young man could survive a lot of cold and dampness, as the men who went through the H-Blocks in the North of Ireland had shown. It made a difference when you were a bit older. I needed to keep warm and avoid getting the flu, as in these conditions the flu could be a killer. One of the most valuable possessions that I had left was the thick pullover I was wearing. I settled down in the bed for the night and was soon asleep. I did not even think of the Colombian prisoners shivering in nearby cells without warm clothes.

The light coming on in the pre-dawn darkness woke me up. The first priority was to do something about the runners I was wearing. The laces had been taken so they flopped up and down on my feet, making walking difficult. I looked around the cell for some substitute for laces. Would I sacrifice a pair of socks? No, the bin liner I was given my blankets in would do the job. I rolled the top of the bag down to form a thick rim and then bit through it. I was able to tear it off from the rest of the bin liner as the plastic tore at the rolled-up rim. I twisted the cord of plastic and stretched it until it formed a usable lace to tie the runners with. I was just finished when the door of the cell was opened by the guard.

We had five minutes to get a shower. I stripped off, wrapped the towel around my waist, took the soap – there was no shampoo, and no hair to wash either – and I ran the short distance to the shower. There were three taps and three men having a shower. As soon as one finished, I hung up my towel and got in under the spray of water. It was freezing cold. After a quick lather of soap and a rinse down, I grabbed the towel and tried as best I could to do a lightning drying job. Back in the cell I got into bed until I had warmed up a little. I got out of bed again and organised my clothes and the bedclothes, then brushed my teeth and shaved using a disposable plastic razor. Shaving had to be done by touch, as there were no mirrors allowed.

Later in the day I was taken from the cell for an examination by the prison dentist and doctor. Both were women. There were also some women guards. One of the guards was attempting to rush me so I decided to delay by trying to make conversation with the medics. Niall was there as the translator so it ended up with him doing most of the talking. The guard was annoyed but it was important not to hurry when they wanted you to. It set the relationship at an early stage. When

I got back to the cell, I had plenty of time to think about these things. I could not do much else without something to read, or something to write with, or someone to talk to.

The three of us, and our Colombian friend, were brought out for our hour of sun. Our faces were white from rarely having been outdoors in months. There were three other prisoners in the exercise cage. We all shook hands. They had been in reception since last Saturday. Niall asked them about using the telephone. It could only be used when you had a special 009 phone card. We did not have one, or even the money to buy one until the money for our accounts was sent to whatever *pabellón* we would end up in after our time in reception.

One of the other prisoners gave Niall a 009 card – an extremely generous thing to do, for we were total strangers to him, although he had seen us on TV. Niall then asked the guards to arrange a phone call and he pointed out to them that neither our families nor our lawyers knew where we were or if we were all right. Remand prisoners had a legal right not to be 'disappeared' or held incommunicado. The senior guard said that he would arrange a call later that day. Meanwhile Martin got a light from a guard who kept a box of matches in the office for just that reason. It seemed that they made no fuss over prisoners having cigarettes but strictly controlled lighters and matches. The guard said that it was to stop prisoners setting fire to other prisoners that they disliked.

Each *pabellón* had 102 cells and each cell was supposed to hold two prisoners, but when they filled up, I expected that three or even four prisoners would be held in each cell. We were taken back to the exercise cage to wait. While waiting, the guard in charge of reception told Niall that our papers had not arrived from La Modelo and that we would remain in the reception cells until it was sorted out.

A little later we noticed a woman and man in civilian clothes outside the exercise cage. The woman approached us and said that Patricia had sent them here as the local representatives of the Defensoría del Pueblo. Patricia Ramos had met us before, in the DIJIN with the European human rights woman, and later in La Modelo. We had a good working relationship with Patricia, who was very good at her job. They told us that the Irish Embassy had been in contact and had asked the Colombian authorities not to put us in any unsafe location and not to have us held with sentenced prisoners or paramilitaries.

It was really good to hear that the Embassy was on the ball. It was also clear now about the supposed papers not arriving. We were to be kept in the reception cells until they figured out what to do with us. Another bit of information was that our lawyers' *colectivo* had sent an emergency *tutela* to the judge who was in charge of our trial asking that we be returned immediately to Bogotá, as the lawyers could not visit us in Cómbita without a serious risk to their own lives from the paramilitaries on the road over the mountains. The judge would take a few days to give his legal judgment on the matter.

We were returned to the cells but almost immediately were taken out again to make the phone call. This time we were handcuffed in pairs – me to Martin and Niall to our Colombian friend, Marine, who was lively and likable. We were taken out of reception and through a gate to the area containing the *pabellones*. The attitude of the guards had become much friendlier. We were brought along a covered walkway to *Pabellón 8*, where we immediately met up with a friendly man on the food trolley. He was a guerrilla prisoner who had been sent here from La Picota. He had been put into our high security patio in La Picota after their patio had a riot and took eighty guards prisoner, because, among other things, the guards were charging relatives and other visitors an admission fee. The man immediately organised a light for Martin's cigarette. That seemed to be everyone's priority!

There was only one phone for around 200 men so we were lucky that there was only one man ahead of us. When he finished Niall got on the phone and made his call. After Niall, Marine made his call. Meanwhile Martin and I, handcuffed together, went over to talk to a guerrilla prisoner who was looking out through the food hatch of his cell door. The word quickly spread up the long rows of cells that we were *Los Irlandeses*. The guerrilla prisoners shouted welcomes while the paramilitaries went into a state of rage and began shouting death threats.

"*Matar los Irlandeses! Matar los Irlandeses!*" (Kill the Irish! Kill the Irish!)

The noise was deafening. After a while things calmed down a bit and I got my phone call. It was good to get through and say that we were well. I did not mention the storm of threats that we had just received. The story of our transfer had been in the Irish papers and on Irish television news. Martin took his call and then the two of us were taken back to reception. Niall and our Colombian friend, Marine, had been taken back while we were on the phone.

I saw my reflection in the one-way glass while walking past the guards' office. It was the first time since our heads were shaved that I had seen my reflection. I did not look very nice, but then there was no one here to look nice for.

On the way out, Martin got the guard to bring us to the shop in the next *pabellón* to buy cigarettes. We were outside the gate to the shop trying to order biscuits and a biro as well. The guards could not understand what we wanted so they let us into the shop to point out to them what we required. We got two biros, three packets of cigarettes and three packets of biscuits. The two guards took tubs of sweets for themselves – all on Niall's account! That's how the system works. All our money had been put in Niall's account. We were extremely lucky that a couple of weeks previously our visitors had left us in a good bit of money. Here, without money in the account, life would be very bleak.

As we got our stuff in the shop, we saw a few heads in the hatch inside *Pabellón* 7. It was the drugs and extradition prisoners who had been moved from La Picota where they had shared Patio B with us. There were a lot of shouted greetings between them and us.

We were taken back to the reception cells and were locked up for the night but we had given Niall and our friend their share of the biscuits. I thought about the tensions in *Pabellón* 8. If we were moved into a *pabellón* with the paramilitaries, there would be a riot and a lot of blood would be spilled. Cómbita was a powder keg and we were the sparks. We shouted out the news that we had got on the phone so as to share it with each other. By now we had been in so many prisons that we had friends and enemies everywhere in the prison system.

I awoke early next morning because I had gone to sleep very early the previous night. The light went on and shortly afterwards the guard opened the cell door. *Baño!* I came back shivering and got into bed to warm up. When the breakfast came, I got up and took in the food through the door grill. It was coffee, a bun and a tangerine.

Martin was outside the door. How he got out of his cell I don't know, but cigarettes work wonders here. We had a hurried conversation and then he went on to talk to Niall. After a few minutes he returned to his cell, with a lit cigarette in his hand.

Niall was shouting from the cell next door that yesterday at the shop was an indication of how the system works. You let them get stuff on your account or get stuff to give the guards for favours. All went quiet for a few minutes. Then, Niall burst into song.

"The Auld Triangle went jingle jangle
Along the banks of the Royal Canal."

I was thinking about the guard with the video camera, filming me getting my head shaved. I could have made a defiant speech, but I never think of what to say in time – it is always too late when I come up with the good response. Anyway, the use of the camera may just have been INPEC's taking routine film as they often did. I would be at a big disadvantage in this Spanish-speaking environment until I got fluent in the language.

The lights were going on and off at random. Was there an electrical fault or was it just a guard messing around with the switches? Had the jail a generator or did it rely on the electrical power lines? The guerrillas were said to have attacked Cómbita some time ago when it was being built. They had got as far as the outer walls when they came under fire from an army detachment and had to withdraw. If the guerrillas attacked again and overran the prison, would I go with them into the mountains? I would be all for it, but that was a decision for all three of us. There would probably be no choice anyway, and spending years in Cómbita relying on Colombian justice was not a wise idea.

Would my leg hold up to going over the mountains? The army would probably kill any escapees that they came across and the helicopters would be a problem on the open mountainside. I would be happier in the jungle with cover from the air but the jungle was far away. What could we do for the guerrillas? Nothing, but nothing was sufficient. We were now objects of propaganda – the army had built up an image of us as very dangerous Irish rebels who trained the guerrillas to levels of skill with explosives that they had never achieved before.

Our rescue by the guerrillas would be a major propaganda coup against the army and the Colombian state. All we would have to do is try to stay alive and try to get back home to Ireland.

Yesterday, one of the more senior guards had told Niall that we would shortly be moved to one of the *pabellones*. Then we would get back a lot of the possessions that had been taken from us at reception, such as clothes and books, and we would be able to buy things in the shop.

We were told that our papers had still not arrived and so we would not be moved yet but that they would arrange a phone call. We discussed how long it might take to get things sorted out. The judge was supposed to have a maximum of ten days to reply to a *tutela*. INPEC would not take any decision but would refer it to their political boss, who was Señor Londoño, the ultra-right-wing Minister for Justice and the Interior. The diplomatic people would have a say as they had to deal with the Irish Embassy. The next and crucial phase of our trial would start on 5 February. It was now 18 December so we had about nine weeks in which to prepare our defence. Having been moved to Cómbita was a very serious interruption of our trial preparations.

From what we had been able to find out about Cómbita, it seems that while we were in the reception cells we would get one hour of sun a day if that suited the guards. We would then be transferred to *Pabellón* 8 where we would be locked up for twenty-four hours a day until they decided which *pabellón* we would be held in for the rest of our time in Cómbita. That could take up to three weeks. After that there would be a dramatic change because then we would be locked out in an open yard from dawn to dusk, which was twelve hours in this part of the world. Our heads would be shaved every few weeks and sunburn would be a serious problem because at 3,000 metres above sea level ultra-violet radiation is intense.

We discussed the guards through the cell door grills. Which ones were good, which bad? Who would accept a cigarette in exchange for giving Martin a light? We felt we were gradually breaking them down or at least getting to know who might be helpful. Why were we moved from La Modelo? If it was to have better security for us, as it seems they told the Ambassador, then this was the wrong place to send us. I remembered the screaming and abuse of the paramilitaries yesterday. Were they deliberately setting us up? What did they really tell the Irish Embassy? More questions then answers. The man who gave the INPEC Rapid Reaction Force their orders was a general because we heard the calls in the van. Was it an INPEC general or an army general? La Modelo was not safe either. We agreed that the situation had expanded to include diplomatic, legal and human rights elements.

There was a lot of movement by the guards and the rumour was that thirty-four new prisoners had arrived at reception. We had heard helicopters earlier, but they could have been giving air cover to a road convoy or transferring prisoners. We had no way of telling which.

All went quiet again. I had noticed that the towel was still damp from the shower this morning. Nothing dried fast in this dark, miserable concrete cube.

I thought about the possibility of our lawyers making a public call for a whistle-blower from the US Embassy. While only a few of the two thousand employed there would have been directly involved in fabricating the false evidence against us, more would have known about it. A lot of Latin Americans believed that there was a long-standing culture of criminality in the US State Department, directed against them. It is a disgrace to the Constitution, the flag and the people of the United States. Of the thousands of soldiers and civilians who must know what goes on, were there not a few who would put their career and pension on the line to uphold the honour of their country?

All the cells had been filled with new prisoners. Niall called to ask if anyone had been put in with me. I replied that I was still on my own. So was Martin. The guards had put two in every cell except for ours. Niall had been told they had orders to keep us on our own and separated.

My pullover, my most valuable possession in that place, had started to unravel at the seam on the left side. I had intended asking Anne to bring me a needle and thread, but that was when I was in La Modelo. There the guards did not mind what was brought in as long as it was not a gun or drink or drugs. Anne had been very good to me by bringing in small things that made life a bit more comfortable. She brought butter to put on the spuds for an Irish dinner that we prepared now and again. She brought envelopes and nail clippers. On the previous visit, she had brought me a roll of adhesive tape that I used to stick up the Christmas cards. Now that we were far from Bogotá, there would probably be no more of these Sunday visits. To stop the unravelling, I bit off the hem of one of the blankets in order to get a thread. Then I used the top of the biro to push it through the wool so that I could repair the seam.

Looking out from my cell door grille I could see one of the new prisoners standing at his cell door. He was wearing a blanket to keep warm. Many prisoners had been captured in the hot low-lying plains and were dressed in little more than a T-shirt and light trousers and canvas runners. When I was in La Picota in Bogotá, I had shared my warm clothes with poorly dressed prisoners, but La Picota was not nearly as cold as Cómbita was.

Our Colombian friend Marine was telling the other prisoners that he was with the Irish. He seemed quite pleased about that. He said that he was charged in connection with a car bomb that blew up the main police headquarters in Bogotá a few weeks ago.

Niall said that over one hundred prisoners had come in and they were all from Medellín.

It was getting late when my door opened and a guard threw in a black bin liner of clothes. Martin appeared in the doorway with his mattress: good things happened, even on bad nights! There was no room for his mattress except on the floor so we put it there and made up his bed. We settled down to talking and continued long after one of the guards turned out the light.

Next day the cell door was opened and the guards came in and took Martin's mattress. They said that other cells had three or four men and no mattresses for them. Martin would have to share the bed with me. He complained that I snored but I wouldn't believe it – although he was not the first to make that complaint!

A few days before Christmas we heard one of the guards reading our names and details into a phone. Were we about to be moved to the *pabellones*? Or back to Bogotá? Niall succeeded in getting back our book of evidence so that at least we would have a bit of fiction to read. The bad news was that the books they had seized were officially considered to be subversive and would not be returned. *Joe Cahill – A Life in the IRA* might have a few anti-Brit comments, but *Leaving Cert Maths* was a new brand of subversion!

We were going over the book of evidence again, and among the papers included by the military at the last sitting was a training manual in Spanish. Our lawyers had pointed out that it must be a forgery by getting the military intelligence man to admit that guerrillas would address each other as "comrade" or some such term and never as "the subversives". On reading it and a book in English also entered as evidence, called *Weapons of Terror*, we realised that the Spanish was a direct translation from the English language book and that *Weapons of Terror* was an ordinary book available in bookshops. This was a level of incompetence almost beyond belief: they not only gave a direct translation from a book, but gave us the original too! The intention military intelligence apparently had was to make a guerrilla training manual in Spanish with small handwritten notes in English, to indicate the presence of English-speaking instructors.

On Saturday 21 December there was an amazing development: a guard arrived at our cell door with post! After we had arrived at our previous prison, La Modelo, we had been without mail for three weeks, until people got our new address and sent new letters. Now I got a package from my family containing excellent artwork by the kids and a book called *Street Spanish*, which was very useful. I also got a card from Maureen in Co. Meath – an old friend and very good worker in the 'Bring Them Home' campaign. The third letter was from Emmett, a good supporter in *Tar Isteach*. The guard slipped Emmett's letter out of the envelope and opened it. There was a half-tone image of Ché Guevara on every page. I was asked about the image and said that it was of a famous Irishman. The guard did not believe a word of it and took the subversive letter away. (Actually, Ché Guevara had an Irish grandfather called Lynch.)

A bit later, the four of us were allowed to make a phone call. Our hands handcuffed behind our backs, we were brought towards *Pabellón 8*. There were no phone cards on sale there so Niall was brought away over to *Pabellón 1* to get phone cards.

As we stood waiting on the roadway outside *Pabellón 8*, I could see some of the countryside around the prison. We were in a valley surrounded by mountain peaks and there was good farmland around the prison. I could see a farmhouse, quite like an Irish one except for the reddish tiled roof. In front of it on the hills were fields of maize and what looked like coffee bushes. There were some cattle grazing but they were too far away for me to make out whether they were the type we are used to in Ireland or the humped back type that are common in Colombia. The mountains ran down to foothills that were quite near the walls of the prison and there were extensive areas of pine trees.

The guards were having a good time chatting to us about Ireland but occasionally asking about what we were doing in the zone. Everyone seemed to believe that we were training the FARC in the use of explosives: it was a more interesting idea than to accept that we were there to learn about the peace process.

Niall returned with the other guards and, more importantly, with the phone cards, and we went into *Pabellón* 8. The phone was a little out of the direct line of sight and so most of the prisoners could not see us; the ones who could waved to us or gave the thumbs–up sign. There was no repeat of the wild shouting from the paramilitaries that had happened the previous time we had made phone calls there.

Back in reception, we shouted our news between the cells. We told each other the things we had learned from the phone calls. We had mixed feelings about the coming family visits in January. Should they risk travelling from Bogotá?

Another bit of news was that an article in *El Tiempo*, the biggest daily paper in Colombia, had been very critical of Cómbita on human rights grounds and especially about the bad treatment of visitors on family visits. Children could only visit once every forty–five days instead of once every thirty days as in other high security prisons. There was a forty–five–minute conjugal visit once in forty–five days while it had been for three hours once every thirty days in La Picota. Of course, I was aware that with the sex–obsessed form of Christianity in Ireland, the authorities there would not even consider giving a prisoner a conjugal visit at all.

After dinner, we were brought out to the exercise cage for our hour of sun. At the end of the hour a squad of guards arrived and we were told that we were being moved to *Pabellón 6*.

The four of us were taken out of the exercise cage and told to strip naked in the passage beside it. I was getting used to being naked. It was best not to think about it, as feelings of humiliation were no good in helping to cope with life in jail. Another guard came with a metal detector and put it between our legs to see if we had any internal metal objects. Our clothes were searched minutely and given back to us. We were brought back to our cell where we packed our belongings into bin liner bags.

As soon as I came out of the cell door, a guard took my bag from me, and he removed all the contents and searched everything again. I had a pair of laces that I had found in the cage and they were taken. I had all my things separated into the plastic bags that the blankets and sheets had come in. They were all emptied in a heap and the plastic bags thrown away. My toothpaste had been squeezed into a plastic bag and the shampoo into another. I was afraid these would leak on to my clothes so I had wrapped them up well in a piece of plastic. They were taken out and thrown on the heap. I had to put everything back in the black bin liner. Finally we were marched away. I was not sorry to leave reception.

Chapter 13

Pabellón 6

W E REACHED *PABELLÓN* 6, handcuffed and carrying our bags. Inside the big door made of solid steel, there was a space of three or four metres and then another big door made from steel bars. We had to repeat the whole performance of ten minutes earlier, of strip and search. This time they went a bit further: they confiscated the black bin liner too. Each of us piled all we had on to one of our blankets and carried the lot to the inner gate.

There were two familiar faces among the crowd of prisoners who greeted us. One was the ELN guerrilla El Chino who had been in Patio B of La Picota. He was a model prisoner with a six-year sentence now down to two years to go. He had owned the guitar that we took with us to La Modelo. The other prisoner was the M19 guerrilla who had taken part in the big riot in La Picota and as a result had spent time in a punishment cell with Niall, who had been there over our refusal to attend court for the opening of our trial. Afterwards both of them were moved on to Patio B. The M19 man's name was Manuel. He was about fifty, medium-built and weathered-looking, but he still had very dark hair and a big moustache dominated his cheerful face.

It was nice that these prisoners remembered us as comrades and were glad to meet us again. It also eased our way on to this *pabellón* and we had the paramilitaries pointed out to us, so we did not find out who they were the hard way.

There were only around twenty prisoners in the *pabellón*, with more guerrillas than paramilitaries. We were probably not in too much danger but the numbers could change very rapidly. Apart from some old hands who were in the patio to do maintenance work, everyone here was on charges and due in court. The Colombian diplomats were probably telling their Irish counterparts that we were not in with paramilitaries, only with prisoners who were not yet sentenced, because they had to be presumed innocent until proven guilty.

The four of us were allocated cells on the second level, well away from the other prisoners. Martin and I were in cell 28, the others in 27. Inside the cell were two concrete slabs sticking out of one wall, with mattresses. There were two smaller slabs sticking out of the opposite wall that served as shelves. At the end was a sink and draining board, also made of concrete. In the corner there was a stainless steel toilet.

We went back down the steel stairs to the patio to meet the other prisoners and shake hands with everyone, and be shown around. We were shown the invention that Martin had been searching for. Two men unwound about ten feet of toilet paper and doubled it over. This was then twisted to form a 'rope'. When the end was lit and it was smouldering it was hung on the wall for everyone to light up their cigarette from.

Martin brought a 'rope' back to the cell for lock-up, which was around 5.30pm. He hung it from a small barred window high up on the cell wall. After a while he lit up a cigarette. An hour later I started to cough in the white fog of smoke from the rope and the cigarette that filled the cell. The 'rope' was evicted so that it hung down the wall outside and could be pulled in when it was needed to light up. Martin went to bed happy. We had both just settled down when the light went out. Our first night on *Pabellón 6* was starting.

In the morning, ten minutes were allowed to have the shower. I had to walk the whole length of the *pabellón* to get to the showers. The concrete was cold on my bare feet, but not as ice-cold as the steel stairway. The best way to cope with the cold was to move as fast as possible, and minimise the time spent exposed to the cold air. Clouds moved in over the prison at night, covering everything in a cold fog, which often did not disperse until the mid-morning sun evaporated it.

These showers were different from any I had seen before. There were six spaces between head-high concrete walls, and each space had a hole above it that the water poured through from a tank above. The tank was flooded each morning for ten minutes. I hung my towel on the rail and went into the concrete cubicle with my soap. The shower was like an elephant pissing on you. It was a thick jet of water that came from two metres above and hammered on your head and it was cold! On the way back to the cell, Martin passed me on his way up. In the cell I dressed and gathered up what I thought I would need during the next thirteen hours while locked outside: my spoon, a notebook and biro, the book of Spanish slang, the letter from Maureen and the drawings by my kids, and of course, some toilet paper. That was it. We were out in the patio and the cell doors were locked in ten minutes.

The patio was a concrete space about fifty metres long by twenty-five wide. In the roofed end there were twelve concrete tables with concrete benches on each side, all set into the concrete floor. Breakfasts were passed out through a long narrow slit that joined the shop to the patio and we ate at the tables. There was a TV set high up on a shelf near the tables that we could watch, but it was difficult to see the picture because of the daylight.

Even before breakfast was finished, men were queuing for the phone. The phone was in the space between the entrance gates. You had to reach through the bars and lift the receiver, but you could not see the numbers clearly from that angle, so it was difficult to key in the correct numbers. I got my turn after waiting in line for about an hour.

I phoned home to let them know that I was out of reception and into a fairly permanent place – depending on whether our lawyers' request to the judge resulted in us being moved back to Bogotá or not. Later in the day I got another call in to my brother, Gerry. We talked about possible arrangement for the January visit and what he should bring over for me.

I spent a good bit of the day walking in the open patio, talking Spanish with other prisoners and getting to know them. The day was cloudy with short bits of sunshine. There was a football match between a five-a-side selection and I watched that too. I began to realise that the top of my head was being burned, even though there was not much direct sun. The Irish head is not made for sunshine, especially when it is shaved. The hair was growing back but was still far too short to provide any protection. I tried to avoid being in the direct sunlight but even in the shadows the high altitude sun burnt into my scalp and arms. It was a long time since I had spent so much time in the open air.

I had not dressed for a day of bitter cold in the morning and burning sun for the rest of the day.

After the mid-day meal, the three of us were talking on the top level where we had gone to look at the mountains. The guards came into the patio and up to where we were. After speaking with them Niall said that we were moving again. Where to? Another patio? Bogotá? The move was only to cells across on the other side of the patio and on ground level. Our new homes were to be cells number twenty-five and twenty-six. Martin and I threw all our belongings into a blanket and completed the move in about fifteen minutes; Niall and Marine were even faster. There are travellers in Ireland who have not shifted home as often! Most of the other prisoners were watching a soccer match on TV. Colombians are really keen on soccer. When the four of us had finished moving, we sat and talked with the few guerrilla prisoners who were not watching the match.

After a day out in the air, we were tired – especially Martin who had played in the football match. Martin had his 'rope' out the window but fell asleep without using it.

The routine of *Pabellón 6* soon became apparent. Back in the cell after the shower I packed the same few things that I would need for the day and a vest to put on my head as protection from the sun. I had a quick shave by touch. The disposable razor was damaged in the move and gave a bad shave, cutting my face, but looks did not matter here. I took my own white towel and the prison issue one out to wash them along with most of my spare clothes. There was a large concrete sink and wash-board beside the toilets, and I had bought a bar of blue soap for washing clothes.

After a while, one of the paramilitaries, a big black man, came over to me and patiently explained that there was an arrangement for sending towels to a laundry every Saturday. We had just missed it. I thanked him and hung my towels and clothes on the handrail outside the cells to dry in the sun.

Breakfast was at 7am and was a bun, a boiled egg and a mug of hot *panilla* to drink.

I got a telephone call in for 9am but there was no one at home. They were on holiday. I made a call to Huila in the south of Colombia where Anne lived, and got a telephone company reply that the dialling code was not correct. The move from Bogotá to Cómbita had brought us into an area with another dialling code for reaching the south of Colombia. So I did not get to speak to anyone. I had lost all my numbers in the frequent searches and could only call those that I could remember. I booked another call for 2.30 in the afternoon, which would be 7.30pm in Ireland.

The music of *Ultima Hora* came from the TV. That meant there was an important newsflash. All of us made for the TV. The government was announcing peace talks with the paramilitaries, and the paramilitaries announced that they were on ceasefire. This had been coming since the election of Álvaro Uribe as President. Uribe had a history that put him quite close to being a paramilitary himself. He had been advocating a seat at any future peace talks for the paramilitaries and this move was a big step in that direction. They wanted their child at the table!

I was getting a bit of help with my Spanish from one of the Colombian prisoners. We were using the book of Spanish street slang as our textbook. He was doubled over laughing at how I pronounced some of the words. One of the other prisoners came over and we found that while the English and Spanish letters looked the same, the correct way of pronouncing sounds were very different. I ended up teaching them the English alphabet. Afterwards, he told me that he was doing nineteen years for homicide. I had been under the impression that this patio was for men awaiting trial.

We filled out a form with the help of the M19 guerrilla prisoner who was the *Pabellón 6* representative. The form was officially asking for the return of our books and for permission to get my painting materials in here. Such forms are filled out in very formal Spanish.

Later, when I was making a phone call to Ireland, the prisoner who said that he was doing time for homicide approached me and told me to leave money on my phone card so he could make a call. It was an order rather than a request. Of course I continued the call until the cash on the card ran out, which was only a few minutes altogether. After the call, he came to me again and explained about getting the people outside to call the prison, so saving on phone cards. Then he wanted me to give him the other card I had, so that he could make a call. I said, "No!" There were no cards in the shop and I needed the one I had to call Ireland on Christmas Day. I suggested he talk to Niall who had better Spanish. I told Niall what I thought was happening.

Niall talked to him and it was just as I thought. The prisoner was one who pressured others into buying things for him and giving him the use of their phone cards. Niall said that we needed the cards we had for home and legal calls and not to continue asking for the use of our cards. Niall then approached one of the guerrilla prisoners to find out a bit more. The man was a social prisoner in for murder, who had killed another prisoner for one of the *Caciques* or bosses. He was caught for that, and the *Cacique* who ordered the killing had refused to pay him. Now his original sentence was finished, but he was broke and awaiting trial for the second killing. That explained why he was in this *pabellón* for unsentenced prisoners. It was obviously very dangerous to have him anywhere near us, and the best way to handle such men was not to give them an inch.

As the sun was setting, it lit up the third-storey landing. The three of us climbed the steel stairs to sit in the last of the sun's rays. Martin was trying to compose another song. He had sent one out from La Modelo that he and a FARC prisoner had put together. The words were Martin's and in English. The two of them had worked on the guitar music, which was Colombian with a little Irish influence. It was judged very good back in Ireland, but seditious and libellous, not suitable to be sung in the company of lawyers. They asked for another song – one about our experience in the prisons of Colombia that would make a good impact in Ireland. Here in Cómbita, there were no guitars or other musical instruments of any kind, but we could always hum or whistle it.

Martin said to us. "I can't wait for lock-up; I want to get to bed early."

We rounded on him. "A weekend in Cómbita and the Yanks have you acclimatised!"

"You mean he's institutionalised?"

"Yes, he's institutionalised!"

We had a great laugh about that as we went down the stairs for the evening line-up and head count. A few minutes later we were locked up. The light in the cell was very poor. It was a 15-watt bulb behind a frosted plastic cover and it did not give sufficient light to read or write by in comfort. We knew that we could not continue to sleep for ten or eleven hours a night and we would have to find a way of passing the time until lights out. We could talk to each other but after a full day of talking together in the patio that was not much of an option, there was nothing left to say. However, we were not yet used to a full day out in the air and in a few minutes we were asleep in bed.

On Christmas Eve Niall and Martin brought blankets out to sit on and wrap around themselves while watching TV. It was against the rules so they wrapped the blankets up in towels. Martin hung his over the handrail beside the steel stairs while Niall left his on one of the seats beside the concrete tables, an area that the guards would not be likely to look at during the morning locking of the cells. The guards generally stayed out of the patio and watched events from behind one-way, bullet-proof glass in watchtowers at both ends. These glass observation posts resembled the bridge of a battleship.

Because we were in such close proximity to all sorts of prisoners, we used code words when referring to the FARC ('the boys') or to the paramilitaries ('the Billys'), so that it would not be apparent who we were talking about. Niall told us that another Billy had come in the previous night. Almost every day more men arrived in. The balance of guerrillas to paramilitaries was fairly equal but could change dramatically, and we felt that the tension could build and explode, probably over an issue such as access to the telephone. As the *pabellón* filled, access to the one phone would become an issue of major importance.

Talking about the new Billy, we thought that we had been sent here, not to increase our security against attack, but to lower it. We were shoulder to shoulder with paramilitaries and social prisoners here, as well as with guerrillas. The paramilitaries being on ceasefire did not make a real difference, as they would simply pay social prisoners to carry out an attack anyway. As the patio filled up over the weeks and months, an attack would become easier because of the crowds of men everywhere. The cameras would not be able to see who stabbed any one of us, especially on a wet day when everyone would be crowded into the area that was roofed over.

The mid-day meal was quite good, the best chicken and rice we had had since arriving in Cómbita. Things were looking up! Martin said that he was really looking forward to tomorrow's Christmas dinner. He thought that today's dinner was an appetiser for the really good one we would get tomorrow. It was our second Christmas in a Colombian jail.

My solicitor, Pedro, arrived at the prison, having come from Bogotá across the mountains to see us. In the visiting area near the reception block we spoke to him through a small steel grille in a glass window, the three of us gathered into a bunch around our side of the glass because it was difficult to hear what was being said. Niall translated. There was no privacy, which made it impossible to prepare a defence in confidence; four guards stood beside us listening to every word we said. Pedro told us that the danger involved in his coming to visit us would not be considered a legal reason for returning us to Bogotá. However, it appeared to our lawyers that we were moved to Cómbita without the knowledge or consent of the judge in charge of our case, and that might be a legal ground for our return.

Pedro had taken a considerable risk in coming. His reason, he said, was to see for himself that we were okay. We thanked him. On the way out he gave Niall a book about their collective's work in helping the indigenous Nasa people defend their rights. After a rigorous search, the guards allowed Niall to take the book back to *Pabellón 6*.

The indigenous people had suffered terribly from massacres and harassment. These were usually carried out by the regular army, because they suspected the indigenous tribes of supporting the guerrillas. In the past three years the paramilitaries had taken over this role to allow the army to have a better human rights record. Human rights now mattered to the army, because some good North American political figures had succeeded, against heavy opposition, in tying military aid to a particular military unit's human rights record. Equipment such as helicopters were to be used only for anti-drugs operations. It was about money and weapons, not morality. The lawyers who documented the crimes and collected the evidence were army targets because of their work.

We received another call from the guards. What was it this time, a move to different cells? Was it a move to a different *pabellón*? A move to a prison in Bogotá? None of these: it was a visit from Padre Andres, the prison chaplain who had been very good to us and to our families. He and another man had travelled for three hours to visit us on Christmas Eve. This was real Christianity. He and his assistant were given a little room which was between the gates, and they had fifteen minutes to talk to us. It was very good for our morale. He had the great foresight to bring some telephone cards so that we could ring our families on Christmas Day.

After lock-up I had letters to write to people in Ireland and to Anne to tell about our situation and to ask them to replace the lost phone numbers. When that was all done, I really was keen to get to bed. As a bonus, INPEC had increased the voltage to the cell lights so that they were at their proper brightness, which was a great help in writing the letters.

In the morning the light went on, then off. Then, after a few minutes, it went on again. The sound of a diesel generator starting and stopping in harmony confirmed that the prison had its own power source.

While the lights were acting up I decided to take the mattresses down to air them. Under the mattress on the top bunk I found a copy of *El Tiempo* with a photo of Cómbita and an article about one of the biggest drug barons in Colombia, being held here. In the article it said that there were eighty soldiers and one hundred police guarding the prison.

Pabellón 6 was one of the four that would have a special conjugal visit on Christmas Day. The other four *pabellones* would have them on New Year's Day. For the rest of the year, conjugal visits were every forty-five days. As the prisoners were taken out through the cold mist for their conjugal visits, their hands were handcuffed behind their backs. It hardly set a romantic mood!

There were eleven prisoners still inside at 9am. The sun shone down from a deep blue sky, sending us into the shadows for fear of being burned.

I got in an excellent bit of Spanish practice with the M19 guerrilla. He was telling me about the time M19 took over the Palace of Justice in Bogotá in 1985 and took a lot of senior members of the judiciary hostage. The military stormed the building and over one hundred people were killed, including eleven members of the Supreme Court. Since then most of the M19 guerrillas had changed sides and joined the government. My friend did not agree with their changing sides.

The Christmas Day dinner was one of rice, beans, banana and vegetable with fruit juice afterwards. Martin was not happy. He had been looking forward to a big leg of roast turkey. Niall said that yesterday's meal, which had included a leg of chicken, was the Christmas dinner. Martin thought that it was an appetiser. Christmas, it seemed, was celebrated on 24 December in Colombia.

All the men came back from their conjugal visits smiling and happy in spite of the handcuffs and the short time. It was supposed to be a visit from 7am to 11am, which included a forty-five-minute conjugal visit, but some of the men were not taken out of the *pabellón* until around 9am. Their wives and girlfriends would have travelled very long journeys and paid a lot of money to get to Cómbita and home again, and they only got half the visiting time allowed. Even so, prisoners were so glad to have a Christmas visit that they did not complain.

I had a phone call booked for 12.30pm. The idea was that I would ring home and when the phone was answered, I would hang up so that they could ring the phone here in *Pabellón 6*. It would enable me to make several calls on my phone card. The reason for the call and the return call was that the phones in the prisons had the bell disconnected so they did not ring. It was very difficult to get and hold on to a phone at any exact time, so it often did not work out if they said they would ring at an agreed time. Around Christmas, they were quite likely to tell you that all transatlantic lines are busy anyway.

All the lines across the ocean were busy so I was lucky to get through at all. The phone rang and rang, but no answer. What could have happened? My kids were to be in the house all day with the family. I tried again and by great good luck got through. Nóra had heard the phone ring the first time but the party was in full swing and by the time she got to the phone it had stopped ringing. She was ready the second time. We had a good chat and instead of her trying to ring back we just let the card run out. Niall had news from one of his many brothers that Christy Moore would be ringing us at 3pm. Niall was trying to get Christy's number because of the uncertainty of him being able to get through.

I was reading a bit of the lawyer's book about the massacres of the indigenous Nasa people. The word 'immunity' was frequently mentioned. The paramilitaries had immunity, which meant that the state would not charge them with any crimes committed in relation to killing guerrillas or guerrilla supporters. They considered the Nasa tribe to be guerrilla supporters. Immunity was not a formal thing; it was more a fact that was evident to the legal observers and to the victims. It struck a chord because only a matter of months earlier President Bush had been insisting that not only US soldiers in Colombia but also his government's civilian employees must have immunity from criminal charges on a range of serious crimes. The Colombian government granted it for the next seven years.

Christy Moore did not get through. Martin spent fifteen minutes on the phone but no call came in. He would hold down the lever for ten seconds, and then release it for ten and so on. With every release he would talk into it and listen.

By the time lock-up came I was feeling tired and had a touch of sunburn on the top of my head. The light had reverted back to a dull 15 watts. Christmas day was over in Cómbita.

The next day we learned from Niall's brother that Christy Moore had tried for hours but could not get through to Cómbita. Later we found out why: INPEC had blocked all incoming calls.

We had an interesting talk with one of the better-off prisoners who was here on a drugs related charge. It seems that the Federal Bureau of Prisons rules have no standing in Colombian domestic law and that they are being challenged in the courts one by one. The government is fighting in the courts against its own laws and in favour of North American laws. INPEC is afraid that they may end up having to pay compensation to some well-represented prisoners and then have to change the rules back to the original ones. In the meantime, as always, there is one law for the rich and none for the poor but if the rich win out in this case it will benefit everyone.

There was a five-a-side football match in the really hot sun. The teams included Martin (in goals), guerrillas, paramilitaries and drugs prisoners and, of course, the harmless-sounding 'social' prisoners. They played hard on the hot concrete patio while the rest of us watched and cheered.

The 'social' prisoner who had wanted my phone card made two attempts to get in touch with me again. As I was walking with Martin, he joined us and put his arm around my shoulder in the 'old friends' manner. I bent over so that his hand passed over my head. I told him that I had a lot to talk about with Martin. He went off but returned later offering to teach me Spanish. Again I said that I was busy in a conversation. I felt he might be tempted by the big money offer from the paramilitaries.

Other things came and went but there always seemed to be a game of parquets in progress. They also played chess or cards and quite a lot of dominos but parquets was the clear favourite. The board was like a ludo board and was played with two dice; each player had four pieces. The objective was to get all four pieces round the board before anyone else could. If you landed on another player, they had to go back to the start, and if you failed to take another player when you could have, then

CHESS PLAYERS   COMBITA COLOMBIA   Sé 10°

you went back to the start. Good players were extremely difficult to beat, and the game was a lot more difficult than it appeared at first sight.

I started playing dominos with one of the prisoners, and we were joined by one of the paramilitary chiefs. One game led to another, and I was also learning a few words of Spanish. Suddenly, it was past 2pm. Past my time on the phone! When I got to it, I was relieved to find that it was free. The shortage of phone cards had worked in my favour. I dialled and got in touch with Anne, who told me that on the Sunday morning we were moved, she had been in the visiting queue and later spent hours phoning prisons to find out where we had gone. We were effectively 'disappeared' for three days; only then had she found out that we were in Cómbita.

On Saturday 28 December we learned about an article that had appeared in one of the US papers reporting that two witnesses would be brought to our trial under heavy military protection on 5 February. The witnesses were guerrillas who had deserted and were now in the hands of the army. One of them at least had been in prison since December 2001 and had refused to appear when called to give evidence earlier this month. The army intelligence men would be schooling them on the evidence they should give, because they now had access to the entire range of defence statements.

The normal procedure was that witnesses were cross-examined by the prosecution, the defence and the *Procuradora* in the early part of the trial process. All that should have been completed and handed over by *Fiscalía* to the judge who would conduct the trial. This was not done in the case of the witness held in custody since December 2001. The judge had for some reason accepted that it could be left until during the trial to do it.

We were aware that our case was causing a division among the judiciary between those who insisted that the verdict be based on the evidence, and those who wanted to deliver the verdict that the Colombian and US governments clearly wanted. It seemed to me that our judge, who was respected as an honest man, was buckling under the pressure.

The last night of the year was a night of broken sleep. The lights came on during the night and woke me up. Eventually I went back to sleep. The morning was very dark and colder than usual, and the lights went out again while it was still dark. Martin and I were walking around the patio to keep warm, with Niall following about five paces behind singing:

> "Tie a yellow ribbon round the old oak tree.
> I'm giving up the smokes and telling bad jokes.
> Will you still want me?"

Martin was on his last day before he was to give up smoking for the New Year.

Sometimes there was something worth watching on the patio TV set, such as the news or a film. However, this day's news was mostly a list of new taxes to pay for the war. Colombia was sliding into a situation like that of Argentina where it might have to default on its foreign debt – thanks to the war and the neo-liberal economy. *El Tiempo* had reported that the diet of most people in Bogotá had deteriorated and that many children were going to school hungry. The gap between the elite and the ordinary people was increasing.

The items left in by visitors on Sunday were delivered to the prisoners in a wheelie bin. They were mostly clothes and some books, magazines, newspapers, phone cards and stationery. From seeing what was allowed in for other prisoners we had a better idea about what to ask our visitors to bring us next month. I could tell them by phone.

The New Year's Day breakfast was a special Colombian dish consisting of corn and chicken boiled in a banana leaf. It was better than the Christmas dinner, I thought. The day started with the cold morning mist that gave way to a beautiful sunny sky.

Martin was on the phone to home and came back with the word that his wife, Cristin, would be visiting on 12 January. I was pleased for his sake, but it did indicate that there was not going to be a simultaneous visit by members from all three families this time. I could see that it would be difficult or impossible to co-ordinate three families every time that there was a visit, as people had work and babysitter problems. We got a family visit about once in three or four months. Being in prison in a different culture made family visits all the more precious. I tried to phone Gerry to find out when he planned to come, but he was not at home.

This was Martin's first morning in twenty years without a cigarette. He was walking around kicking a football in front of him. It was lucky that we had no patio cat or it would have got kicked too!

On the news, they said that of all the staple foods in Colombia, potatoes were now the most expensive. Last year, 30,000 small farmers who grew potatoes were put out of business by subsidised imported potatoes that Colombia was forced to allow as part of the neo-liberal open market. Having destroyed the local producers, the importers put up the prices to everyone.

The main reason why *campesinos* or small farmers in Colombia took the very real risks of growing drug crops was that neo-liberal economic policies had ruined the markets for their food crops. They had to sell some crop to survive. The crops mostly grown were cocaine and opium poppies. The indigenous people and *campesinos* often grew the crops in jungle clearings created by burning the trees. North American mercenaries flew light planes to spray chemicals similar to the 'agent orange' that did so much harm in Vietnam. It killed all the food crops as well, but while the food crops died, the cocaine bushes could be cut back to ground level and would have grown back in five or six weeks. The 'fumigations' were wiping out cultures that had survived the brutality of the Spanish conquest and the neglect of the Colombian elite. Even the right-wing Colombian government was not keen on the 'fumigation', but they were puppets in the hands of Washington and did as they were told.

A tiny amount of cocaine was enough for a user to get high. Over 500 tons of it a year went to the US. If it were alcohol, would they be justified in spraying poison on French wine-growing areas? It was their citizens who were taking the stuff – who were paying the big money. If the buyers were not there, then the poor countries would not have the problem of the producers. Killing all around them in Latin America was an immoral and politically easy cop-out.

A *campesino* got €0.30 a bag for cocaine leaves and so they made around €25 for a family-sized clearing. They could get two or three crops a year, but after three years the land would be exhausted and they would have to abandon it and burn more jungle to make a new clearing. Out of the money they made, they had to pay for things that they needed, such as a chainsaw and petrol and an outboard motor for their canoe to get the bags of leaves to a buyer. As well as all their other problems, drug traffickers exploited them, and paramilitaries tried to take over their land. The guerrillas taxed the buyers, but the buyers passed it on to the growers. The big money was made after the drugs were refined.

The vast majority of the suffering caused by the anti-drugs part of Plan Colombia was caused to the poor and unimportant growers in remote areas of Colombia. No crops were poisoned by aerial spraying in paramilitary controlled areas, only in guerrilla controlled or disputed areas, because the main objective was counter-insurgency, not counter-drugs. It was an excuse to devastate areas of support for the guerrillas. The goal was to destroy the economic base, destroy the food, and poison the water.

If the anti-drugs war had been genuine, it would have concentrated on the supply network within the US and on rehabilitating drug users. Both of these are far more cost effective than trying to destroy drugs supplies in the source countries, according to US studies, yet the vast majority of funding was for attacking drugs in source countries. By operating as it did, the anti-drugs war had given the US immense influence in the police forces and military of Latin American countries. It was a mechanism of counter-insurgency, of intelligence gathering and of control, aimed at foreign policy objectives; it was not a serious attempt to deal with the drugs problem within the United States.

Niall asked one of the paramilitaries why he had joined them. His story was that he was a soldier in an army unit that had carried out a massacre of suspected FARC supporters. The guerrillas found out that he was a soldier in that unit and they killed all his family and grandparents, so he joined the paramilitaries for revenge.

Niall was told by the FARC prisoners that Robinson, who was in *Pabellón 5*, had sent word that he was giving his protection to the Irish. This was very good news for us because he was giving his word that he would deal with anyone who attacked us. Robinson was not to be taken lightly.

Martin was back to his normal twenty cigarettes a day. He asked one of the guards to lend him twenty until the shop opened at 3pm and amazingly the guard did. Cómbita was not the place to give up smoking.

I got through to Anne on the phone and learned that she had spent Christmas Day in La Modelo talking to some prisoners who did not have anyone to visit them. She said that almost every single prisoner had asked about us and about our conditions. It was a very kind thing that she did.

Niall had phoned home and got the news that legal observers from the Brehon Law Society in the US would be coming, and that Steve McCabe, the president of the society, would personally attend the trial on 5 February. I had spoken to them when they had visited La Modelo and I had no doubt that they were good people, concerned about injustice and the very real possibility of a serious miscarriage of justice in our case.

A shortage of phone cards was a source of anxiety for Martin, as he needed cards to keep in touch with his wife during her journey to Cómbita from Ireland. The main danger she faced was at Bogotá as her visa read: 'Purpose of visit – To visit a prisoner'. There were very few Irish prisoners in Colombia so it would be easy for any official to guess which prisoner. A lot of state officials supported the Billys and would pass on information to them. She could be kidnapped and held for ransom as a result.

I read the December issue of *Semana*, a popular Spanish language magazine that was left in for some prisoner on a visit, which was being passed around. I could manage reading a bit better than speaking. We got two mentions in it, although not by name. The first was the mischievous piece by Colin Powell.

The second article was from army sources and said that there had been a rise of 500 per cent in deaths of security forces from land-mines. Their casualties from land-mines had risen from 30 in 2001 to 141 in 2002. They downplayed the fact that the end of the peace process brought a massive increase in the level of fighting, with the invasion of the peace zone.

An official in the Colombian Justice Ministry had promised to notify the defence lawyers and the international observers on 7 January if the army witnesses would be attending the trial, and which other witnesses for the prosecution would be attending. The judge in the trial had also given an undertaking to supply the same information to the defence. That left the defence with four weeks' notice if our witnesses would be required to travel from Ireland.

The army witnesses against us were teenagers or in their early twenties, deserters from the FARC. Two of them seemed fairly sure to appear in court and another seemed to have disappeared.

The FARC and ELN guerrillas, we had learned through our dicussions with fellow prisoners, were organised in 'Fronts', each of which fought in their own area of the country and was self-contained. The 'Front' recruited, trained, financed and fought almost independently of the rest of the country. The advantage of this loose organisation was good security against infiltration by enemy intelligence that could result in harming the whole struggle. It also had the advantage that any local military disaster would not bring down the whole struggle. The main disadvantage was that central military control and political development is made very uneven and difficult. The 'Front' system of organisation had proved durable over decades of conflict in the jungle and mountains.

The FARC seemed to have problems transferring itself from rural to urban guerrilla warfare, however. Over the last forty years there had been a spectacular growth in the population of cities and towns, so that now about 70 per cent of the people lived in urban areas. It followed that in future guerrilla warfare would have to adapt to the cities.

Life for the guerrillas was tough. Marching over mountains and through the jungle and swamps or across the open plains was difficult and dangerous. Even when there was no army, no helicopters or bombers, no paramilitaries, there were blistered feet, mosquitoes and snakes. Before putting on Wellington boots in the morning, they had to check for scorpions inside. They wore Wellingtons because of the wet conditions, but these caused fungal infections of the feet. Some guerrillas eventually couldn't take it any more and deserted. The army captured some of them and squeezed any useful information out of them.

They ended up in jail while the army checked them out. They might face charges of rebellion or more serious charges, especially if army intelligence felt that they were holding back information. They were putty in the hands of army intelligence. They could be schooled on the evidence they might give against captured guerrillas. While there were some good honest judges, in general the judicial system was just another part of the state's repressive apparatus.

Our lawyers assured us that they were very well practised in breaking down false witnesses and did not expect much difficulty in that aspect of the trial.

On one day each week men from *Pabellón 6* would join a group who were brought to the football field. I watched prisoners playing football. Even though I didn't play, I enjoyed the bit of time away from *Pabellón 6* and walking barefoot on the grass. The day was so hot that in fact I spent most of the time lying on the grass.

As I was watching, I could see that both Niall and Martin were trying their best, not the most skilful on the field but always where the action was. Marine, our Colombian pal from the move to Cómbita, was very fit, very quick-witted and game. A good guerrilla of his age would be like that, and so would a good intelligence man. It struck me as a possibility that he could be here to guard us, to see that we came to no harm, or possibly to see that we did not escape.

On balance, I think that he was a very capable FARC guerrilla sent into Bogotá to carry out a very difficult attack on the police headquarters. Still, you had to think about things, to consider possibilities without getting paranoid. After all, a general had ordered the move that brought the four of us together in the van that morning, when we were on our way to the helicopter that brought us here.

Chapter 14

Raids, Conditions, and a New FARC Leader

O N TUESDAY 7 January we were subjected to a sudden raid. We had
gone over to watch the news on TV at 7am. Just then a crowd of
guards came in through the front gate, then more and more guards
arrived. Instead of the usual head count, it was a search. They switched
off the TV and ordered us to stand in two long lines in the patio. A
guard armed with a very long baton with metal ends faced each prisoner. We were told to strip off. It was freezing cold and I had more
clothes on than most of the other prisoners. I took my time at taking
off my clothes to minimise the time that I would be naked in the cold.
The guard in front of me was okay in that he saw what I was doing and
did not pressure me to go faster. Eventually, I had everything off.

Men on each side of me were being ordered to squat down and I
knew that I could not do so because of my injured knee. The guard did
not push it and I put on my clothes again. I was shivering with the
cold. We were all herded into a space near the TV while the cells were
searched. All the time the activity was being filmed on video camera by
one of the guards.

As suddenly as they had arrived, the sea of guards withdrew out of
the patio. I went and checked my things and the wet towel drying on
the railing. Everything seemed okay.

Martin received disappointing news. Cristin could not come on
the visit. Her family were just too worried about her travelling to
Cómbita. A visit meant so much when there were so few of them. The
news that it was not to happen was hard to take.

Martin was walking around in the mid-day sun while everyone
else was sitting in the shade. He was still preoccupied by the visit
being cancelled. About an equal number of prisoners were playing
parquets or dominos. There was one man on the phone and two

watching football on the TV. I had washed a towel, a T-shirt and a vest and hung them on the second floor railings to dry. It was exactly like every other day in Cómbita.

We had discussed all the usual topics so much that there was nothing new that could be said. On the 12.30pm TV news they showed the scene of an ambush by the FARC that killed five soldiers and injured the remaining three in a patrol not far from Bogotá. We wondered were the guerrillas really on the defensive in the face of the army build-up, or were they forcing the army to go into the jungle after them.

We got word from our lawyers that our appeal to the judge against getting moved out of Bogotá had been turned down. Before they could appeal that decision, we had to be officially notified by the judge's office. This has not happened yet. Judge Acosta would be back from holidays during the week. There seemed to be a level of trust between our lawyers and the judge.

The cell doors were opened about fifteen minutes early. When we went to our cell, we saw why. Everything was thrown in a heap on my bed, the bottom bunk. It took the full fifteen minutes to sort everything out and tidy up. At the head count, Martin said that he would find out if this morning's strip search were open to legal challenge. It was very likely that mass strip searches were classified as inhuman and degrading treatment under the UN Charter of Human Rights that Colombia had signed up to.

Shortly after the 7am news the next morning about fifty guards came in. Here we go again, I thought. They made us line up in the two lines. Some guards went around and took all the blankets that men had taken out to the patio to keep themselves warm. They also opened and then shut all the ground floor cells for some reason known only to themselves. I did not bring out a blanket so I did not lose mine. The nights in the cells without blankets would be extremely cold, and Niall had lost one of his blankets.

The mail that should have been delivered on Saturday arrived. We got a load of Christmas cards and two or three letters each. In all, I got thirty-two items. I was delighted. It had all been posted to La Modelo and forwarded. In among Niall's mail was a letter from Padre Andres containing four 20,000-peso phone cards. Niall kept two cards because he also had to phone the lawyers and Caitríona. Martin and I got one each. A 20,000-peso card would give about ten minutes to Ireland.

I got through on the phone to Ireland. My ten-year-old son Dónal took the call. He told me that he would photocopy the comic strip that he had made and send it to me. It was based on *The Lord of the Rings* characters but with his own plot. It was seven pages long. He had drawn and coloured the pictures. Usually it was my daughter Nóra who drew comics for me and they were based on *Buffy the Vampire Slayer* or on her own imagination of haunted castles. She was good at art for a twelve-year-old. Both of them in quite different ways had good imaginations and liked to draw pictures and even comic books of what they imagined.

A guard on the front gate returned the confiscated blankets. I was glad to see that they were not being vindictive. After lock-up, there was no shortage of reading material with all the post that I had got for Christmas. As well as the post from Ireland, there were cards from Australia and Canada and quite a lot from Philadelphia in the US.

Niall was on the phone to the lawyers' office. There were no new developments about us getting moved back to Bogotá, but the first legal opinion was that mass strip searching was against the human rights law that Colombia had signed up to. If further legal investigation confirmed this, then we could set the stage where demands could be made that the prisons have to be run to the standards of the United Nations Convention on Human Rights and not to the inhuman and degrading practices of the US Federal Bureau of Prisons. The next move might be to get the Defensoría del Pueblo involved.

If we were going to have to live in Colombian high security prisons, then it was worth getting a few blows of a baton or months in solitary to improve conditions. Strip searching in open patios, abysmal visiting conditions and no constructive training or education were issues to start with. Lack of adequate mail for foreigners and lack of adequate access to the telephone for prisoners awaiting trial were other issues. Perhaps the most important issues in terms of the right to stay alive in prison were that there be separate patios for guerrillas and paramilitaries.

A newly arrived Billy, known as Cat's Eyes, wasted no time in taking them over. The older leader seemed quite content to hand over the reins of power. The new man was dynamic and had taken on a lot of the small jobs that no one else wanted, but which made the place run smoothly. He was not hostile to us, but that would count for nothing if he were to get an order from outside to have us killed.

Niall was on the phone again and told us that the legal opinion of the *colectivo* was that the mass strip searches were illegal and they had notified the Defensoría del Pueblo. In the next few days we could expect Patricia or her local representative to visit us looking for statements about what had happened.

We were expecting our lawyers to come to Cómbita on a visit that afternoon. The question of risk for them in visiting us was very real, but they were willing to chance it. The three of us had spent hours preparing a list of the topics that we needed to cover. We needed to consult in relative privacy and not on the telephone with the prison service, INPEC, the DAS and military intelligence all listening in. This was a great country to have a persecution complex in, because the bad things that you imagined were only the half of it; reality was always worse!

Niall showed us a beautiful moth that had landed in the patio. It was a light green colour on the wings and gold on the body, but it was definitely a moth because of the heavy body. It was about three centimetres across. A few days ago, there was a big one about six centimetres across the wings. It was a speckled brown and black that looked exactly like two large eyes looking from between two leaves. The leaves were the wings and it had a spine in each, just like a real leaf.

As evening came, it was clear that we would not get a visit from our lawyers. Perhaps they would come some day next week.

After lock-up, the lights were working normally on mains electricity. The light holder had a bulb and two fluorescent tubes. The two tubes were on. We felt tired after the day so there was not a lot of talking between us.

Niall watched the 7pm news on the TV. That was quite a feat as his cell door is a good 35 metres away from it. The Defence Minister, speaking on the topic of recent guerrilla attacks using new technology, such as the radio-controlled cars that carried explosives to their targets, had spoken about Irish and Spanish influences being involved. It seemed that there was a shift in emphasis away from the three of us and towards a generalised Irish and Spanish (Basque) influence. It was not exactly a climb down, more a backing off.

Anne came on a visit. She had a really bad time getting in, and was strip searched, but she persisted and eventually got two hours out of the four she should have got. She had asked the guards for a letter I sent out but did not receive it. (Items for exchange are not passed directly between prisoner and visitor. They have to go through the guards in advance.) The letter was opened and eventually returned to *Pabellón 6*. No blankets were allowed for the visitors but fortunately it was not a cold day.

An escape attempt was discovered in *Pabellón 7*. A guard was caught bringing in a hacksaw blade. On follow-up searches, a hacksaw and blades and a heavy insulated wire-cutter were found. There was an electrified fence all around the prison. It seemed that eight men were to have escaped. There was news that a new prison director, a serving military officer, was about to be appointed.

For me, it meant I would not have the pleasure of walking on grass again. In future only the players would be allowed visit the football field. I was banned from going because I could not play football.

I was told that the guards had a needle and thread with which I could repair my torn trousers. I asked for them on Monday, and was told to wait until Wednesday. On Wednesday I was told that they would be available on Saturday.

The next morning I was having another visit from Anne and I wanted to send a letter out for posting on to Ireland. I went over to the notices giving the rules to check that it was all correct for sending out. I had the letter in an envelope with my visitor's name on it, as well as my own name and number: Jim Monaghan TD 873 to Anne Barr, visitor, in Spanish.

The visits were held in the visiting block, about 200 metres away from *Pabellón 6*. I walked around the patio talking to Martin while waiting to be called out for the visit. Seven o'clock came and went, then 7.30.

Some men were called to the gate. They were handcuffed with

their hands behind their backs after being frisked. They were then escorted out the gate and down the covered passageway to the visiting block. I got tired of walking and stopped to watch the cartoons on the TV. Eight o'clock came and went. Eight-thirty came and went and still I got no call to the gate. I was sitting down at that stage as the severe cold had gone out of the morning and I was starting to worry that Anne had not been able to come, or she had had a row with the guards and was not allowed in. At 8.50am a guard came to the gate and shouted '*Irlandese!*' I took the letter and went to the gate.

I was frisked and handcuffed but with my hands in front instead of behind my back. There was a lot of confusion about the letter, but eventually they let me hold on to it. A guard took me outside the gate where we met several more guards and the whole conversation about the letter was repeated. Again I managed to hold on to the letter. At the visiting block the guard removed the handcuffs and let me into the area where we met our visitors. Anne was not there. After waiting ten minutes or so I asked one of the English-speaking prisoners to find out if she was outside. The guard confirmed that she was and a few minutes later she appeared at the gate. She had been waiting since 5am in queues to get in. She had queued to leave in letters and newspaper cuttings and phone cards for me. She had queued again to get an entry docket and be searched and finally had to queue to get into the visiting area.

The area was about 30 metres square with a grass triangle in one corner on which there were children's swings and slides. Along the opposite sides there was a covered part with seats made of concrete, like practically all furniture in Cómbita. The sun was just breaking through and was shining on the grass triangle so we went and sat there. Anne's feet were freezing as she was wearing sandals.

The search had not been as bad this time as on the visit two Sundays previously when she had had to strip completely. She had written letters of protest to the prison authorities about the long delays and the strip searches of visitors, but this time someone pointed out to her the officer who was the director of Cómbita. She tackled him directly. He answered that it was all necessary for security reasons, but Anne pointed out that while there was one or two guards looking after each queue, there were several more just standing around, so the cause of the delays was the inefficiency of organisation by the prison staff.

We settled down for a good chat. After a while, we went over to the gate where the guard who runs the shop on *Pabellón 6* was with a selection of crisps, biscuits and milk or minerals to drink. Anne had not eaten since leaving to catch the bus to Cómbita, so she was not only cold but also very hungry. We bought food and something to drink and settled back in the sun. When the sun did come up, it was really fierce so we headed for the shadow of the wall. A family from Huila, near where Anne lives, came over and had a friendly chat with us. Before long the visit was over and it was time to go.

The families and observers would take up the next visit. I arranged that if she were still in Bogotá and we were still in Cómbita, Anne would visit again in four weeks. She had been refused a renewal of her visa, even though she had lived in Colombia for over fourteen years. She had to keep trying to get it renewed and did not know how long that might take. Her trouble seemed to be in retaliation for the visits to me in prison.

Anne could make some money in Bogotá as an astrologer. In Colombia, astrology is very popular, especially around the New Year. I often joked with her that she should have known which would be a good visit and which one would be bad. She was a high-tech astrologer, using computer print-outs of all the relevant planet positions corresponding to the birth date and the present day. We wanted to know the outcome of the trial, but the planets were keeping that a secret.

After the visit we prisoners went to the front of the building, eleven at a time, and we had to strip down to our underpants. Then we had to sit in a metal detecting chair. A guard in front of each of us searched our clothes. We then returned to *Pabellón 6*. On the way, we passed through a small checkpoint where I noticed the figures for the various parts of the prison. There were a total of 1,033 prisoners. At the rate that the prison was filling up there would soon be three or four to a cell in Cómbita. Anne had said that another 150 prisoners were coming from La Picota and from another smaller prison.

I got through to Anne on the phone the next day and she told me that they had been kept an hour in the hot sun on the way out after the visit. Several children had got sick, vomiting up their crisps and cola because of the heat. She had avoided the special bus with its maniac driver, taking the slower but safer regular bus back to the city. The mountain roads tested the nerves of the best passengers, and it seemed from her description that the maniac driver of the first bus had scared even the most seasoned of travellers. The visit had taken her from 1am on Saturday night to 4.30pm on Sunday evening with no sleep. She was exhausted but happy that things had gone well.

After breakfast, a meeting of all prisoners was called. The first man to speak was the new FARC leader. Yesid Arteta had arrived a couple of days ago from Valledupar. We were impressed with him. He had quickly gone around all the guerrilla leaders in the *pabellón*, then all the paramilitary leaders and the narcos. Now, after three or four days, he was impressing on everyone that he was in charge while giving due recognition to all other factions. He did it with style, with no hint of aggression or hostility to anyone. It was just natural and an aspect of his personality and experience.

The guerrillas had lacked a credible leader as the *pabellón* filled up. There were now eighty-two men here, and fifty-four of them had arrived in the last ten days. The M19 guerrilla had been the leader, but his authority was not fully accepted by either the ELN or the more numerous FARC prisoners, and certainly not by the narcos and para-militaries.

The paramilitaries had been dominant, partly because they were allied with the narcos and social prisoners and partly because they were better led. But they had a problem caused by the influx of new prison-ers. They now had four different leaders. The man who led the narcos and his second-in-command had won a *tutela* that they were to be moved to La Modelo prison in Bogotá, and they expected to be moved soon, so they were not in the race for leadership in *Pabellón 6*.

The meeting was conducted very democratically with everyone who wanted to contribute being given an opportunity to talk and be listened to attentively. The outcome was that the various activities in the *pabellón* were divided between the various factions; no one was iso-lated or embarrassed, but power had shifted to a collective leadership. Each faction was represented by one or two of its chosen leaders. It was made clear that the *pabellón* would be run for the common good and not for any one faction. Since the telephone was the most likely cause of conflict, a system was agreed where each man would be allotted a ten-minute space to make calls and could trade with other men for more time or for goods in exchange for his own time. As between fifty and one hundred more men were expected in very soon, it would mean that each man would only get to the phone once in three or four days depending on the availability of phone cards.

Most of the new prisoners were coming from the military law area of Arauca where the army were arresting scores of people, but still taking a hammering from the guerrillas. It was an oil-rich area in which the US government had paid the Colombian military $100 million to protect the oil pipelines. On the morning's news, six soldiers had been killed and a further eight injured in an ambush. The prisoners from Arauca were generally very poor and often could not buy phone cards, but the new *pabellón* leadership was getting a larger number of cheap cards ordered by the shop to help in this situation.

We were sitting up on the steel staircase getting a bit of sun when Niall called us. The three of us went to the front gate. We were searched and handcuffed. We had visitors from Defensoría del Pueblo.

We were brought into a little room that had been intended as a classroom but never used. The chairs still had the original plastic covering on their legs – real chairs not concrete ones! Patricia Ramos and the acting head of the Defensoría del Pueblo were already there. In the talk that followed we discussed conditions, visits and our application to be returned to Bogotá, which was influenced by questions of danger for us here. Patricia said that the mass strip searches were illegal.

Patricia asked whether I had my painting equipment here and wrote out a request to the director of Cómbita requesting that I be given the art material. She asked whether I was getting medical attention for my knee problem. While I had been getting attention in La Picota there had been no treatment in La Modelo or here. The most important outcome of the meeting was that they would send an emergency letter to Judge Acosta supporting our return to Bogotá because of the problems for our Irish family visitors and foreign observers, and the bad conditions for legal contact by visits and telephone in

Cómbita. It was also important to us that the Defensoría del Pueblo agreed that mass strip searches were illegal under the UN Charter that Colombia had signed.

Niall had got word from our lawyers. The judge had issued an order that we were to go to Bogotá to consult on our case with our lawyers. The date he gave was 5 February, the same date that the next session of our trial was to be held on. We had already made clear that we would not be attending the trial on the 5th by letter to the judge. What was happening? Was it a mistake or an attempt to force us to appear? If it was deliberate, then for what purpose? Niall was to ring again after the lawyers had spoken to the judge.

Niall told us that the Irish Minister for Foreign Affairs was backing our lawyers' request to the judge that we be returned to Bogotá on much the same grounds as the Defensoría del Pueblo. That was good news. The more worrying news was that our legal team did not understand what was going on with the judge fixing a legal meeting on the 5th.

He was saying we should consult with our lawyers on the same day that he knew they would be busy in his court. There was also the question of interviewing the army informer who said that he had personally seen us training the FARC guerrillas in the former Peace Talks Zone. He had refused to come to the court in Bogotá in December and the court had since arranged that the lawyers go to the city of Medellín to interview him before the next session of our trial on 5, 6 and 7 February. There was only about a week to go and yet the judge had not sent the orders to set a date for the interview. This meant that the interview would very likely clash with the trial dates so dividing our legal teams while we were on trial. Was it a case of dirty tricks? Was the judge under so much pressure from the Uribe government that he was causing problems for the defence? We would learn a bit more when our lawyers spoke to the judge, but the judge was not available to talk to them.

In the cell that evening, Martin and I talked quite a bit about all the possibilities and twists that were emerging in our case. Martin talked to Niall through the cell window but he had no clear ideas either.

I had not received the letters and press cuttings or the phone cards and pencils that Anne had left in for me on Sunday's visit. I had given Niall the last bit of credit on my phone card to ring the lawyers. The shop had no phone cards on sale and possibly would not have any until Friday. We expected that the coming week would be eventful and we needed to keep in touch with lawyers, family and friends. We could be moved at any time to Bogotá. INPEC liked to move people in the days well before they were due in a legal process for security reasons.

The following morning, while walking around the patio, we discussed yesterday's news of the judge saying we could consult with our lawyers on the same day as the trial was on. Niall thought that he just wanted to give us a date that we would have to refuse and so he would not clash with the government over moving us from Cómbita. We were strongly of the opinion that our being moved to Cómbita was a decision taken at a higher level than INPEC, probably by the Minister for Justice.

Around that time, we got a copy of *Semana* magazine of 20 January. In it there was an article about the US Ambassador to Colombia, Anne Patterson, being questioned about three US mercenaries (civilian contractors was the term used) who had directed the bombing of the town of Santo Domingo, in the oil-rich department of Arauca in 1998. (Santo Domingo was the equivalent in Colombia of Crossmaglen in Ireland, a small town that was a symbol of resistance.) The article was of interest to me because it was more evidence of the culture of criminality that had led to the forensic evidence in our case.

The helicopter attack had killed seventeen civilians including several children, and injured many more. US-based human rights groups had heavily criticised the Colombian military for the attack and had forced a situation where the US State Department had reluctantly imposed sanctions against the Colombian Air Force base involved.

After years of delaying, the case came to the point where the Colombian helicopter crews were charged, but no mention was made that US mercenaries were involved. The Colombian military were enraged and, in retaliation, they had revealed the identities of the three US contractors who directed the cluster bombing of the town, and also that they worked for a security company employed by Occidental Petroleum. The Embassy got their three men out of Colombia and safely home. No charges could be brought in Colombia as they had immunity for such crimes. Because all the witnesses were in Colombia, it was extremely unlikely that any conviction could happen in the US in the unlikely event that they might be charged there.

One day the three of us were called to the gate. It was for the doctor. We were searched and handcuffed together: me, Martin and Niall and another man. We were brought to the medical centre where there were about twenty other prisoners. We knew four or five of them from previous prisons. It was strange to see men shaking hands while their hands were handcuffed behind their backs. After a time my handcuffs were removed and I was led into the doctor's room. Niall came too as an interpreter. I asked for treatment for my knee. The doctor made an arrangement for the next day. Martin needed sun cream as his nose was burnt to a cinder. While we were having the *craic* with the lady doctor and the guards, we were told that we were wanted for an *inter vista* – a legal interview. Who wanted to see us?

A guard took us across to the pharmacy. The prison did not supply sun cream but they would give permission for a visitor to bring it in. We were taken to the visiting block to see who it was that wanted an interview. When we entered the building, there were three heavily built plain-clothes men from the intelligence service, DAS. They were based in Tunja and wanted our fingerprints and photos. We discussed whether to co-operate with them or to phone the lawyers. Our judge had ordered them to come and we knew about it, so we decided to co-operate.

While they were taking down our details, Martin remarked that one of them looked just like Hugo Chavez, the president of Venezuela. The DAS man was mortified. Hugo Chavez was not a popular man with Colombian intelligence. You might as well have said that he looked like the devil! The other two were laughing at the idea of it. When the photos were being taken, the senior DAS man told Niall to adjust his collar and smile. Niall asked him to lend his jacket for the photo. When we were finished and leaving the building we shouted back to one of them: "Hasta la vista, Hugo."

Back in *Pabellón 6* we ate our food and spent a while talking about the morning's events. Niall was given back the form he had filled in for us to do education – we were to teach English. The three of us had signed it, but they wanted three separate forms, each signed and a duplicate also signed, and all of them fingerprinted. There was also a letter to the judge, pointing out that the date given for us to consult with our lawyers conflicted with the date of our trial, and requesting a different date. That letter had to be done out three separate times, duplicated and all six copies fingerprinted as well.

We got another call to the gate – it was a busy day! This time it was the *Procuradora* – the agency that looks after the interests of the state and sees that state institutions such as prisons obey the state's laws. The guards let us in between the main gates where we were searched and handcuffed but this time the visitor gestured to us to follow him into an office. We did so while the guards were confused about what to do. We went to the disused classroom where the three of us sat down. Opposite us was the man who turned out to be the representative of the *Procuraduría* in Tunja and the woman who was their person in charge of prisons in Bogotá.

Both were tense and distant as if expecting the worst from us. Niall did most of the talking in Spanish with Martin and myself making some comments or suggestions as they occurred to us. The Tunja representative did most of the talking from their side, asking whether we had complaints about how our trial was being conducted and about our access to lawyers and so on. We covered a wide range of issues, including the mass strip searches and the difficulties here for us preparing a defence and the bad visiting conditions. The woman looked a bit sad and very quiet but as the conversation went on she took more part in it. A guard came in and said that there was another prisoner that needed to talk to them, so the man left to deal with him.

The woman said that she agreed the main thing for us was a return to Bogotá, and that both of them would recommend it. She asked a bit about us – were we married? had we children? – and so on. When she asked what we worked at, Niall told her that I worked in *Tar Isteach* as part of the Irish peace process, helping ex-Provisional IRA prisoners with re-integration into life outside prison.

She said that it was a key wish of hers to get a similar project going in Colombia. She became much more lively and interested, and by the time the meeting finished she was on friendly terms. On our way out the man left his meeting to shake hands with us and assured us of his support. He said that we must be sure to send our request for transfer to Bogotá for his endorsement. He had also listened to our views about the terrible conditions that visitors, especially the women visitors, suffered and the very minimal visits – two hours instead of the four which were supposed to be allowed.

When we were in the patio talking about what had just taken place, a general meeting of all the prisoners was called. The new FARC leader addressed the meeting. I thought that Yesid Arteta was probably a future president; the Nelson Mandela of Colombia.

The collective leaders had also met the *Procuraduría* for a discussion on how things were in *Pabellón 6*. The agenda had covered a range of topics: that the INPEC guards, especially regarding visits, did not respect the rights of the prisoners and their families. It was also about men left to suffer in the cold with completely inadequate clothing, in cold cells or outside on chilly mornings.

When Yesid finished, Niall addressed the prisoners and told them that the Irish had spoken not only about the specifics of our own case but also about matters concerning all the prisoners, and that the *Procuraduría* had agreed that mass strip searching in the patio was inhuman and degrading treatment and illegal. Searches had to be conducted in conditions of privacy in a cell or room and not with fifty or sixty guards looking on. This was laying down the foundations for a legal challenge to the Federal Bureau of Prisons that the prisoners could possibly win or at least pit Colombian and human rights groups against the US for control in Colombian high security prisons.

It had been a full day – the judge was not yet available to meet our lawyers on what he was up to regarding our case.

As a follow up to the *Procuraduría* visit, Niall wrote a letter giving our reasons for wanting a return to Bogotá. We each signed and fingerprinted it and then it was sent out to the woman from the *Procuraduría* we had talked to. We also sent a letter asking that Caitríona from Ireland be allowed a special visit on the coming Sunday because we were not due a visit here until 9 February. If she could visit us then we could have some input into the events of next week or at least get a rundown on developments that could not be talked about on the phone.

Cómbita did not stay dull for long. INPEC had sent in a written notice that phone cards would not in future be allowed in by letter or by visit. They would be available solely through the shop – which never has near enough cards to meet the demand. So, they have deliberately made all the remand prisoners incommunicado. We had visitors coming for the next part of our trial, due in five days. There was a lot happening that vitally concerned us, but we were cut off and without communication. We believed that the move was in retaliation for newspaper criticism of the terrible conditions and maltreatment of families visiting here. Our first reactions were that we would inform the international observers who would be here next week, and hopefully turn the prison authorities' 'retaliation' against them. The one thing the US hated was publicity about what they were doing in Colombia.

The guards came yet again with stuff left in on last Sunday's visit. I went over to the gate. There was a whole bin full of parcels and some large letters. Things were looking hopeful! The guard said, "*Irlandés*" and I started to move forward, but then he said "Martin McCauley". Martin was not expecting anything and was sitting at the table furthest away. He came over. Another name was called out. Martin and the other man were handcuffed and led in behind the gates to the disused classroom. I waited a while, but nothing happened and neither of them reappeared. I drifted away disappointed and mystified.

Martin reappeared with both arms full of cards and envelopes. He had to open each Christmas card in front of the guard who does the post. There were cards for me, for Niall and for Martin and others addressed to all three of us. It was the Christmas mail to La Modelo, which they had sent on to Cómbita. Among the items that we got was a copy of *The Irish Times* dated 9 December. It was very pleasant to catch up on the news from Ireland. It was really great to receive so many cards mostly from Ireland but some also came from Belgium and Canada and from the US.

After the evening head count, I gathered up all my stuff and went into the cell to read the rest of it. It was a good end to another day.

The next day the director of Cómbita sent word to this *pabellón* asking the Irish not to send him any more letters about the visits as it was being discussed in Bogotá and he was waiting for their directions.

Most of the morning passed reading the cards and newspapers and writing down return addresses. I would be able to send some thank-you notes when our visitors came. Because we had been without a reliable mail service, I had got out of the discipline of writing letters.

The three of us went to a quiet spot on the third level to have a talk with Yesid Arteta. We asked him about the previous peace process in the mid-1980s – how it came about and why it failed. The talk widened to cover the history of the FARC and of the other revolutionary movements in Colombia such as the ELN and the M19 group and the much more recent rise of the right-wing paramilitaries. We had already heard a good bit of Colombian history but it was particularly interesting coming from a man who had Yesid's experience and grasp of politics and history.

I asked Yesid where he got his name, as it did not sound Spanish or indigenous. He told us that he was descended from Arab immigrants who came to the Caribbean coast of Colombia in the mid-1800s. Around the same time Jewish and Irish immigrants also arrived there. The large numbers of Afro-Colombians living along the Pacific and Caribbean coasts were the descendants of liberated slaves.

Afterwards we were sitting at our favourite concrete table talking when there was a commotion behind us with everyone rushing to form a queue. It was for phone cards! We had been keeping an eye on the shop expecting that if there were cards going on sale it would be about this time of day and we wanted to get some badly. We rushed to join the queue. Niall was ahead of Martin and me and after a while he came back to where we were to tell us that he had got our three names down on a list – there were no actual cards on sale yet.

Yesid had been telling us that there are quite a lot of people of Irish decent around Barranquilla on the coast. They came around the time of the famine in Ireland. He was writing a book about that period and one of the characters was an Irish immigrant who organised the dock-workers. He had studied the Irish situation and the IRA as part of a series of political lectures he had given in another prison. He was very impressive in the breadth of his knowledge about Colombia and the wider world. He asked us about James Joyce's *Ulysses*, but none of us had read it.

We were walking around the patio with Yesid when he said to us: "You Irish have become a symbol for the FARC." It was nice to hear, but it was also a source of danger. Any enemy of the FARC would consider us to be good targets. It was not the first time that we had been told that some Colombians admired us. Some months ago, in La Picota, university students who had been arrested for subversive political activity had said: "You are a role model in the university."

We had just enough money left in our combined shop accounts for each to buy a ration of phone cards. We had stopped buying peanuts and potato crisps. We would only buy the essentials such as toilet paper and soap and razors until we had a visit to top up our accounts. A few weeks ago, we had started drinking the tap water without any bad effects.

Niall called the lawyers and Ireland and was told that Caitríona had been refused entry to Cómbita on Sunday but she could get an *inter vista* on Monday – that was a visit behind a glass screen where she could talk through a small grille to the three of us on the other side of the glass.

Under the new arrangements for phone calls, each man was asked to pick from a deck of numbered cards for their turn. I picked No. 17, which gave me a ten-minute call at 8.40am Later on I exchanged this for No. 9, which gave me my call at 7.20am. Niall would use some of my ten minutes to call the lawyers. Rationing out my calls, I would make each call about one or two minutes, because I expected a gap of two days or more before we would get more phone cards. By using part of each other's time we could get in more short calls.

I was thinking of the weeks and weeks that went by while we had money and the shop had no cheese. Now the shop had the most delicious looking white cheese, but we had no money to buy cheese – only phone cards. Martin still bought the odd packet of crisps on the grounds that it was the nearest thing we could get to Irish food. We paid so much attention to food because it helped put in the day. One day Martin came back from the shop with cheese, bread and crisps! We could worry about tomorrow after we had eaten today.

Yesid Arteta gave an order that in future everyone was to queue for his own food. We were among the culprits because it was our practice that one of us collected the meals for the other two. I could see the justice in the order because some men, especially the big narcos and paramilitaries, were having their food brought to them by prisoners who were treated as servants. That was one of the political lessons I had learned here – the FARC were not much into revolutionary talk, but they implemented practical things that said more than hours of talk.

Everyone queuing for his own food resulted in a faster service. The quality of the food was so low that it was hardly worth queuing for; always cold, the liquids were mixed in with the solids to form a dog's dinner. The US Federal Bureau of Prisons seemed to be a totally incompetent organisation at running visits or kitchens or education. The only thing they put any effort into was security. The quality of the food in La Modelo, where we cooked it ourselves, was much better. In La Picota it was cooked in a kitchen for around fifty men and we had some control of the prisoners who did the cooking, so again the quality was good.

We got word that Caitríona and another woman were outside the prison trying to get a visit in the afternoon. They were our legal contacts with Ireland and should have been allowed in because they had the judge's authority to visit us. We would just have to wait and see whether they did get in. We had sent the usual letter, fingerprinted and signed, asking for the visit.

Caitríona and her sister Therese Ruane succeeded in getting a half hour visit. We were brought to a corridor in the building where conjugal visits are held and had our meeting sitting on some plastic chairs while a guard stayed a few metres away. It was great to talk to Caitríona and Therese and it was very good for us to hear the news of how things were shaping up for the trial, and about the observers and so on. We were given the observers' report to read afterwards. The half hour passed very quickly. When it was over, we had our hands handcuffed behind our backs while we were saying goodbye. The two women had done very well in spite of heavy intimidation by the director and the guards. We felt that the guards themselves were okay but they were under strict orders. We spent most of the rest of the day and evening discussing the report by the political and legal observers who had attended the trial in December.

The report was an interim one, as the trial was still going on. Among other things the lawyers pointed out that state officials such as President Pastrana, General Tapias, commander of the armed forces, and Dr Luis Camilo Osario, the head of *Fiscalía*, had breached the necessary presumption of innocence. All had said publicly that we were guilty. The judge was appointed for a term of four years by the President and Congress and so depended on them for reappointment. In terms of a fair trial, all the observers agreed that so far it had been very unfair, and one of them had said that it was in breach of the Universal Declaration of Human Rights. The meetings with the United Nations Commission on Human Rights and with the Red Cross were confidential but apparently supported the ideas that the observers put in the report.

The whole issue of phone calls exploded in a meeting called just before lock-up. Some of the prisoners, especially the ELN leader, were very strongly in favour of a ballot system where each man picked a number from a bag and that number was to be his turn for a ten-minute call during the day. Under the surface of these moves about phone calls there was a power struggle going on. The Billys had been in charge of the ordering of phone calls and were working with the leading narcos. It seemed that other Billys and narcos were being heavily favoured, so the demand arose for a lottery of times that could then be swapped if the time did not suit. I picked No. 57, which by chance was within ten minutes of the previous time I had been given. The Billys had been pushing for a simple queue system because they had plenty of money, as did the narcos. They could pay a social prisoner to queue and then take the phone call while that man queued again.

The Irish Ambassador, Art Agnew, was due to visit us. All the assurances he had been given about us had been broken, so we needed to write a letter in formal Spanish for him which he could use in talks with Colombian officials. We had got Manuel, who had some experience at writing these formal letters, to help us. We worked out what we wanted to say, then Niall told him in Spanish and finally he put it into the formal language.

The letter covered a range of topics such as the very bad communication by phone, the bad visiting conditions for our relatives, and our being subject to inhuman and degrading mass strip searches. We decided not to put in anything about our safety here because such a comment could lead to us being locked up twenty-three hours a day "for our own protection".

A guard called out some orders in Spanish, which I did not understand, but I saw everyone lining up as if for a morning or evening head count, and I just did the same. A big number of guards came in the front gate and I realised that it was a general search. They fanned out on to each landing and started searching the cells. I thought that next they would order a mass strip search, but when they finished searching the cells, the guards lined up at the end of the patio and then left the *pabellón* as suddenly as they had arrived.

The three of us had agreed that we would only strip to our underpants and then insist on being brought to a cell or room for a full strip search. The guards had three-foot batons and would probably not listen to our point of view, so I am not at all sure how it would have gone from there. In the end, we felt that we would win the legal battle, but they would get revenge on us one way or another.

Every day brought its own problems and opportunities. The last thing to decide before going to bed was how to dress for our meeting with the Ambassador. The arse was gone out of my white trousers; after sewing up the holes, they had simply torn again alongside the stitching because they were worn so thin. My blue jeans had a big hole in the right knee, but at least the rest was okay, although very threadbare on the arse – they would have to do!

Around 10am a Blackhawk helicopter appeared overhead and circled the prison. Soon afterwards we got word that the visit with Art Agnew was about to start. I collected some papers from the observers' report that we wanted to have with us. Niall took the letter that we had prepared the day before. The three of us were handcuffed and taken to the visiting block where we sat in an open yard and waited for our visitor. Within a few minutes he arrived. The plain-clothes men stayed discreetly at a distance, as did the uniformed INPEC guards. We all shook hands with Art and settled down to talk.

Niall led off, describing the situation as we saw it, then Martin spoke and finally, I said my piece. I asked him to convey to the Irish government that we felt the international observers were our best assurance that we would not be steam-rolled by the Colombian state. I said that in the event of serious delays in the case, we might be left without any observers to look after our rights. We wanted the Irish government to appoint their own observer or at least ensure that there would always be an observer whom they trusted at the trial. I said that eventually our campaign might not be able to afford the cost of bringing distinguished observers to Colombia. His answer was diplomatic, but I took it as positive, that we would always have observers present.

My purpose was to try to ensure that the Irish government would be kept informed of the legal twists and tricks of the Colombian prosecution, as they grew increasingly desperate. It was also to block the Colombian and US governments' option of using long legal delays as a substitute for proceeding with a trial where they had no credible evidence.

One of the things that Art told us was that he had arranged with the director that all of our visitors should get in on Saturday, instead of dividing them as was usual into men on Saturday and women on Sunday. That was excellent news as the whole party could leave Colombia together on Sunday instead of the women being left in Bogotá until Monday. The point was very relevant to their safety, as there was serious fear over links between the Colombian security forces and the paramilitaries. The last thing any of us wanted was the kidnapping or shooting of any of our visitors.

Art had also raised the family visits with the director and had got an assurance that the prison would be flexible to ensure a good visit. Overall it had been a successful visit by the Irish Ambassador and hopefully progress would soon be made on our getting returned to Bogotá to be near our lawyers during the critical parts of our trial.

There was to be a meeting of the observers and the Ambassador with Vice President Santos on Friday. Santos was also in charge of human rights and as a member of one of the ruling families in Colombia, he would be acutely aware of the damage adverse publicity was doing to the future of the oligarchy.

The time for our food came, and we ate it amid all the usual chatter. Just after we had finished, Niall was called over to the gate by a guard and he arrived back to the table with three nice jam pastry rolls. "The director has sent us these for dessert!" After all the bad things I had said about the director, here I was, bought off for a jam roll. It was delicious!

Later, there was another meeting of all the prisoners called to vote to elect the men who would go to the kitchen to prepare our food. Naturally we voted for guerrillas. We hoped that the selected prisoners would improve the quality of the food.

In the time between the evening food and lock-up, we were asked did we want haircuts. As the visitors would be in next weekend, the three of us opted to have a haircut. The guard giving the haircuts was okay and would cut the hair in the way we wanted it. We went into the disused schoolroom one at a time and when I went in I told him not to take any off the top of my head because I needed the hair as protection from the sun, but to cut the sides. He cut it as directed and when he finished I thanked him. He then got me to sit back in the chair while he perfected his work. I think he did his best to give me a really good haircut. The top of my head was still painful with sunburn, even after six weeks of exposure.

Just before lock-up a FARC guerrilla came to the three of us and gave us detailed instructions about what to do and where we were to go in the event of serious trouble with the paramilitaries. He said that they had agreements and did not expect any trouble, but experience had taught them to be prepared. All of the guerrillas in the *pabellón* had a place to go, and a person to report to for instructions. Each would have a cake of blue laundry soap in a stocking as a weapon. We were impressed at the level of organisation they had. We would be put in an area protected by a ring of trusted men. That was reassuring.

Chapter 15

Our Trial Resumes

WEDNESDAY 5 FEBRUARY 2003 was to be the first day of our resumed trial. We would be watching the TV news carefully and also calling Caitríona on the phone for updates. Nine observers were to attend; these included Sinn Féin TD Seán Crowe; Senator Mary White of Fianna Fáil; Paul Hill, one of the Guildford Four; and six lawyers, Pat Daly and Ronan Munro from Ireland; Steve McCabe and Natalie Kabasakalian from New York and Shaun Kerrigan and Ian Latham from Australia.

The defence lawyers were objecting to the judge's ruling that a FARC deserter was to give his evidence in the city of Medellín, because the prosecution said they could not afford the cost of bringing him to the trial in Bogotá. It meant that the defence would have the cost of going there instead, and it would be difficult for the observers to attend.

Meanwhile, Gerry Adams had confirmed that Niall was the Sinn Féin representative in Cuba; there had been some confusion at first over that.

A guard gave all three of us a call to report to the front gate. "It's for the dentist." None of us had asked to go to the dentist so we were a bit worried that it might be a trick to get us to the court – although it would be late in the day for that. Later, the guard came back with papers to take Niall and me out to the dentist. We decided it was genuine and went with him. Once outside *Pabellón 6*, I realised that my eyes were affected by continuously seeing everything at short distances, and I felt dizzy when I looked at the mountains visible over the prison walls.

When we got to the medical block, we found that we knew quite a few of the prisoners that we met there, or to be more accurate, Niall knew them while I vaguely recognised them. The woman dentist was pleasant and helpful. She took out the root of a missing tooth for me and gave Niall's teeth a polishing. As we returned towards the *pabellón*, we met some prisoners whom we knew from La Picota as well as more from the reception cells here in Cómbita. It was becoming the case that everywhere we went in the prison system we knew some prisoners and some guards.

Back in the *pabellón*, we had barely finished discussing with Martin the various men we had met, when the mail came in. We got the correspondence that Caitríona had left in, but not the new clothes. There was no word of the things that Anne had left in ten days ago.

Later on, I was reading a copy of *El Tiempo* that was on a table where the Billys sat. One of the Billys came over and asked, in Spanish, if I could read the paper. He was learning English and soon the two of us were stuck into reading and translating an article in the paper, me reading it and him correcting the pronunciation and explaining words. Then he went and got a book in English, *The Kingdom of this World*, and started reading it. Martin joined us and when some of the language was beyond us the big man who had spoken good English to me when he had come on to the block joined us.

The language lesson was interrupted by one of the guards addressing the whole patio. He was the guard in charge and he was giving out about men hanging their damp towels from the cell doors. He had confiscated a number of towels the previous evening and now he was giving them back. Immediately he had finished speaking, a number of prisoners demanded that he show a book of rules instead of punishing men for breaking rules that no one knew existed. Yesid, the FARC leader, got stuck in about the arbitrary rules and within two minutes there were dozens of guards flooding into the patio. The argument broke up and the extra guards left.

We got talking to the big man. He offered to teach us Spanish, as he was a teacher with a lot of experience in languages. He explained that he was friendly with everybody, paramilitaries and guerrillas and narcos, but that he wanted to leave Colombia as soon as possible. The country had no future and was beyond salvation. His story was that when he was young he had been the friend of a rich man who had helped him get on in business. He financed his business by going to the Panama Canal where he would meet Russian seamen with suitcases of watches. He would buy the watches and sell them again in Colombia. He graduated from watches to drugs and was selling them in the US. He was caught and had been in several prisons in the US.

Unlike me, he was full of praise for the Federal Bureau of Prisons, saying that the prisons were very good and provided him with excellent educational opportunities. I pointed out that the same Federal Bureau was running the prisons here and that they were a disgrace. He agreed but blamed lack of funds and the Colombians. It seemed that in the US the prisons were well run. I would have to revise my opinions. It reminded me of the reputation of British justice – it was great as long as the accused was not Irish or black.

The 12.30pm TV news came on. There was a brief bit about us on it. One of the witnesses, Edwin Giovanny Rodriguez, who had refused to turn up in December, was there as promised – but he refused to testify! He wanted a deal with the Witness Protection Agency. The outcome was that he would testify on Friday. Another prosecution witness would not have to testify in court but a special commission would go to him. We wondered whether this was all stage-managed by the prosecution.

The next witness had been the army officer Captain Pulido who was in charge of our arrests and interrogation. He was also present when the US Embassy had taken the forensic tests that were the basis of the charges against us. We had no information that the subject of the forensic tests was to come up or had been subject to cross-examination. The key things about the tests were the highly irregular circumstances in which they were taken and their effect in damaging the Irish peace process and the talks that were then in progress in Colombia. A purely technical cross-examination would not expose the political manoeuvring that was fundamental to this case. I was worried that by not raising these matters then, we could be manoeuvred into a position of being unable to do so on Friday, if the witness talked about us during the time that we actually were in Colombia – previous witnesses had talked about times that we were not, and we had alibis for those times.

To get the latest news on our trial, we had to resort to phoning Ireland. Niall had got early reports from Caitríona in the court during the lunch break, but mobile phones had to be switched off during sessions.

We needed to watch the evening TV news at 7pm. It would not be easy as we were in cells about 30 metres away from it. We did get the TV turned in our direction and there were two of the cleaners who would listen carefully and tell us what had been said. Unfortunately, they were not likely to be very accurate.

Niall was in the queue at 4pm to ring Caitríona after the court case was over. The Billys were hogging the phone – two of them in particular because it was a day when most prisoners had no phone cards and a queue system was in operation. It came close to Niall having a fight with the worst of them, but eventually he did get on the phone. Caitríona and all the lawyers had their answering machines on! With every answering machine, he lost phone card credit and got no news.

The wait for the 7pm TV news was long. When it came on, we were not mentioned. That could be seen as a good sign. A guard told us that the judge had made an order that we be returned to Bogotá. This was good news, but every bright silver cloud had a black lining – would we be moved before, during or after our visits at the weekend? Would there be problems and confusion?

The next day started as usual with a cold shower, and then there was a rush to the phone. I got there first and got in a call to Anne to tell her that the judge had said we would be transferred to Bogotá, and since we did not know when it would happen, she should not plan to visit. We did not know where we might be held in Bogotá but we hoped that it would be in La Modelo. Martin regarded La Modelo as his second home. We were all hoping to go there. It had the roughest living conditions and was the most dangerous, but the guerrillas there were friendly and good *craic*. We felt safer because we had the guerrilla prisoners covering our backs and also Martin and I learned Spanish there faster than anywhere else.

Niall joined me in the queue just behind his favourite paramilitary – the one he nearly had a fight with over the phone queue. After a bit of trying, he finally got Caitríona and got the latest news. Both the military intelligence man and the GIAT explosives expert had finished their testimony. The next witness was the informer who had deserted from the FARC. He would testify on Friday morning. As there were no more witnesses for the prosecution to appear before then, there would be no court proceedings until Friday.

We spent the time walking and discussing the developments in our trial. Now the big question was, what was the deserter going to talk about? He was the one who was not subject to questioning by either the prosecution or the defence. The judge had allowed military intelligence to hold this ace card until the very last day of the prosecution case without committing him, so that they could school him up to the last minute. If they had got away with it, they would have held him until after the defence had testified also, but our legal team had objected and refused to give the defence case before he testified.

Yesid Arteta, the FARC leader, joined us. Yesid's opinions were always very much to the point. I had not realised that he had written a book while in Valledupar, one of the worst prisons in the country. He showed us a copy of it and asked us to sign it. We signed the cover for him.

After our discussions and the morning meal, Martin and myself settled into a bit of good-humoured talk with six or seven of the guerrillas from Arauca. We were doing very well with our Spanish and having fun at the same time. Niall was called to the main gate and we thought that it was for the stuff left in by Anne eleven days ago or else the clothes left in by Caitríona last Sunday. It was neither.

"Pack your things, you're moving out."

It was the response to the judge's order given yesterday. We were going to Bogotá! In a bit of a daze, we went with the guard, who opened our cells for us. As we gathered our belongings and put them in the centre of a blanket, a huge crowd of prisoners gathered. They wanted to shake hands, to say goodbye. Prisoners always gather around anyone leaving out of curiosity or to get some of their belongings. These prisoners were different. They pushed cards and books at us to sign. They were emotional and concerned. I gave Loco, my amigo, everything that would be of use to him and his guerrilla friends. We had an emotional farewell from Yesid and from the Workers Defence man who had spent hours teaching Martin and me Spanish slang from the book that I had been sent. Some of the paramilitaries came over to shake hands. The big man who was offering to teach us Spanish also came over to say goodbye. I gave him two books in English, including the one we had read passages from.

We were brought between the main gates and to the disused classroom where we had our property searched and we were then handcuffed and led out again. There was a big crowd of prisoners gathered at the gates shouting their goodbyes. With a last wave of farewell, we left *Pabellón 6* and headed for reception. The guards were good-humoured. Another three prisoners were taken to reception with us, one at the same time and two later. We were put in the open air cage at first but then three more prisoners arrived from outside to reception so they locked us in the cells.

We knew several of the prisoners in the reception cells as they had just come from La Picota, and they included the university computer students. When we had been moved to La Modelo in November last year, they had been moved from the high security patios to the normal patios in La Picota. Among the prisoners was one of the indigenous people who had responded to the *gringos* drilling for oil on their lands by kidnapping and ransoming the *gringo* oil workers. As the oil industry's 'private security' mercenaries had killed many indigenous people, they had killed oil workers in retaliation. I had a lot of sympathy for the indigenous people of Colombia responding to genocide as best they could. They could not hope to be successful against the professional gunmen who worked for the big international oil companies.

About mid-day Niall was brought back to where our things were, to collect our spoons so that we could eat lunch. While there, he saw that Yesid was also there in the cage. Yesid did not know where he was being sent to or why.

After we had eaten, we were taken from the cells to an area in front of the cage and strip searched and had our things searched by guards from the unit of INPEC who move prisoners. Yesid and the two with him and a fourth man were also strip searched. We were all put into a big prison van. Martin had his heart set on another ride in a Blackhawk helicopter. I had been telling him that after the trial, our status would be such that INPEC would move us to Bogotá in the local bread van.

We made frantic enquiries about where our property was. We were presented with a sheet of paper to sign, saying that we had got our belongings, even though we had not set eyes on them. If we did not sign, then our property would stay in Cómbita until someone from outside came to collect it. In the end, we signed. The van started out with two armed guards in the back, both carrying automatic rifles. It was dark and the van smelled strongly of diesel and exhaust fumes. The van was followed by a truckload of INPEC guards in their dark blue uniforms and wearing US style black painted helmets. They were heavily armed with automatic weapons.

As the truck and van sped along the bumpy road to Bogotá – a three-hour journey – the man I was handcuffed to collapsed on to the floor. He was sick and gasping for breath, and I was wondering what to do for him. All I could do was cling to the seat and extend my arm so that the handcuffs did not cut into his wrist. The van was in darkness and swayed violently as it sped along the mountain roads. We could not see the dangerous turns or the ravines and mountain rivers far below, but we imagined them. Just up the seat from me, one of the prisoners got sick into a plastic bag several times. I could feel waves of hot and cold sweat sweeping over me. It was like seasickness so I closed my eyes. I held out for over two hours but eventually I grabbed the other man's plastic bag and got sick into it three or four times.

We eventually stopped. The back door opened and we looked out on buildings that none of us recognised. Were we at La Picota or La Modelo? Two of the prisoners in our van were transferred to another van and then we were told to get out and collect our belongings – our bags from Cómbita were there and everything was intact. We were video filmed and asked for our names, and then we were loaded back on to the same van. It went a short distance around the buildings to the front gate. It was La Modelo! We were told to get out with our things. I had been hoping that Yesid would be coming with us, but he and another prisoner were going on to La Picota. We said goodbye for the second time in one day. I was convinced that Yesid would be an important leader of Colombia when it wins its freedom from the tyranny of the oligarchy.

We went into the familiar entrance of La Modelo and were fingerprinted and photographed and we were led up the long corridor
towards our old haunt on Piso 1, *alto seguridad*. We stopped at the
junction of the long corridors, where there was an INPEC guards'
office. The man I had been handcuffed to was giving his details to
the guards.

"Occupation?"

"I am engaged in commerce."

"What branch of commerce?"

"Narco trafficking!"

Well, he was direct in his answers.

When we got to the high security Piso 1, where the guerrillas were
held, there was a tremendous welcome for us. We were greeted as long-
lost comrades and surrounded by well-wishers. Each of us was taken
around and shown all the changes to the place. They had built sleeping accommodation and a place for artwork and crafts. We were given
coffee and soup and chocolate and generally made a fuss of. The pity
was that by 8pm we were falling asleep – the effect of the routine in
Cómbita. We were as happy as prisoners can be, here among our
friends in La Modelo. It was a full day. I was sleeping on the floor again
but who cared when you were among friends.

Things were different in La Modelo. For a start, I could not get to
sleep at my usual time of 8pm. The man whose floor space I was sharing was making a model car out of wood. He was at the finishing stage
of lacquer-painting the parts of it. The sound of a radio and the smell
of the lacquer were strange and my stomach had not recovered fully
from the journey. So, eventually I got up again and dressed. The man
making the car offered it to me for 20,000 pesos – about €10. I said I
would buy it but that all my money was still in Cómbita. I expected
that on the visit on Saturday I would be left in some money so I would
pay for the car and send it home with our visitors. The car was an old
1920s open-top type with a boot and engine compartment that opened,
and it had spoked wheels.

I went out into the main room and found Niall and Martin, who
also could not sleep and were sitting there talking. Luis and El
Comandante Alfredo joined us and the five of us sat talking until late

at night. I had been told that El Comandante had been released, but his sitting opposite me contradicted that story.

There had been publicity on his case as a result of our observers saying they had met a man imprisoned for ten years without being convicted. He had been convicted of rebellion, and should have been released after about three years. They kept bringing spurious charges, which they withdrew just before coming to the end of a trial, as a means of keeping him in prison.

I woke up at 5.30am as I had been programmed to by the routine in Cómbita. After trying vainly to go back to sleep, I got up and had a shower. When I went to the main room I found that the other two were also up. We passed the time watching the TV. One of the ministers in Uribe's government was missing. His light aircraft had crashed in the mountains after they flew out from Tunja Airport (the town nearest to Cómbita prison).

Caitríona had earlier told us that a witness against us was being held in La Modelo. We guessed that he was the same man who had been in a cell opposite Niall when we were held in the DIJIN.

The 12.30pm TV news did carry a bit about the case and even repeated bits of what the witness had said – in spite of the judge ruling in December that there would be a heavy fine if they did. The key element was the dates on which he accused us of conducting the training, and these he had now said were between 5 and 25 February 2001. Now that we had that information, we could set about proving that we were not in Colombia at the time. Videos made by *Tar Isteach* and my work record as well as Martin's job sheets would cover that whole period.

In between all the trial stuff, the TV news, the phone calls and discussions, we had to get ourselves included in cooking groups so that we would get fed and we had to be integrated into the structure of the prisoners in La Modelo.

Each morning we went up on the roof for sunlight and exercise for two hours. On the roof there was a big cage in which there was a small football pitch, a bank of four telephones and a nice little shop/café. Through bullet holes in the corrugated iron sheeting, we could see parts of the prison below us. The ordinary patios were grim-looking places, dilapidated buildings, wires strung across asbestos roofs, gaping holes in the roofs, barrels of rubbish and lines of washing, partly hidden groups of men standing around or sitting on the concrete. Our life was much better in the high security area.

Further out, beyond the prison walls, was the city. It was vast and grey; it climbed up the mountainsides and disappeared into the trees. Bogotá had eight million inhabitants, most of them desperately poor but some were richer than the richest people in Ireland. The skyscrapers contrasted dramatically with the slums. The Chinese once said that it was not the splendour of the wealthy or the desperation of the poor that bred revolution – but the contrast between them. Here it was spread out for miles all around us.

When we came down from the roof after exercise, we three were separated out of the crowd to have our photographs taken. The guards were relaxed and friendly and they were joking with us. The high security area was relaxed overall because there was an agreement between the guerrillas and paramilitaries about access to exercise and other outstanding issues that had been a cause of tension. For instance, the prisoners in the shop on the roof were paramilitary, but they had no problem with serving guerrillas.

Outside the jail in the cities, towns and countryside a life and death struggle was going on, with the state and paramilitaries on one side and the various guerrilla armies and militias on the other. The trade union movement was becoming both desperate and more militant as the state cut back on public service employment to fund the war – 70,000 more workers were to be made idle in the coming months. All these conflicts could feed back into the prisons and a local agreement could only be viewed as temporary.

I was trying to get my things and living space in order. I was sleeping on the floor but had nowhere to keep my clothes. The observers would be coming in to see us in the morning.

About 8pm, as I was getting ready to go to bed, an *Ultimo Hora* newsflash came on the TV. A car bomb had exploded in north Bogotá, the rich area. Our visitors had gone out for the evening to enjoy themselves after the long day in court – where had they gone? Could they have gone to the north of Bogotá? Most of the nightlife was in the rich areas of north Bogotá. As the news came in, we saw that the target had been a large building, about twelve storeys high, which was seriously damaged and burning.

Eventually, Niall made contact by phone, using a mobile phone number for Caitríona. They had gone to the south of Bogotá and they were okay. All evening and late into the night more details of the bombing came in. Somewhere between nine and twenty people had been killed and over a hundred injured. The police were blaming the FARC but there was also the possibility that it was done by one of the drugs cartels, angry at the extradition of their leaders by the Uribe government to the US.

Next morning at around 10am Caitríona appeared at the gate and spoke briefly to us, saying that the rest of our visitors were on the way in. Then she went back to help the visitors with the many checks they had to pass through. A while later they all appeared at the final checkpoint – the guards' office just outside the iron bars that separated our living space from the guards' offices. We waved and called across to them while they were being processed.

There was a great welcome for them when we met. The legal observers had seen enough of the trial to know that there was no credible legal case of us training the FARC. The political observers seemed to be convinced that we were suffering an injustice by being held in prison on the evidence that they had already heard. Mary White spoke to each of us in order to make a formal report back to Irish Prime Minister, An Taoiseach Bertie Ahern. We circulated to make sure that everyone was included as we felt that on the previous visit by the observers, some of them may have felt that they got less attention than others.

Although the visit lasted about two hours, the time passed extremely quickly and our visitors were on the way out while there was still much to talk about and to show them. Because of the lack of opportunity to do any craft work or painting in Cómbita, I did not have much to send home with them – only two or three fairly thin letters and some wristbands with tiny pictures of Ché Guevara on them, made by men here in La Modelo.

I felt that this latest part of the trial had gone well for us even though the feedback was that some of the Colombian and foreign newspapers were running with the FARC deserter's version of events. Caitríona would be back tomorrow to give us a blow-by-blow account of what had happened in court, as we had needed to give all our attention to the observers during the meeting. It was very important to us that they were satisfied about our innocence of the charges, and they were not only listening to the evidence in the courtroom but were able to ask each of us any question they wanted to, face to face. They were also in a position to watch us interact socially and judge what kind of characters we were from close observation.

There was one big change from the last time that we were in La Modelo. In their usual sensitive way they explained to me that I was considered an extremely bad cook. By popular demand, I would not be cooking in future.

Next morning we were ready for Caitríona with a list of questions about what topics had come up in court and, equally important, what had not. We were trying to analyse the state's strategy. We wanted to know how the judge was behaving towards the defence as compared to his behaviour towards the lawyer from *Fiscalía* – cutting through the words to the actions. What kind of comments were coming from the journalists? There was no such thing as a non-political journalist, either in a newspaper or TV station. Knowing their political slant, you could make judgments about what they knew from the comments they made. They often knew things from sources that we did not have.

When Caitríona did arrive, we brought her to a little table and asked all the questions we had. She gave us some of the papers covering new evidence offered in the court so that we could study it and offer suggestions to the lawyers. Only now, eighteen months since we had been arrested, had the dates on which we were accused of training the FARC been given to the defence. She would have to go back to Ireland and look for witnesses who could testify that we were not in Colombia on those dates.

Caitríona was pale and feeling sick. She blamed the tensions and exhaustion of the past week as much as any bug that she might have picked up. One bug in particular had affected her, however. She had returned to the hotel early the previous day and gone straight to her room. On opening the door she found two men had removed the mirror that was on the wall and were busy with exposed electric wires. She challenged them to explain what they were doing but was far from satisfied with either their answer or their nervousness so she went to the management and got a change of rooms.

The whole party of visitors had stayed in the hotel instead of going out shopping or sightseeing because they were worried about hostility. The state had constantly linked the Irish with every bomb and mortar attack over the past year. It was understandable that some of the more ignorant might link the Irish visitors with the big bomb at the Nogal Club in the north of the city. The casualty figures were now at thirty-two dead and 170 injured. The observers would be leaving for the airport around 6pm and until then things would be very tense.

We asked Caitríona to give our good wishes to all the people in Ireland who were doing so much good work to get us home as quickly as possible, and to give us a run-down on how things were developing in the peace process. After a good discussion, it was time for her to go. When we had finished the goodbyes, there was a strong sense of anticlimax. The turmoil of the past weeks was over. We could look forward to a quiet and relatively relaxed few weeks ahead. In Colombia, we had learned that the unexpected is always just around the next corner. We would take it as it came. The next part of the trial would start on 25 March when the defence would put its case.

On 4 March 2003, John Alexander Rodriguez Caviedes gave his testimony before a commission in Medellín. In it he said that we had given the FARC training in the manufacture and use of explosives in December 1998 or January 1999. He also said that we returned to give further training in February and December of 1999 and again for six weeks in December 2000 and January 2001, all at Los Poses in the demilitarised zone. We did not arrive in Colombia until June 2001.

The trial resumed on 26 March when defence witnesses were to be heard, but the prosecution had not finished. An official from GIAT, an army unit dealing with explosives, testified that FARC and IRA technology used in mortars and other weapons was similar. He was unable to answer questions from our lawyers regarding technology used by other Colombian and Latin American guerrilla groups, and he looked up every question in a laptop computer before answering. Eventually he conceded that the technology could have been obtained from anywhere in the world and in particular it could have come from Asia. This concession made his evidence more or less irrelevant.

Edwin Giovanny Rodriguez testified next. He claimed that we trained members of the FARC in April 2001. When questioned about the meaning of some of the words he used in his evidence to the court, he admitted that he did not really know. Our lawyers were making it clear to the judge that the witness had simply learned a script supplied by military intelligence, and was incapable of answering questions about what he had just said.

On 8 April the defence case started with the testimony of Ros O'Sullivan. He said that he worked with Concern Worldwide, a humanitarian emergency agency with an annual budget of 60 million euros. Mr O'Sullivan knew Niall Connolly socially in Ireland and also met him in San Francisco. He visited Niall and his family in Havana, Cuba, at Christmas in 1999 and again in 2000. He was able to produce photographs and airline tickets to confirm that both he and Niall were there.

Doctor Seán O'Domhnaill testified that he was a frequent caller to the McCauley household during 1999 and early 2001. He would have been aware of any absence by Martin and said that he could not have been gone more than a few days during that time.

Caitríona told us that Mike Ritchie, a director of *Coiste na nIarchimí* in Belfast, had given very clear evidence about how ex-prisoners were playing an important role in the peace process, involving their communities who would otherwise remain hostile to negotiations and compromises. Most of the current Sinn Féin leadership were ex-prisoners. He gave a lot of documentry evidence showing my attendance at meetings and his own account of having been at a *Coiste* Christmas party with me in 1999 when the deserter said that I was in Colombia.

Dr Keith Borer was an international expert specialising in explosives and forensic testing. His evidence was very detailed on IRA and FARC technologies, and the thrust of it was that each had developed weapons and mortars to suit their own particular circumstances and there was almost no sharing of designs or methods of use.

His evidence on the forensic tests taken on a machine called an itemiser by the US Embassy official was scathing. He was too diplomatic to say outright that it was false, but he came as close as possible.

Natalie Kabasakalian summed it up: "He explained the machine's operation and the evidence presented in the embassy report. He stated that many of the purported positive results did not comport with the machine's calibration, and it was technically impossible for the machine to recognise many of the readings as positive. The tester's documents demonstrate that the machine was running smoothly at the time the tests were run, so anomalies cannot be explained by machine malfunction. Accordingly, many of these positive results could only be explained by tampering."

Natalie was a court attorney in the appellate division of the Supreme Court of the United States. She had extensive training in international law and human rights. She worked for Amnesty International USA as the country specialist on the United Kingdom and Ireland. She could certainly follow and understand evidence presented in court.

Síle Maguire and Mike Ritchie testified early on Thursday, 10 April. Mike was in the box from the afternoon until late on Thursday night, and again on Friday morning. The court watched three video tapes showing me at *Tar Isteach* in Dublin on 7 February 2001 and at a training course in Belfast on 21 February 2001. These were accompanied by sworn affidavits. Catherine Murphy and Michelle Devlin, who had made the videos, were in court, ready to testify and answer any questions. The judge did not call them to give evidence, saying that he was satisfied that the videos were genuine.

Dr Laurence McKeown, himself an ex-prisoner, gave the court evidence as to why ex-prisoners, peace activists and Irish republicans might travel on false documents. These included the risk of exclusion from certain countries, being subject to harassment and delays. He himself had been harassed and detained by the London Metropolian Police while travelling to Colombia during this trial. All the people who were convicted for playing a part in the Irish struggle were listed as security risks on computers used at airports worldwide.

Mike Ritchie, who had finished giving evidence, was in to visit us for a short time and, just in case anything went wrong with Saturday's visit, I sent out what I had ready with him.

The final visit was on Saturday 12 April. The witnesses and observers would be going home on the plane in the evening. The arrangements for the visit were that only the men would come in, because Saturday was a men-only visiting day. The women who made the video would unfortunately not be able to get in. As witnesses they could not have visited us before they gave their testimony and they would need to stay until Sunday if they were to get to visit us.

The visitors arrived and there were hurried signings of flags and plaques. Caitríona was there as part of our legal team, so we had a private meeting with her to get the inside story on what had happened in court. Our hope was that the proceedings would force the media to focus on the evidence – or lack of evidence. It had paid off over the months.

After our briefing on all aspects of the case in court, we joined the witnesses and observers to talk to them. They understood our need for a private chat with Caitríona and there was no problem, even though we took about an hour to complete it. Once we were finished, I immediately started to talk with Mike Ritchie. Mike had been impressive in court according to all the reports that we had got.

He told me that the judge seemed to be really interested, not just in the evidence relating directly to where I was on the dates in question, but in the whole concept of conflict resolution. The whole idea of *Coiste na nIarchimí* and the involvement of ex-prisoners in the peace process was very relevant to Colombia. The idea of militants in the war being militants for peace also should have given the judge a new perspective on us and our presence in Colombia.

It was a terrible pity that Laurence McKeown had not been able to come in on the visit, but he would be required to give evidence at the next session in eight weeks time.

I spoke to Steve McCabe, the New York lawyer who was an observer, asking what he thought. He was concerned that during the eight weeks the prosecution would conjure up a new witness or two against us. It was a worry: there was an endless supply of potential 'eye witnesses' who would say anything that they were paid, bribed or threatened to say. I had great respect for Steve's opinion, himself and Natalie Kabasakalian were proof that there were very good key people in the US. The army intelligence or *Fiscalía* problem was not getting 'eye witnesses' but getting credible ones, smart enough to stand up to cross-examination. As usual, the time just flew to the end of the visits. I said goodbye to Paul Hill, to Ronan and Shaun, Steve and Ross, Seán and everyone else.

After the visitors had gone, I felt drained. The week was over, for good or ill; everyone had done their bit and nothing more could be done at this stage.

Chapter 16

The Law's Delay

O N 25 APRIL Martin came and warned me that trouble was coming because a paramilitary had tried to escape and had got as far as the front gate. The telephones were off and there would be searches. Later in the day we were told to stand by our beds as the INPEC guards were coming in to search. When they did arrive into the room – where four of us were sleeping – there were so many of them it was standing room only. They did search, but it was not as bad as it could have been. Searches were often punishment exercises, rather than serious attempts to find something. The guards would wreck the area and leave you standing in the debris. This time they just searched but left things more or less as they found them.

The following day, Saturday, should have been men's visiting day, but the visits had been cancelled as a collective punishment for the escape attempt. There would be no women's visits on Sunday either and we were not sure how long the punishment would go on. Word came later that the women's visits would go ahead, and they would bring in food as usual, but the weekday visits were stopped.

One of the other prisoners asked me for a loan of my bed as he had a visit from his girlfriend and I had no visit. I had seen him the previous week with her and they had had nowhere to go. Even though he was not really a friend of mine – and he played his radio far too loud – I said okay. That meant that after 9am I was homeless for the day, until 4.30pm.

After the visits ended, the man I had lent my bed to arrived with a gift of a big plastic bowl of dessert. I put it in the fridge for later when I could share it with Freddy and Milton, who often shared meals with me in the evenings.

Word was coming through on the telephone about the end of the

Irish peace process; about Tony Blair's rejection of the Sinn Féin position and the cancelling of the elections. One of the reasons that Blair gave for cancelling the elections was that Sinn Féin had not "come clean on Colombia". Another politician saying that we were guilty even before the trial took place!

We discussed all that but we lacked hard information about what was happening so we could not come to any definite conclusions. Apart from its obvious effects in Ireland, the British move could have implications for us. Up to now the British had played our case low key because of the implications for the peace process; now they might take a more openly aggressive stand, especially in supplying so-called 'intelligence information' to damage the good strong defence that we had. The Colombian state was desperate for a new line on how to make a credible case against us, and the Brits might cook up something for them to work on.

It looked like the current phase of the peace process could only limp on until Tony Blair was defeated in an election or was otherwise replaced as British Prime Minister. Cancelling an imminent election, or saying it was postponed with no definite date fixed, was a political position hard to justify or defend, and it seemed that three out of the four main parties in the North wanted the elections to go ahead. It was by no means certain that David Trimble's Ulster Unionist Party would get enough votes to be the majority party in deciding who the new First Minister would be, so cancelling an election on that basis was to presuppose that the results would not suit British policy. Some democracy!

In the evening there was a general meeting. It was May Day and the staff wanted a little political discussion and then to announce what had happened in relation to the weekday visits. The discussions started off with the ELN leader – Tito – giving a brief history of the origins of May Day and he talked a bit about the trade unions in Colombia. He was followed by another ELN speaker –El Chino – who gave an anti-capitalist talk, which I found difficult to follow with my limited Spanish. Niall spoke about James Connolly and Ireland. I spoke in English with Niall translating about our project of helping ex-prisoners, some of whom are helped to set up in business. That gave us practical experience from which to discuss the problems and the running of the economy. Martin spoke, again through Niall, about what had been won in labour struggles for the working people in terms of hours per week, social insurance, sickness and maternity benefits. He also spoke about the Irish land war origins of the term 'boycott'. One or two others spoke as well and then El Commandante Alfredo and Luis the OC had their say.

Luis then told us that there were indicators that the weekday visits would be reinstated as the heat from the escape attempt died down.

On 2 May a meeting was called and a group of seven people arrived from the Defensoría del Pueblo, the state human rights organisation. We sat in a big circle and one of the women in the delegation told us what the purpose of the visit was. They had had a look at our living accommodation and were pressing the prison authorities to give us the next floor above as well as the one we were on. There were about forty of us and we had twenty-four sleeping spaces, sixteen of which had two sleeping in them.

On the second floor there were eleven cells, which would certainly ease the overcrowding. They would look for access between the floors because the kitchen and eating spaces were on the ground floor. They wanted us to get fresh air and sun every day as well. If these things actually happened it would make life here a good bit better. Of course, the main thing most men wanted was that the weekday visits be restored.

A billiard table was set up in the open space between the cells. It had been arriving here in bits. It was a business venture by one of the prisoners. The prison was probably benefiting as well. The prisoner would charge for playing time and so be able to pay the rent on the table and turn a profit for himself. The prisons allowed little businesses to be run by prisoners, such as small shops and the telephones and the billiard table. There were even stalls in the lower security patios which I pictured as something like Moore Street in Dublin. I had never seen them but I could hear people shouting their wares in the morning, on the other side of our kitchen wall. I had even heard one of them calling "Marijuana! Marijuana!"

We bought a tin of white emulsion paint. I wanted to paint my cell walls on Monday. The cell had only three walls and a curtain. I moved everything for the day to do it. I had been thinking of painting a window on a blank spot of wall – with a horse looking in from its field!

Freddy, who slept in the next bed to mine, was carving a wooden plaque of Venezuela. I drew a picture of Ché Guevara on it for him. He carved around the picture, leaving it to stand out on the map. Out in the kitchen, Niall was making himself a bed out of heavy wood. He was cutting joints for the end posts, using woodworking tools that we had bought to supplement what was available for doing craft work by the prisoners..

On Sunday everyone was up very early because they wanted to have everything ready for the restored visits. The first visitors were women from the women's prison, and then the ordinary visitors started to arrive. The three of us Irish sat at the big food table talking. None of us was going to have a visit.

I brought twenty-five blank cards and the paints to give myself something to be at during the day. I also had a copy of *Peace News* which Anne Barr or Jenny James of Atlantis had sent me. The cards were a very useful thing for me during the couple of weeks that I had the tummy bug because it was a mechanical task that could be done without inspiration. Some of the cards turned out quite nice, which was a bonus. I hoped that people in Ireland who got them would think they were worth keeping on the mantelpiece for a while.

On 5 May news started to come on the TV about a spectacular rescue attempt by hundreds of Special Forces soldiers. They had tried to rescue ten prisoners held by the FARC in a camp deep in the jungle. Three helicopters had dropped off the soldiers at different points about a half hour from the camp. When the Special Forces arrived at the camp the FARC were gone and the prisoners had been shot. One survived.

In the afternoon of 6 May we got word that El Comandante Alfredo was going to be released later in the day. Immediately, Jimmy, the man who was sleeping on the floor in our room started to get excited and wanted me to move my stuff into El Comandante's place so that he could move his stuff into my place. I told him to be calm and that as soon as Alfredo went out the gate I would move my stuff. El

Comandante came into the room and there was an emotional goodbye for everyone. After the goodbyes he went all around the patio having a final word with all his comrades. He was on his way, after many false starts and rumours of release.

As soon as he went out the gate, and the last cheers had died away, I started to move my things. I had to be reasonably quick as items disappear like magic when a man gets out. I was satisfied that I had ended up with most of the good stuff that Alfredo had left.

Niall got the plank of wood for under the bed so I used the other to set up a low platform to hold those things that I did not use often. I put the things needed more often on Alfredo's shelves. After a couple of hours I had everything laid out where I wanted it. It did not take long for me to get used to the new bed and sleeping space. The bed was a proper bed – a bunk-bed had been sawn in two and it was the bottom half. It had a foam rubber mattress which was a lot more comfortable than the lumpy, hard, horsehair one that I had left behind.

The news that evening was all about the FARC shooting ten prisoners. The FARC had repeatedly said they would shoot the prisoners if there was a rescue attempt so the outcome was not hard to predict. The relatives of the prisoners were apparently very much opposed to a rescue attempt as it was widely believed that a prisoner exchange was not far off. The government could use the incident as a reason not to go ahead with the prisoner exchange.

On 8 May I got dressed for going to the judges' offices to see what was new in the legal process. We expected that the transcripts of the defence witnesses' testimony would be there, but there could also be other additions of interest. We reviewed the process every couple of months.

Our names were called at the gate. We went out to the guards' office where the 'moving squad' were waiting. Each of us was fingerprinted – twice. The first time was our own guard checking that the correct prisoners were going out the gate, according to their paperwork. The other fingerprints were for the 'moving squad' to make sure that they were collecting the prisoners who were to be moved to the judges' office.

We walked down the long corridor, handcuffed and escorted by several guards dressed in flak jackets. At the front of the main building we stopped for more fingerprinting. This time it was the prison administration that wanted to be sure we were the correct prisoners. We were searched very rigorously. As things were removed from my pockets they were checked and handed back to me, but I was hand-cuffed. When it came to putting the stuff back in my pockets I dropped my glasses by accident and luckily they survived. Martin's cigarettes and lighter were taken from him. From there on the attitude of the guards moving us was tough.

We were put into the van outside the door and one of the guards moved to put leg irons on us. We had agreed that we would cancel the trip if they made us wear leg irons. There was a tense few minutes when we said the trip was off and we wanted to return to the prison. In the end it was agreed that the leg irons would be taken off at the court buildings before we left the van. They then chained both of Niall's legs together and I had one leg chained, through a metal opening, to Martin's leg. If there was a traffic accident both of us would have a foot ripped off. On the way to the judges' office there were six heavily armed guards in the back of the van, separated from us by a wire mesh door.

At the court buildings, we were unchained and rushed up four flights of stairs to a holding cell. The guard in charge refused to return Martin's cigarettes and lighter, so he was left without a smoke all the time we were in the cell. It was at times like this that he most needed a smoke. After an hour or so we were taken out of the cell and rushed down the four flights of stairs to an empty courtroom where we could read the transcripts. There were twenty-five guards with us, fourteen of them in the room, all heavily armed with automatic rifles and sub-machine-guns and pistols. That was in addition to the police guards in the court building. They refused to take off the handcuffs.

The court clerk came into the room with a huge armful of paper. We found the latest transcripts but also found it extremely difficult to manage them with handcuffs on. One of the guards started to read from the remaining heap of our case papers. Niall objected strongly and there was another stand-off. After a few minutes a guard came over to me and removed my handcuffs, then Martin's and Niall's. The other guard moved a little away from our pile of evidence. They had no right to read any of it.

We read through the headings fairly quickly and noted what we wanted photocopies of. After a while we had the page numbers for each of the witnesses and how they had answered the questions put to them. We did not require the long legal arguments, as these had been judged on anyway. The court secretary made the photocopies that we wanted to bring back to the prison and then we told the guards that we were finished. All the transcripts of the court proceedings were in Spanish. Both Martin and I could read Spanish enough to get the drift of what was going on and then, if it was important, we asked the meaning of particular words or sentences.

While waiting for the van to bring us back to La Modelo, we were left sitting in the courtroom near the guards. A conversation started between them and us and the tension eased. On the way back to the prison there were no guards at all in the back of the van and only Niall had leg irons. The guard who was putting them on us was called away before he finished his task. Back in the prison things were more relaxed as well.

I had felt sick in the van because my stomach was acting up; it had been doing so for two weeks to some extent, but now it seemed more severe. So, immediately after I got into our living area I asked that my name be put down for the doctor. I phoned Jenny James in the Atlantis Commune and asked her opinion. She told me that for the first year or two that they were in Colombia they were plagued with stomach troubles until they built up a resistance to the local bugs. She thought it might be an attack of parasites. I was ready with the Spanish words to explain my symptoms to the prison doctor.

The doctor arrived in the living area that same evening. I was about to launch into a Spanish explanation when he took off his white coat and grabbed a billiard cue. He played a game – and lost – before putting on the white coat again. Luis said something brief to him and he pointed at my stomach.

"Pain?"

"Si!"

He pulled out a notebook and scribbled something. I had to sign the page and the duplicate.

"Listo." (Finished.)

That was the end of my medical examination, and my Spanish explanation of weeks of suffering. It was obvious that my condition was very common and did not require much diagnosis. I thought that now I was almost cured, all I needed was the medicine he had written down. I asked Luis about it and he said he would look after it for me.

We had another outing to the court building the next day – this time to talk to the lawyers. When the guards came for us we went to their office and went through the process of fingerprinting and being handed over to the moving squad. Things were a lot more relaxed than the previous day. We had three paramilitaries with us. Possibly because of that we were not handcuffed until we got to the main entrance.

There was a bit of relaxed talk with the guards, and one of the paramilitaries went out of his way to be friendly to me. In the van there were six guards with us but they were simply carrying revolvers. They had left their Galil automatic rifles and Uzi sub–machine–guns behind them. I almost got sick in the van with the constant jolting and the bad driving and no vision of the outside. There was a little light from air holes in the van, but not much.

When we arrived at the court buildings, the attitude suddenly changed for the worse – probably because of who was in charge. We were rushed up the four flights of stairs to the holding cell and locked in. After a long time had passed they came and rushed us down the stairs again to the empty courtroom. The judge's secretary gave us the evidence papers that we asked for. After a while one of our lawyers arrived. We discussed various aspects of the case with him. Another lawyer arrived, saying that the third one could not make it.

One of the lawyers said that it was necessary to have a delay of four weeks after the prosecution summed up their case, so that it could be examined in detail. This produced an adverse reaction from Niall and Martin who wanted things to finish up quickly – on the basis that we were going to win. I was breaking ranks by agreeing with the lawyer.

A little later the same lawyer said that win or lose, there would be an appeal, which would take another couple of months. If we won against the *Fiscalía*, the *Procuradora* would almost certainly appeal. This produced an even worse reaction, because it meant extra time in prison, but the reaction was lessened by him saying that we would get bail. It all demonstrated the tension that being held in prison created. It would have been much worse, of course, if we had been still held in a prison like Cómbita, far away from visitors and lawyers.

When it came time for the dinner break, I was feeling a lot better, and more able to concentrate. I wanted to ask a few more questions. After the dinner break the other two wanted to return to La Modelo. When I insisted that I ask the questions, because it would be weeks before we saw the lawyers again, the result was more tension. The guards put us back in the holding cell upstairs and, in a vindictive move, took away the book of evidence that we wanted to use the two hours reading.

There were two women prisoners in the cell already, both of whom had lived in New York and spoke fairly good English. They were being held on drug trafficking charges in Buen Pastor, the women's prison. After a half-hour, a messenger arrived from a local restaurant with three takaway meals sent by the lawyers. Niall offered the women a meal but they declined, taking a cup of fruit juice that came with the meal. I ate my chicken and vegetables because now that I was recovering from the sickness, I was hungry.

At 2pm, we were taken downstairs to the empty courtroom. The lawyer who would have given better answers was gone. We asked the other lawyers the questions, which led to more questions and answers. It took perhaps fifteen minutes to go through what I wanted. It had emerged from my questioning of the lawyer that the US Embassy had probably got away with their crime and would only be subject to a mild criticism of incompetence in making the forensic tests that had produced the evidence of explosive contamination of our clothes. Without that false evidence there would have been no credible case against us.

The guards, as usual, took a while to get the van. We were put in the back with the lightly armed guards and no chains on our legs. Even so, the violent motion soon had me feeling that I was going to get sick again.

When we got back to our place, I immediately asked Luis, the OC (officer commanding), for the medicine. He told me that he would have to give the prescription to his wife on Sunday, and that she would buy the medicine on Monday and get it back into the prison – it might be next Saturday before I would get it! I would probably have cured myself by then.

On 10 May, as soon as the men's visits were over at 4.30pm, Luis announced a general clean-up and decoration of the living area. The next day, Sunday, was Mother's Day. We started cleaning the plastic tables and chairs. Others mopped the floors and cleaned out even behind the cookers and all the hidden corners that usually did not get cleaned. They had bought coloured plastic bags which were cut into strips. The strips of different colours were made into rings by stapling them and joining the rings to form long chains.

Other men inflated balloons and wrote messages with markers on them, such as "Salute to the mothers of the world". By 8am the place was like an Irish Christmas party. There were big disks of folded news-papers on the walls and arches of balloons near the gate. Niall and Milton were writing out a message on a large sheet of cardboard. They were using woodworking glue and brightly coloured small pieces of aluminium foil. When they had a piece written they would sprinkle it, so that the bits of foil stuck to the glue.

Later in the evening things went very quiet because everyone had done all that they could and were now just waiting for tomorrow morn-ing. The strips of plastic left over from the long chains were used as decorations on the doors and plywood walls of the sleeping areas. They were hanging down in multi-coloured clumps that were full of static electricity. They stuck to each other and to the walls.

Mother's Day started with noise! In the opinion of some it was music, but it was so loud that it was just unbearable to me. I stayed out of the kitchen area, except for a quick foray to get my breakfast, which I brought out to a quieter place to eat. At about 9.30am the mothers and kids started to arrive and there was soon quite a good gathering.

A band of six or seven came into the living area with a range of small guitars and a really big harp. Some of them sang while accompa-nied by the harp and the other instruments. It was a nice change from the CD player and had some stuff worth listening to.

After the visits ended, we took down the decorations but the band music went on. We had a meal of chicken and chips for me, Martin, Niall and Flaco. I enjoyed it! For the first time in several days I was feeling better.

There was a document that I had not felt up to reading for a few weeks, so I took it off the shelf. It was the 2002 US State Department report on human rights in Colombia. There were fifty-three pages of type in it. I read a bit more than half. In the section about the courts, it went into the intimidation of judges and witnesses resulting in acquittals of suspects – implying very strongly that guilty people were getting off by intimidating witnesses. As an example, the report cited our case. "Two witnesses failed to turn up for the trial saying that they were afraid to do so." The inference was obvious – and this in a case where the US Embassy was directly involved in perverting the course of justice by supplying false evidence. The entire report was a whitewash job for the Colombian government and its forces, heavily biased to show them in the best possible light in spite of a lot of condemnations from independent human rights bodies and the United Nations. The good report was used to justify increased arms supplies to repressive governments, while bad reports were there to build up some credibility for the State Department's human rights report.

There was an article in *El Tiempo* about Comandante Alfredo getting out. 'Alfredo' was an alias and not his name at all. He was José González Perdomo, and he had been the single most important FARC prisoner, according to *El Tiempo*. Sentenced to ninety-five months for rebellion, he had thirteen other charges against him which were used to prevent his release by bringing yet another spurious charge. In Colombia you would expect to do around half the ninety-five month sentence, which was about four years, but they held him for ten.

He had been moved very frequently from prison to prison in case the FARC tried to rescue him. It was unfortunate that my Spanish was only now reaching a standard where I could sit and talk, because he was there all that time and would have enjoyed talking. We did have some conversations with Niall interpreting, but that never developed into a conversation about all the small, interesting things. It tended to be about the big issues.

Luis was an interesting man as well, but until I was better at Spanish I could not bridge the gap – and even then, he was a reserved kind of man. I did not want to know anything secret or important, but I would have liked to get to know them as people – what they thought,

MUSIC IN
LA MODELO '0

what they hoped for, the kind of country they wanted to build or if they had a vision of the future.

Luis came in with a small package – the long-awaited medicine! There were two kinds of pill, one to be taken every eight hours and the other every twelve hours. I took one each of the pills in coffee. I might have got the bug in the first place by washing down multivitamin tablets with tap water. The heat of the coffee would kill at least some of the less tough bugs that swim in the water.

I was writing in bed at about 11.30pm when the electricity failed. There was total darkness, with a lot of shouting. I immediately got up and dressed in case it was a prelude to a paramilitary attack. In previous attacks they had run through the area shooting people who were still in their beds. I felt a bit vulnerable without a weapon of any sort. Other men had knives and wood chisels for defence and I hoped that there were some pistols concealed somewhere. The INPEC guards simply withdrew to their offices and then from the building in the event of fighting.

Someone got two small candles and lit them in the main living area. It was safer to stay away from the light until it became clear that it was not an attack but a power failure. After an hour or so I decided to go back to bed. Niall came and asked if I had any batteries so that he could listen to the local radio. I gave him the batteries that I had. He might be able to find out from the radio whether it was part of a larger blackout or confined to the prison. I removed my runners again and lay on the bed, fully dressed – ready for any alarm. Gradually the talk from nearby beds died out and I drifted off to sleep.

On the mid-day news a couple of days later, Uribe said that instead of a prisoner exchange, he was considering the system used to release prisoners in the Irish peace process. Martin thought that we would be out of here in the not too distant future. Niall thought that it was very good in that it was an official recognition about the Irish peace process involving prisoners, which must set a better climate for our case. I, as usual, was the pessimist, but I did take Niall's point. I thought there was a strong possibility that Uribe had thrown in a red herring to buy time and deflate the campaign for a prisoner exchange.

In the Irish peace process, the releases came as a result of a much wider agreement on a whole range of topics. There was no such agreement in Colombia, and no open negotiations towards an agreement. If I had been a FARC negotiator I would not have been inclined to welcome this initiative by Uribe. It meant, at the very least, months wasted in clarifying it, when it was not likely to be a serious attempt to deal with the prisoners on both sides. It was a case of 'Talk Peace, Make War'.

A possibly useful aspect of Uribe's speech was that it focused attention in Colombia a bit more on the Irish peace process and might in time lead to more contact between Irish and Colombian people and institutions. To some small extent that had already happened between the human rights lawyers involved in our case and their counterparts in Ireland.

People like Irish solicitor Peter Madden met and got to know Agustin Jimenez, the president of the Foundation for Solidarity with Political Prisoners, and the others who travelled to Ireland – and Peter came to Colombia. There was also a delegation of Colombians who went to Ireland to study the peace process and meet people from the various political parties there. It could only be to the good that contacts were built up and each nation learned from and helped build on the experience of the other. The downside was of course that the corruptos in both countries would also love to exchange ideas and I could just imagine how the police forces might compare methods. The US would not be pleased at all as they needed a cloak of ignorance around their historic and present behaviour in Latin America.

The three of us had quite a long session going over the defence evidence that was given at the last court session. We were dealing with the evidence given by Keith Borer, who was the defence expert on forensics and explosives. His testimony was documented in Spanish and Niall had to translate it for us. Legal stuff was difficult enough in your normal language – in another language there was enormous scope for misunderstanding. Still, we did get the general drift of it. There were two areas that seemed to be of enormous importance.

One was the accusation that the US Embassy made of having found traces of drugs and explosives on our luggage. They did not press charges on the drugs but their finding of explosive traces was what gave credibility to the whole case against us. The evidence was false and the US Embassy was aware that it was false – if not right from the start, then from the time a couple of weeks later when Niall said so on TV. They would have checked from ambassadorial level whether there was truth in what we said.

The second aspect was the accusation that – as a result of us and IRA training previously – the FARC's use of mortars and other improvised weapons had changed dramatically. Our man showed clearly that there was very little similarity between IRA and FARC weapons. This should discredit their case that the evidence of IRA training was in the changed technology of the FARC. It was important because we were charged with training and they needed some evidence to support that. The FARC deserters who said that we trained them had been discredited, so indirect evidence was needed, but Borer has also discredited that.

I had grown up in Rathmullan in County Donegal until our family moved to Dublin, and on Saturday 24 May 2003 the 'Bring Them Home' campaign was having a solidarity walk in Rathmullan to show support for us. There was probably a huge gap in politics and understanding between me and the people that knew me there as a twelve-year-old. They would be in their fifties or sixties now, and I had taken many choices during my life that left us worlds apart. I rang Eileen Sheils and she was on her way there. She did great work, along with her sister Maureen Fanning, in organising events to raise money for our campaign. There were several others who also did a lot for us. I would make something for each of them.

Late in the evening I was watching Freddy making a belt from string. He had a nail in the wall and a wooden gadget that was tied around his waist which had attachment points for the strings. There were five groups of strings, two strings in each group. The string groups were attached two or three at a time to the wood and the loose strings woven around them, then the groups were changed and woven again. It took an hour to do twenty centimetres. He was willing to teach me how to weave belts. He had learned from his grandfather. They were cattle herders in Venezuela and spent a lot of time making woven things.

Our case would come up again on 16 June but we didn't expect anything dramatic, so it was not a cause of tension. It was expected to be the last in the series for taking evidence. If it was, then the next stage would be a series of dates on which the various parties would sum up the case.

It was possible that the Irish Foreign Affairs Department would back the observers' report. Foreign Affairs gave us the feeling of being weak and compliant – tugging the forelock to their perceived betters – but Brian Cowen, the new minister, might break that habit. In a recent letter I had been told that Cowen had stood up to the British media on his choice to use Irish rather than English – that was a hopeful indicator. If the Irish government voiced its backing for the observers' report that said that we did not get a fair trial, that would embarrass the Colombian and US governments internationally.

Some days later we heard from Ireland that the observers were meeting Bertie Ahern, the Taoiseach. He had made a speech which included remarks harmful to us, implying strongly that we were guilty of something and demanding that "there will be no more Colombias". He did not apologise or say that it would not happen again, but did say something to the effect that his remarks were "inappropriate". I was sure that if Tony Blair were to tell him to do it again, he would. But at best he was embarrased.

One of the prisoners had asked me to paint two flowers on a bit of woodcraft work that he had done. I sealed the wood with the shape of the flowers in white and then painted the yellow and red flowers and dark green leaves and stems. I was almost finished when the prison psychologist – a big Russian woman whom we had met in La Picota – arrived into my cell and asked me to come out to the main living area.

Chairs had been set up and everyone moved to where a four-man Colombian band was ready to make music. There were also several visiting people for the performance. The band consisted of two men with long Indian pipes like very big tin whistles, and two others with drums. One of the drums was the normal kind, about forty centimetres in diameter, which he had tied to a chair to play with drumsticks. The other was the long conical type of drum that the man sat with between his knees and played with his fingers. The man with the pipes also had a small drum that he held in his lap and one of them had a sort of rattle which was a ball filled with dry beans which he shook to make the sounds. They played for about twenty minutes.

I asked Niall whether it was Indian or Spanish music. Niall asked the band leader, who said that it was music from the north of Colombia, from the Caribbean coast. It had strong African and Indian influences and, of course, a lot of Spanish. Martin thought that in the basic arrangements there was an Irish influence as well. The band went upstairs. The paramilitaries and the drugs prisoners liked the music too.

Late in the evening I was going past Martin's cell and I saw Milton playing the guitar. I sat beside him to listen although he was just strumming away. Mario, 'the real Irishman', was passing and dropped in as well. (He got his nickname because he looked like a caricature of an Irishman: he was big and well built with red hair and freckles.) He got down the other guitar and they both played bits of Indian-type music. Mario then went to his cell and returned with the Irish tin whistle that Niall had given him. They played some lovely Andean music from Peru. The tin whistle gave a reasonable performance in place of the Indian flute. After that they moved on to Simon and Garfunkel music; 'The Sound of Silence' had a special meaning for me as it was constantly on the radio in the summer of 1970 when I was doing my first time in prison, in Brixton, London.

Next day I was told that one of our lawyers, Pedro, was in the living area seeing another man; he had said he would talk to us shortly, so I got Martin and Niall.

The main business was an update on what was happening and the technical reasons that might cause a delay of several months in our trial. We did not get as agitated about delays as we used to because they seemed inevitable in the legal process here – all that changed was the reason for the next delay.

Later Padre Andres and the big Russian psychologist came in. We had a chat and the priest had some money and e-mails for us. They asked about my health and I explained the problem with my stomach. Our Russian friend said she would return with a doctor. Sure enough, about an hour later she did.

The doctor asked me what was wrong and I started to explain. His English being about as good as my Spanish, we got into total confusion in two languages. After we called in Niall as interpreter, things went a lot more smoothly. We went to a cell where he gave me an examinaton. All that we established was that the focus of the trouble was at the bottom left side of my stomach and a secondary point centered under my ribs, at the front.

He said that he would arrange for a more detailed examination, and in the meantime gave me a lot of pills and multivitamins – and a prayer book. He was religious and told us a Bible story about Egypt and the prophesy of the seven years of plenty and seven years of famine. He was humorous and had a pleasant nature. After dealing with me he spent a lot of time seeing other men and had the same good-humoured sort of chat while he dealt with their medical problems.

At about 5pm another doctor arrived in. He said that the test on my stomach would be available in about fifteen days. With all the pushing and prodding it was acting up again, but if they really did the test in fifteen days that would be okay. Hopefully it would clear up itself before that – if it was a minor problem like parasites.

Martin told me that the body of Yesid Arteta's lawyer, who was

MUSIC LESSON
MARTIN OCT '02   Se

'disappeared', had been found on a roadside near Huila, which was not
far from where Anne and the Atlantis commune were. That was probably a job subcontracted out to the paramilitaries by military intelligence. We couldn't miss the implications for our lawyers. The price of
successful defence of a person whom the military wanted condemned
was often torture and death on a lonely roadside. Meanwhile Uribe,
the President, was congratulated in an editorial in *El Tiempo* for his
diplomatic triumphs in getting pledges of support from the G8 countries and for a resolution from the Grupo del Rio countries calling for
a ceasefire by the FARC with possible military intervention if they
refused.

   You only half believe what any prisoner said about themselves.
Time and events show a good bit, but not all about anyone. Freddy said
that he was medically trained in the Venezuelan army. He did seem to
know a good bit about minor ailments all right, so I asked him to look
at the pills that the doctor had given me. They certainly seemed to

work for me – I was eating and feeling fine. He said that they were for ulcers, that they formed a protective layer in the stomach.

Food rations arrived in and I was put with a group of men taking beans out of their pods. Other men were doing the same job with peas, while others were cutting up green beans. There were sacks of spuds and sacks of yucca roots, scallions and onions. A couple of men were cutting up meat and chickens and there were even two turkeys there.

Patricia Ramos from the Defensoría del Pueblo and her assistant came in to have a look at conditions and to talk to prisoners. Martin pointed out that each time in the past when she appeared, we got shifted.

This evening the men were sitting around watching the TV news. Among them was a man called Ballastras, accused of hijacking an aeroplace and flying it to Venezuela for the ELN. There was no real evidence against him, just the usual *testigos*, or eye witnesses, that the army have such a supply of. One of them had said they saw him in a café near the airport where the hijacked plane took off from. As he watched the news, his case was mentioned and they said he had been sentenced to thirty years.

On the phone, my young lad Dónal told me he was reading a book called *The Civil War in France* by a fellow called Karl Marx. I asked him what was good about it and he said he liked the history and the descriptions of the battles. I had *Peter the Great*, a really big book on that period of Russian history and when I finished it I intended to send it back to Dónal with the visitors on the 26th of next month. Irina Malenko, a Russian friend of the family, sent it to me because I enjoyed the videos she showed us one time about Ivan the Terrible.

I decided that I would do a self-portrait. It was a good fallback because you have a model who has a bit of patience and an interesting face. The drawback was that everyone was looking over your shoulder and accusing you of making the painting younger looking or better looking than the reality. I hung a mirror on one of the stands for making hammocks. I had to paint in the kitchen where everyone was, because it was the only place with good enough light – and then only in the mornings. I did a pencil sketch with the pad in one hand and the pencil in the other, standing in front of the mirror. It was a shaving mirror so I could only have the face and shoulders. It took about an hour to paint in the face and the surrounding area. I took the picture and hung it up at the end of my bed to observe any corrections that were needed.

I was looking at the self-portrait trying to figure out what a stranger would make of the man looking out of the picture. The expression was intent, neither smiling nor cross, but concentrating. I had just painted what I saw, not intentionally with any particular expression. When you observe as a painter, you do not look in the normal way, you do not see the overall person. You see a pattern of shape and colour, a bit of the overall. Every detail was interesting but no judgments were made at all, except for the shapes, edges and colours. That is why, to a painter, every face is interesting, even fascinating for its patterns; notions of conventional beauty don't come into it. What shocked me was that the portrait was of someone older and thinner than I imagined myself.

After the visits were over Niall came and got the three of us together. Luis had come to him and pointed out that both Martin and I had lost a lot of weight, especially me. He said that we should make up a diet that we would eat to stay healthy. We got together and decided that on three days of the week – Monday, Wednesday and Friday – we would have meals that we would finish and so get enough nourishment. The doctor had said I needed more fibre, but he had not thought that I was underweight – at least he did not say that.

We would put vegetables, spuds and porridge in the diet as well as dairy products like milk powder and cheese. We would make sure to have enough meat, chicken or fish, as well as eggs in the diet. We actually did get sufficient fruit as fruit juice in our present diet, and meat or chicken. What we needed to buy more of was cheese, eggs and milk powder and oat flakes for porridge. We had spuds, but not often enough. On the other four days we would be eating Colombian grub, which was mostly rice, beans and yucca. It tended to have too much fatty meat, rather than not enough.

There was an article in *El Spectadore* which said that Uribe had already studied the Irish peace process while studying in England before he became President. The Minister of Defence said that they were using the Irish process as a model to develop in Colombia. Only guerilla deserters would benefit from the measures, not prisoners who were captured and sentenced. The main beneficiaries would be paramilitaries wanted for massacres; if they deserted they would not serve time for what they were accused of.

There was a policy of imposing large sentences on guerilla leaders for actions carried out by men under their command. For instance, when Ballestras was sentenced for hijacking the plane, they also sentenced several leaders of the ELN in their absence. In the context of Uribe's explanation of the Irish peace process it could be a powerful inducement to desert and have the charges wiped out, or at least not have to serve time for them. The idea was that 'on the runs' would go through a nominal trial but serve no time, unless they commited a further offence, and in that case they would serve all the time they had been sentenced to.

We got a phone call from Jack Crowe and a group from the 'Bring Them Home' campaign who were doing a sponsored parachute jump to raise money. The weather was too windy for the jump but they were hoping that the wind would drop in the afternoon. When we rang back in four hours to find out how things had worked out, we were delighted to hear that they had made the jump.

I phoned Eileen Sheils and Maureen Fanning on their way home from Castlerea prison in Ireland, to thank them for the great work that they were doing for us. The prisoners in Castlerea had undertaken a sponsored run which had raised around €6,000 for our campaign. It took a lot of money to get the legal and political observers out to Colombia – but they were essential. It also took money to get family visits.

The two men in the room with me were sitting reading the Bible to each other. In all the years I spent in prisons, I never saw that happen in Ireland or England, but here among the Marxist FARC and ELN there was actually more personal religion – not the 'seen the light' sort of guilt trip that is common among loyalist prisoners in Ireland, but a quiet personal sort of thing. One of them, Milton, played the guitar and sang a religious song. Maybe they were both feeling a bit desperate. Freddy was down in the dumps a couple of nights ago. I got out some of my cheese and other food and I cheered him up with a wee snack.

On a Sunday visit, while I was working on a painting, two women were sitting nearby talking to Tito and one of the cooks, José. The women were curious to see what I was at, so Tito called me over. I explained and got talking to them. They were visiting the ELN prisoners and were training to be lawyers. I had a very pleasant couple of hours talking to them and drawing their portraits, and putting on an art exhibition of the fourteen pictures that I had painted for the visits. I explained what I considered important in each of the pictures, what the picture was about and the technical bits of how and why I painted it. I got in a lot of excellent Spanish practice. Unfortunately their visit was a one-off.

Niall had some of the men helping with making stuff for the visits. Next weekend we expected to have the legal and political observers over for the trial. As well as them, we would have Caitríona and Therese from the 'Bring Them Home' campaign. On 26 June we would have more visits, this time from our families. We liked to give gifts both as tokens of thanks to those who had done so much for us and also for our families and friends. I sent paintings to be used in fund-raising on each visit. This time there would be wooden plaques and harps as well as Ché Guevara wristbands. Martin and Niall were working away at the woodwork while I painted.

I phoned Anne; she was busy: Alice, another member of the Atlantis commune, was having her first baby at home and it was a difficult birth. When I had phoned last night she was already in labour, and twelve hours later she still had not given birth. I told her that I would ring again in the evening. Anne had told me that Alice was a big, strong teenage girl and should have had no problem.

During the 'hour of sun' today I went to the roof. I was watching the volleyball when one of the guards came over and told me that a doctor wanted to examine me. I went downstairs with him and met the doctor. We went into the guards' observation room and he did the examination. Between his bit of English and my bit of Spanish we managed okay. He was not satisfied that it was a gastric condition brought on by tension; he wanted an ultrasonic examination. That was

WHEN I GIVE FOOD TO THE POOR
THEY CALL ME A SAINT,
WHEN I ASK WHY THE POOR HAVE NO FOOD
THEY CALL ME A COMMUNIST

SÉ LA MOTELO 03   DOM HELDER CAMARA

to take place in two or three weeks time. I had worked on ultrasonic machines so I understood the principle – they were looking for a cancer growth. It was 'precautionary' but that was not what his body languge said.

I tried to phone Anne to find out if the birth went okay and how Alice was. At 8pm no one answered the phone. I waited forty-five minutes and phoned again. Again no one answered. I was worried that the birth did not go well and that they had to bring her to hospital for emergency attention. I was delighted to be told the next day that both Alice and the baby were okay.

Chapter 17

Our Trial Resumes Again

THE DEFENCE WAS now, in June 2003, putting its case to the court, and the international observers were watching everything that went on. The evidence for the defence was to rebut the statements given at the previous sitting by Edwin Giovanny Rodriguez and John Alexander Caviedes, in which Rodriquez had said that we were training FARC in February 2001, while Caviedes said that he had seen us training in 1998, 1999, 2000 and 2001 – he had given three very contradictory statements with different dates and details.

Our lawyers produced three witnesses. Síle Maguire, first secretary in the Irish Embassy in Mexico, had been allowed waive her diplomatic immunity to give evidence about a meeting with Niall on 17 January 2001. She testified that she was in Cuba with Irish parliamentarians Jim O'Keeffe, Madeleine Taylor Quinn and Ben Briscoe, who had dinner with Niall on that date. She had also spoken to Niall four weeks before that date.

Dr Sean Ó Domhnaill gave evidence that he had attended one of Martin's family on a weekly basis during the time that the army informer said he was in Colombia. Martin was present during these sessions.

Ros O'Sullivan, an aid worker with Concern Worldwide, gave evidence that he had spent Christmas 2000 (from 23 December to 5 January) with Niall.

Work records and affidavits from people shown in the videos with me were also supplied to the court. The prosecution tried to argue that the videos had been tampered with but experts would have been able to tell fairly easily if the date shown on a video had been altered.

We had decided to attend the trial itself and make statements to the judge, so we informed the judge and INPEC. Each of us put on our best clothes; I was wearing a sky-blue shirt, a dark tie and dark trousers. Martin looked well in his slate-blue shirt and dark-coloured tie. Niall had a white shirt on. Each of us had a fresh haircut. After the usual procedure for leaving the prison we got in the van and were taken to the court. Security was exceptionally heavy; they were taking no chances at this late stage! There was an atmosphere of nervous anticipation as we waited in the reception cell to be brought to the courtroom. We had each made out a statement to read to the court, which our lawyers had looked at and approved. I read mine once again, but I found it difficult to concentrate.

Finally the INPEC guards came and handcuffed us for the short walk to the courtroom. Outside it the handcuffs were removed and we entered a side door to the seats on the right of where Judge Jairo Acosta sat. Pedro, my lawyer, was sitting right behind me along with José Luis and Eduardo, Martin and Niall's lawyers. The courtroom was crowded. I could see Gerry, Cristin and Johnny, Niall's brother, sitting near the back of the small courtroom. The international observers and Art, the Irish Ambassador, were all there as well. There were a lot of media people around the main entrance, and a lot of police as well. We spoke to our lawyers until the judge indicated that proceedings were starting.

The court called Martin first to give his statement.

Following the signing of the Good Friday Agreement an International Commission headed by Chris Patten, a former British government minister and former British Governor of Hong Kong, was established to make recommendations for the creation of a new police service that would be acceptable to all sections of the community. I gave evidence to this Commission based on my own experiences at the hands of the RUC. As a result of my court case and the publicity it received I was subjected to a campaign of vicious harassment by the RUC and the British military. A bomb was placed at my home. At that time I was legally represented by Rosemary Nelson, a human rights lawyer. Rosemary was threatened by the RUC. In 1999 the same death squads that had killed Pat Finucane, killed Rosemary Nelson.

I was in genuine fear for the safety of myself and my family. I moved from the North of Ireland, which is under British occupation, and went to live in the South.

Prior to moving South, I had been involved with former political pris-
oners in Lurgan, Co. Armagh. When I had settled into my new home I
became reinvolved with work for former prisoners. I re-established contact
with Jim Monaghan, who I had met previously. Through this work I became
involved in discussions and debates on conflict and conflict resolution.

I met Niall Connolly through Jim, following a discussion on Latin
America. When the idea of the trip to Colombia arose I agreed to travel
with Jim and Niall. I had never been to Latin America, and I was inter-
ested in visiting this continent and seeing their peace process.

I have lived openly, North and South, for twenty years. I have been
in regular employment. Part of my employment involved me adapting
motor vehicles for use by people with disabilities. I have travelled openly all
over Ireland. I have not been charged with any of the offences alleged by
the RUC or the British Embassy. I am not a member of the IRA. I am not
guilty of the charges laid out against me in this court.

Like my two friends, I was using another name. Each of us had expe-
rience of threats, harassment and violence in shared and different situations.
There is nothing more than a desire to travel unhindered in the fact that I
was travelling on another name. I have explained how my life and those of
my family have been threatened. I have explained how two human rights
lawyers who have worked on my behalf were murdered by pro-British death
squads.

I am a supporter of Irish republicanism. I have worked within my com-
munity to help give a political voice to their views. I am not a member of
Sinn Féin. I have worked for Sinn Féin candidates in elections. I believe
in the right of the Irish people to control their destiny free from foreign occu-
pation and interference.

The peace process in Ireland continues to survive but it has been under-
mined and attacked by elements within the British political and military
establishment and from pro-British forces in Ireland. Our arrest in
Colombia has been used by these and other elements to further undermine
the peace process. Elements in the Colombian military and the political
establishment have fed lies and misinformation to the media to serve their
own interests. The Embassy of the United States cannot escape criticism for
its role in this affair. Their so-called forensic evidence against us is fraudu-
lent and misleading.

I wish to directly refute the evidence given by Captain Pulido. At no stage did I speak with this man. At the airport I was not asked for my passport nor was I asked my name at the time of my arrest. Captain Pulido's testimony is wrong.

In conclusion, I wish to thank my family and friends, the legal and political observers who have travelled great distances to help us, and everyone involved in the 'Bring Them Home' campaign.

I was next. I walked up to the stand and when I was within a comfortable distance from the microphone I started to speak.

Former political prisoners have always played a central role in Irish republican politics. Today many of the political leaders within Sinn Féin are former political prisoners. The role of prisoners and former prisoners was recognised as crucial to the development of the peace process within the community at local level.

An organisation called Coiste na n-Iarchimí *was established. Its primary aim was to help former prisoners reintegrate into society and to enable them to use their abilities to shape the new society that will emerge from the Irish peace process.*

In 1999/2000 I was granted a position within Coiste. *It was a full-time paid position. I was the director of a new sub-unit in Dublin called* Tar Isteach. *My job, indeed the project, was funded by the Irish government as part of the peace process. Similar projects were and are funded by the British government in the North of Ireland.*

Many of the discussions that we had during the course of our work in Coiste *identified the need for social justice and how that could be achieved. We recognised the need to study other situations and see how conflict resolution processes were developing. To do that we knew that it was necessary to meet face to face with others in different countries who were engaged in broadly similar processes.*

Witnesses have already explained in detail the problems facing former prisoners, including travel restrictions. With these problems come dangers. Because of these and previous experiences in travel shared by each of us we felt it wiser and safer to travel by legitimate means but using a different identity.

I came to know Martin McCauley through the ex-prisoner community;

our friendship developed when Martin and his family were forced to move near Dublin following threats to their lives. I have known Niall Connolly for a number of years. He is a native of Dublin and returns there on his regular trips home from Latin America. I knew Niall worked on humanitarian projects in that region. The three of us share the same broad political interests. Niall and I travelled to Nicaragua together a few years ago.

In the summer of 2001 the three of us travelled to Colombia principally to see the peace process but also to enjoy a holiday. For reasons already stated the three of us travelled with different names. We travelled openly and the way all other travellers would. We visited the peace zone.

We spent several weeks in the zone. We talked to a great many people. We shared experiences about the peace processes in Ireland and Colombia.

We discussed the involvement of outsiders in such processes. From an Irish perspective the advice and experiences of people involved in South Africa, Palestine, East Timor and other regions in Latin America were very important.

We discussed the process of becoming involved in a political system seen as hostile and the gains and the problems that resulted from such a course of action. We talked at length about the role of former prisoners in political developments in Ireland and the Irish peace process.

We met with members of the FARC. We learnt from them about the great number of visitors and political representatives who had visited the zone. This included members of the Colombian government and many people from outside Colombia.

Since we were arrested at El Dorado airport there has been a constant flow of misinformation and false allegations against us. The Embassies of the United States and Britain have both intervened to distort the truth. We were then driven to a military barracks; North American officials were present. After this we were brought to the Prosecutor's office. Everything was happening very fast, there were a lot of soldiers about. We denied meeting the FARC initially because we thought it would make matters worse for us.

The US forensics have been exposed as bogus. The stories of satellite pictures, video tapes and so on have been proven to be false. The British Embassy alleged that I am a member of the IRA. It is illegal in Ireland, North and South, and in England to belong to the IRA. I have lived openly, and travelled to all parts of Ireland over the past seventeen years. I have not been arrested or charged in relation to any of these allegations. I reject them. I am not a member of the IRA.

False evidence has been presented to this court. This is clear in the case of the US Embassy. The British Embassy also presented as factual evidence what amounts to no more than wild claims. Witnesses produced by the Colombian military have been proved to have given false testimony.

The charge of training the FARC is a false charge, based on false evidence. The training never happened, and I and my friends are therefore not guilty.

I would like to conclude by thanking my family and friends who have supported me in every way since my arrest. The work carried out on our behalf by everyone involved in the 'Bring Them Home' campaign has given us strength

Thank you all.

I sat down and it was Niall's turn to speak.

I have been interested in Latin America and the politics of the region since the 1980s.

While living in Cuba I was able to gain employment and put my knowledge of Spanish and English to good use. I worked as a translator. On occasion, as the court has heard in evidence, I was employed as a guide for visiting politicians and media.

I became active in political mobilisation against the British political and military occupation of part of Ireland in the 1980s. In particular, I was influenced by the hunger strike in 1981 when ten Irish prisoners died in a British prison. I participated in campaigns and protests during this period. I support Sinn Féin and wherever I was, at home or abroad, I made myself available to promote the aims of Sinn Féin. I am a supporter of the Irish peace process and the efforts of leaders like Gerry Adams and Martin McGuinness who are striving to bring about a lasting peace with social justice.

I visited Ireland regularly. During one of my visits home I got to know Jim Monaghan. Jim was aware of my work in Latin America and was eager to hear my experiences.

While in Dublin in early 2001 I met with Jim and a number of other people including Martin McCauley, who had been involved in discussions about conflict situations and conflict resolution processes around the world.

As a result of this meeting I agreed to undertake a trip to Colombia with Jim and Martin. I had travelled with Jim previously and my knowledge of Spanish was a primary reason for asking me to accompany them.

I have experienced first-hand the reconciliation process in Nicaragua and El Salvador. I have followed the peace process in Guatemala. I have an interest in the Colombian peace process along with other issues that affect politics in Latin America. When we visited Colombia, the country was trying, through dialogue between the government and the Revolutionary Armed Forces of Colombia, to define positions that would be used as the foundation for a peace process. The government had given political status to the FARC. Observers from around the world came to learn and to offer solidarity in the search for peace with social justice. I was motivated by my desire to see first-hand another process of conflict resolution in motion. I believed that an historic opportunity had been created between the government and the insurgents in one of the oldest conflicts in Latin America. I hope that a new process of reconciliation with social justice will develop in the future in Colombia.

When we were arrested by the Colombian military there were no warrants for our detention.

It became clear that false and irresponsible information was being leaked by the British Embassy. I was described as a member of the IRA. I have never been arrested or questioned about such an allegation. It is false. I am not a member of the IRA.

The intervention of officials from the US Embassy in the taking of the forensic samples and the subsequent media leaks from both the US and British Embassies was an attempt to damage and undermine the Colombian peace process. The so-called forensic evidence has been proven to be false.

Our arrests and the mass of misinformation and false stories that have followed have also been used to damage and undermine the Irish peace process. The Irish peace process is at an advanced stage. Yet more work needs to be done. My friends have spoken about the process of political recognition and status, the process of negotiations between the governments of Ireland, Britain and America and Irish republicans.

Since our arrest the Fiscal, instead of fulfilling his duty and responsibil-

ities to guarantee that justice is done, has arrogantly thrown the presumption of innocence into the dustbin, along with the independence of his institution.

The Fiscal has failed to guarantee that procedures are respected and that the evidence is analysed in a just and impartial way. Confidential details about our case have been given to the media to upset and damage our opportunity to get a fair trial. Fabricated forensics were allowed, while DAS tests that showed that there were no traces of explosives or drugs were kept out.

We have been placed in jails in Colombia under the recommendation of the Fiscal while our lives have been in danger, and in the opinion of one judge, who ordered our transfer, we have been subject to degrading and inhumane treatment. Obstacles have been placed in our way and that of our lawyers when we were trying to prepare our defence. Our lawyers' lives are in danger because of the statements made in the media, many of them by prominent politicians.

Our lawyers from Colombia and Ireland will show that without a shadow of a doubt we are not guilty as charged. They will also show that this case should never have been brought to this court. I am not guilty of the charges laid against me. I come here today to remind the Fiscal of my rights, my international rights of the Presumption of Innocence.

The determination of our families and the 'Bring Them Home' campaign led by Caitríona Ruane, the presence of international observers from Australia, the United States, Ireland and the presence of the Irish government observers at this trial, the messages from all around the world of support and the active support of thousands of people in Ireland has given us much moral support and I thank you from the bottom of my heart.

The trial ended on 1 August; the verdict was expected in four to six weeks. About a week after the trial, Niall Andrews MEP, who was an observer, said in a newspaper interview:

So, what were the three Irishmen doing in Colombia? They said that their purpose was to study the Colombian peace process, which was taking place at the time.

The Colombian prosecutor accused them of training FARC soldiers, an armed, left-wing revolutionary force. The Colombian prosecution team said that they could produce evidence to prove it.

A very open and transparent court case concluded last week in Bogotá. But I believe that the case presented by the prosecution against the three Irishmen was very weak indeed.

The forensic evidence taken by an American Embassy official was discredited by Dr Keith Borer, a renowned forensic scientist.

It was his expert opinion that the forensic tests carried out by the US Embassy official were contaminated and did not follow the usual criteria.

Two 'eye witnesses' gave evidence against the men. One gave evidence on three different occasions, and each time the evidence was different.

The Colombian government failed to produce any credible witnesses. It failed to interview witnesses whose names had been put forward by the defendants.

The prosecution then set about calling into question the integrity of Irish diplomat Síle Maguire, suggesting that she had a "selective memory".

To me, this is an outrage. Not only does it call into question the honesty of Maguire, but also calls into question the written affidavits presented to the court by Jim O'Keeffe TD.

The prosecutor even went so far as to suggest that the video evidence showing Jim Monaghan speaking at meetings in Ireland on 7 February 2001 (Dublin), 21 February 2001 (Dublin) and 22 Febuary 2001 (Belfast) had been tampered with.

The defence team destroyed the prosecution charge that the three men had been "training the FARC".

Following the conclusion of the prosecution case the chief of staff of the Colombian armed forces, General Moro, went on television to demand that they be "condemned".

Colombian President Álvaro Uribe and Vice-president Francisco Santos have made similar statements.

In any normal democracy such intimidation would result in the case being dismissed and the men freed.

Chapter 18

Waiting for the Verdict

A FTER THE TRIAL we waited for the verdict, and waited, and waited! We were delighted to hear that in elections in the North of
Ireland Caitríona Ruane was elected as a Sinn Féin MLA for South
Down. But the weeks and months passed slowly as we went from the
autumn of 2003 through the winter and into the spring of 2004.

A lot of the priosners we knew had been moved to Cómbita and the
remainder of us in La Modelo were moved up on to the second floor,
Piso 2. The paramilitaries had been moved to Cómbita as well. The
only remaining prisoners in *alta seguridad* were ones who were attending court proceedings, or ones such as ourselves who were waiting on
a verdict.

Piso 2, much smaller than Piso 1, consisted of a fair-sized room for
visitors and for eating in, as well as a corridor with five cells on both
sides. Each cell had space for two beds, and had a built-in toilet and
shower unit. One extra cell was used as an office for visiting doctors
and officials.

I was sharing a cell with Martin. Niall was sharing with Marine,
who was also in Bogotá for his trial. José was the FARC leader here
after Luis was moved to Cómbita. There was no ELN leader as there
were only two or three of them left. Freddy was in a cell on the opposite side of the corridor from me. There were no makeshift cells on
Piso 2. Only fifteen or sixteen of us were here at any one time. We were
no longer able to mount guard duty because we were constantly mon-
itored on CCTV and INPEC threatened to lock us up in the cells in
the evening if we carried on with guard duty.

There were no cooking facilities remaining and we had to eat the
badly prepared and half cold 'Wimpy' food prepared in a prison
kitchen. It was served out of three large plastic barrels, a ladle full from
each barrel per prisoner.

Martha was a woman who used to visit the FARC prisoners, and I became friendly with her. When most of the prisoners were moved to Cómbita, she continued to visit the ones who remained and she started to visit me as well. Anne only came to Bogotá now and again, but sometimes I would have both Anne and Martha visiting. That was not a problem as Martha liked to spend time with the other prisoners, and she was in effect the person who looked after their welfare.

One day soon after our move to Piso 2 we were told that we were wanted on the ground floor. There was tension as we made our way down because it could be an official to inform us of our sentence. But it was two human rights lawyers on a routine visit to the prison. They talked with representatives from each group of prisoners to find out if there were problems. Apart from the length of time that we were waiting for the sentence, we did not have serious problems.

The lawyers told us that all the staff in the *Fiscalía* offices were going on strike on Thursday, asking that he resign. Even Dr Osario's own staff were outraged at the total lack of justice in the country. It seemed that it came to a head over the army's killing of civilians recently. A particular case that was in the news last week was the killing of five members of one family.

The army story, carried by the TV and newspapers, was that the family were out on the road late at night and walked into an army ambush set for guerrillas. The dead included a six-month-old baby, both of its parents (sixteen and seventeen), a fourteen-year-old and an adult. The local peoples' version was different – that they were shot after failing to give information about guerrilla activities in the area. There were three other cases of civilians being killed by the army in two weeks. The army were under severe pressure to inflict losses on the guerrillas, with some commanders having been replaced for not being aggressive enough. President Uribe needed results before he ran out of money to maintain the huge military forces he had now. The war in Iraq was probably a big factor as the USA would concentrate its weapons and money to try to win there.

The strike, we realised, might delay the verdict in our case. I rang home and was told that reporter Charlie Bird had been on RTE radio saying the verdict would be announced at the end of the week. Dónal and I had a chat about a new film on Alexander the Great. Dónal had gathered a great deal of knowledge about history from playing computer games such as 'Age of Empires'. He seemed to be following in my footsteps in being interested in things that you didn't need to know.

When I told Martin and Niall about the radio news, it changed the whole day. There was a lot of speculation and phone calls to Ireland, which confirmed the news, with the added information that the verdict would be given on Friday or Monday next.

Freddy left a copy of *El Tiempo* on my bed, so I started reading it; the news written in Spanish was interesting and worth working on to extract the story.

Amnesty International had called on the US and Spain to end military aid to Colombia because of serious and consistent breaches of human rights – especially in Arauca, where the oil fields are. They accused the 18th Brigade of the army of systematic violations of human rights and close links with the paramilitaries, who often had road blocks a short distance from army installations. Between 1 January and 14 November 2003, 47 per cent of the local deaths and arbitrary arrests were of trade unionists.

The strike in the *Fiscal* General's office was set for 5 May. The union leaders said that it was because of his general behaviour and did not mention any particular incident. Osario was in lots of different trouble – mostly connected with corruption but some with justice as well. Even the State Department is the US had found him an embarrassment – they preferred to work on the basis of 'plausible deniability'. They didn't object to his crimes so much as to his lack of effort to cover them up. The State Department went to great lengths to cover up its own involvement in criminality and expected the people it worked with to do the same. Our trial was a good example involving both.

Niall was on the phone to our lawyers and one of them said that he would come to the prison to fill us in on what had been happening over the last couple of days. They didn't usually give advance notice on the phone of their movements for fear of the paramilitaries, and I hoped that he had not made a fatal mistake.

Everyone in Cómbita was down with food poisoning – prisoners and guards alike. That was one of the drawbacks of the centralised kitchens they built. Of course, it was the same here now: all the food was cooked in one place and brought around in barrels; it was a system vulnerable to widespread food poisoning unless there was very good hygiene. When we cooked our own food, any outbreak would be localised and the prisoners had direct control of the hygiene in storage and cooking, and of the dishes used.

My lawyer, Pedro, came in and we were able to talk over the various scenarios regarding what might happen in the coming days. He thought that the verdict could well be delivered the next day. It was possible that Caitríona might not be in on a legal visit because she might have to hold a press conference and also get a good briefing herself before it happened. The Sunday visit would be too late to be useful. We were satisfied by the end of his visit that we had covered all the scenarios that we all could think of. The main thing seemed to be that the Dutch Embassy, which represented the EU, would look after arrangements if we were released immediately. We would not leave the prison until we knew that the car from the Dutch Embassy was outside waiting for us.

Any clash between the government and the judiciary would probably be kept out of the media, but the right-wing senators would make the government's views known. The judiciary had taken the very unusual step of shielding the judge by arranging that all judicial comment on the case would be through a judicial body that the judge was responsible to. That effectively shielded him from direct criticism by the government and forced them to shut up, or take on the entire judiciary. It was one more battle in the war between the ultra-right-wing and the constitution. Uribe wanted a pliant judiciary and was meeting fierce resistance. I never thought that I would be on the side of the judges and the law in Colombia! We were just pawns in that battle, as we were pawns in destroying the Colombian peace process.

The latest rumour on Friday 13 April was that the judicial tribunal would announce the verdict in the Palace of Justice in the afternoon. They were really shielding Judge Acosta from the government, and they would field any questions about the trial and sentence. We read it as good news for us, because if they were going to give us a heavy sentence we imagined that they would not have needed to shield the judge from the government. But naturally we worried that perhaps we had got it wrong.

The latest from the media in Ireland was that a high court judge would announce the verdict, but not until Monday. It was building up nicely. I would be a happy little pawn if, as a result of our trial, the United States, Britain and the Colombian oligarchy got their fingers burnt right up to their armpits. That would be worth our years in jail.

The evening came and nothing happened. The latest news was that the judge personally said it would be on Monday, but I was sceptical, thinking that it could be any day next week. I wondered why it was put back, probably for mundane reasons, but I was thinking that it could be because of disagreements in the tribunal or between the tribunal and the *Fiscal* General or members of the government. It was a very unusual way to conduct giving a verdict.

Both Caitríona Ruane here and Rose Dugdale in Ireland suggested that the timing coincided with a major campaign by the British, the USA and the Irish government against Sinn Féin. The new commission overseeing the Good Friday Agreement consisted of four men, two of whom were active securocrats. Our judge might not be as independent as he liked to say, and dirty tricks were synonymous with securocrats.

Two men arrived from Cómbita and we knew them both. One of them was a heavily built man of about fifty-five who was a *campesino*. He had been sleeping on the top concrete bed when he rolled over in his sleep and fell out. He had two broken arms in plaster and had bad bruising all along his body. The immediate question that his plight raised for us was, who was going to clean his arse? I supposed it was a situation in which you really found out who your comrades were.

One of the visitors told us the latest on El Comandante Alfredo. A video had been shown on TV of three CIA men who had been on a light plane that had crashed in FARC territory. Two Colombian military with them had been killed and the CIA men were taken prisoner. Alfredo was there in charge of them in the jungle.

It was a strange turn of fate to go from being a prisoner who did not know when, or if, he would be released, to being a jailer with prisoners in his care who did not know their future either. They were part of the prisoner exchange deal that the FARC were trying to negotiate with the government. President Uribe said that there would be no agreement to exchange prisoners and that rescue attempts would be carried out by the military.

On the last rescue attempt the FARC shot nine prisoners rather than see them rescued – including the governor of a province. Commandante Alfredo would treat his prisoners well, but if a helicopter appeared overhead, he would carry out his orders to shoot them. I sympathised with the other Colombia Three. They were probably suffering the same sort of boredom and uncertainty that we were – but they were in greater danger than us because of Uribe. If the guerrillas were ruthless it was because Uribe, and the class he represented, made them that way.

Martha told me that my friend Diego had got forty years. He was the ELN man whom I had encouraged to write a book about his experiences – while being careful not to write anything that could be used against himself or his comrades.

What made Diego's book unusual was that he had no hands, and only one eye worked properly. He did succeed in writing a quite large manuscript by holding the biro between the stumps of his wrists. Being a perfectionist, he wanted the manuscript typed up on a word processor. I was to get one copy for publishing in Ireland in Irish, English and Spanish, while he would try to get it published in Colombia. Before the typed version arrived back he was moved to a prison in the Magdelena Valley, far away from Bogotá. I lost all contact with him when Tito and the other ELN men were also moved to Cómbita. I had no idea of how he was getting on and whether the book project was now dead.

I did not have a visit on the following Sunday and I really felt it. I had managed over the past two years to reach a situation where I had a visit on most Sundays. Martin and Niall did not get visits except when people like the observers came from abroad, and of course they got the family visits about three or four times a year. It was a decision they had taken not to look for visitors. I took the opposite view and looked for visits and phone contact and letters from people. I had contact with Anne and the other Atlantis people and with Martha and her family. I shared in their lives and problems and they shared in mine.

Prison life exerted a heavy pressure physically, mentally and emotionally, and the worse the pressure, the more it changed and deformed you as a person. The ones we left behind us in Ireland loved us as we were, and time would change us a bit – but less so if the pressures were reduced to manageable levels. To come out relatively intact was my goal and I felt that if I could maintain a reasonably good social life, then I could do it.

I rang Martha last night to see how the family were doing. They were all sick – whatever was in the soup they ate, it had everyone in the house vomiting, but she said it was not serious food poisoning.

Rose Dugdale sent me over a copy of *New Scientist* and there was an article in it referring to the three of us here as having been involved in the development of fuel-air bombs. It was a bit unexpected to say the least.

One of our lawyers visited and said he was of the opinion that a verdict could well come in around the end of the month and recommended that we hold off on the family visits scheduled for 4 May. He was not the kind to say something unless he felt that he was right, so we had to take it seriously.

While making the bed one morning I realised that I still slept on the mattress of El Comandante Alfredo, and I still used his blanket and big green towel. I wondered how he was getting on with his prisoners in the deep jungle.

On Friday 23 April the verdict was expected very soon. According to our frantic phone calls, Judge Jairo Acosta had said he would give it either today or on Monday at the latest. International media were gathering in Bogotá to hear it. Caitríona and Senator Mary White were coming separately to be present when it was read out. Mary would be reporting to Bertie Ahern, the Taoiseach, and she insisted on maintaining her absolute independence by paying all her own plane fares and hotel expenses.

The procedure for the verdict was that it would be hand-delivered to each of us in the prison and then delivered to the lawyers and the media at a special press conference in the Palace of Justice in Bolivar Square.

I was up early on Sunday and phoned Eileen and Maureen in

Fanad, Donegal, who had been key figures in the 'Bring them Home' campaign. A lot of families in the Meath Gaeltacht came from Fanad, and Maureen and Eileen never lost touch. Maureen had been writing to me in various prisons for thirty years. They said they were keeping a bottle safe for when I got out – hopefully soon!

Caitríona, Therese and Senator Mary White visited us. We had a good general talk about all sorts of things and Caitríona gave us a run-down on possible scenarios for when the verdict was announced. They seemed very sure that the verdict would be announced tomorrow and the media in Ireland seemed to share that view. The media in Colombia had not mentioned the case at all in the past week, and I wondered if this was a good sign. The next morning would be a long one for us as well as for our visitors and supporters.

We were up early on Monday and waiting for something to happen. The legal procedure was that an official from the judge's office was supposed to come with written notification of the verdict and the legal reasons behind it. Once we signed the documents saying that we had received them, other people could be notified.

We had heard by phone from Caitríona that the verdict was to be announced at a press conference in the Palace of Justice. It was 9.45am and so far we had not been notified. We had not gone up to the roof for our hour of sun, preferring to stay on Piso 2 to get the news. The tension rose as we waited; I couldn't face another cup of coffee!

It was a lovely sunny day and I was sitting at the window to get the sun. Just outside the window was a passageway and on the other side of it – about two metres away – was the wall of a patio that holds ordinary social prisoners. A spool of thread had just been thrown over the razor wire on top of the three-metre wall. It was probably for a small consignment of drugs from one of the prisoners (or guards) who worked at cleaning up the passageways. Prison life went on!

The time to be notified was almost up; Niall and Martin were listening to a local radio station in the hope of hearing what our sentence was. I would know immediately, from the curses or cheers, what the verdict was as soon as they heard it.

It seemed that the first we would hear of the verdict might be in a phone call to one of our people in Colombia or in Ireland. We could not afford to keep phoning them – we would need the phone cards for after the verdict. A local station had mentioned the press conference, saying that a conviction would suit the Uribe government.

It was nearly 10.30am. A phone call to Caitríona told us that the press conference had had to be moved to a bigger room to accommodate the large number of press people. They expected it to get underway soon.

Chapter 19

The Verdict at Last

THE WORD FINALLY came by phone: Mary White had phoned Caitríona and she told us the news – we had been aquitted on the training charge! We had got about four-year sentences for the passports, so with time off for work and study, we should get immediate release.

Being found not guilty on the training charge was the important one. We needed to get the lawyers to tell us the implications but it seemed to be all good news; we were really happy with the outcome, and we were all phoning home with the news.

On the 12.30pm TV news, it said that we would be released in the next few days, but that Dr Luis Camilo Osario, the head of *Fiscalía*, was over-ruling his own employee, the lawyer in charge of our case, to personally say that he would appeal the verdict. It seemed that we had also been fined $5,000 each (15 million Pesos). I had been sentenced to forty-four months for the passport, Martin had got thirty-six months and Niall twenty-six months. It did not matter as we had been in prison long enough – with time off for work and education – to cover even the forty-four months.

The official whose job it was to notify us had still not turned up. The lawyers were still trying to clarify matters with the judges as to exactly what the judgment meant; for instance, part of the judgment was that we were to be expelled from the country – did that mean we were to be on an aeroplane as soon as the prison released us or did we have to wait for the appeal? When would the prison release us, and to whom? Would we be handed over to the DAS who deal with matters of visas and travel documents?

I started packing. I wanted to leave as much as possible for Martha and for Anne. I packed two bags to leave at Donni Nelsi's shop outside the gate.

The other prisoners came with buckets of water and soaked the three of us in celebration; they were sharing in our good news. I had a tinge of regret that men like José were facing forty years and Freddy still did not know what would happen to him.

The lawyers were not expected in, so we waited to hear what they made of things as it was far too risky to talk on the phone about future moves. The problem was that in spite of the news saying we would be out of La Modelo in a couple of days, in Colombia plans rarely worked out so neatly. We could be here for weeks or months yet. Nóra said on the phone that it did not matter about weeks or months, as long as it was not twenty years!

The notifier had not come; perhaps he would come tomorrow! We could be released on Tuesday or Wednesday, according to the latest good rumour. If we were released, then where were we to go? It seemed that we were a problem to embassies, but if we had to stay in Colombia during an appeal by the *Fiscal* General, then we needed a safe place.

The verdict that was handed down on Monday 17 April was that we were 'Not guilty' of the charge of training the FARC, and 'Guilty' of travelling using false documents. The lawyers thought that the sentences on the documents had already been served, because we had been so long in prison. But Osario, the *Fiscal* General, had said that an appeal was being put in against our acquital and it would take years before we would be released. However, our lawyers thought that we would be entitled to get bail while waiting for the outcome of the appeal. Meanwhile, we would have to stay in La Modelo until it was all sorted out.

I made an arrangement with Freddy that if we were shifted out before Sunday, than I would tell Anne and Martha to go to him to collect the stuff that I had packed for them. We signed a Tyrone football shirt as a keepsake for Freddy and gave him some stationery and special coloured pens for writing on CDs. Freddy gave me the address of his family so I could write to him when I was free – they would get the letter back to him. He lived for his family and the Bolivarian Revolution. He was good-humoured and helpful and considerate, what a revolutionary should be.

In the evening Freddy and the others prepared a meal that we all shared. After the meal I talked to Caitríona on the phone in Irish, giving the details of our dates and places of birth and so on. The information was needed to prepare travel documents. RCN TV news said we would be released from La Modelo tomorrow.

Niall heard from Caitríona that Mary White had done a very good interview about us. We were all grateful to Mary as she had really worked for our human and legal rights in coming out here and in standing up to the bullies in Dublin political circles who had not wanted her to come.

On the phone Anne said that she had letters for us from Geraldo (Flaco) and Ballastras in Cómbita, but it seemed unlikely that she would have another visit to me. She asked me to put return letters in the bag that she would come to collect next Sunday. I wrote out the letters, and one to her thanking her for all the visits, phone calls, books, e-mails and magazines she and the Atlantis Community had sent me over the past two years. They had been a great help to me getting through the time. The letters in Spanish to Flaco and Ballestras thanked them for being good comrades in hard times. I hoped that life went well for them in the future.

The Defensor del Pueblo came to see us – a more senior man accompanied our usual contact. The senior man explained about the letters they had sent to various officials asking that our security be guaranteed – that no one would get the opportunity to shoot us. He also explained some of the legal technicalities – such as, that in calculating if we could get bail they total the physical time that we have done and the time off for work and education. That came to thirty-two months for me, so I still had another six months to do before my forty-four-month sentence was finished. However, the judge had granted me conditional bail (not a fine).

There was uncertainty both in my case and in Martin's about whether we would be allowed to leave the country, but it appeared that once the bail was paid, we would be released from La Modelo. In Niall's case it seemed that he must leave the prison within three days, and be deported. Our legal team with Caitríona and Therese were negotiating to try to sort something out.

I asked some of the lads about the matter of prisoners being fined:

they were not fined, they were granted bail, but it was so high that their families could never raise it. Since bail was returned later that would not amount to legal ransom – although the state would have a free loan for a year or two from those poor families who did manage to raise the money.

Caitríona and Pedro, my lawyer, came in and gave us an update. They explained about the verdict but they could not be definite about what would happen next. Key parts of the legal judgment were open to different interpretations – especially in the short term, about release and expulsion.

The uncertainty and waiting was a pain, but much less of a pain than the prospect of eighteen or twenty years in Cómbita or Valledupar. All other things were unimportant compared to that.

Anne told me about a radio programme the previous day, in which they were complaining about Irish terrorists being allowed to go free and leave the country. That would be very popular in the upper crust and in the security services. We were worried that Caitríona and Therese as well as our lawyers could be the targets if they couldn't get at us. I did not want to stay in the prison if we could be out, because that would look like we were scared of them.

Our legal team was using the fact that we could not be released until the bail of fifty monthly minimum salaries was paid. It came to about $7,000 cash. The real problem was that outside the prison we would need security. In the lawyer's words, we would be 'sitting ducks' for assassination because we would have to remain in Bogotá while matters were sorted out. That would take at least eight days and could easily take a year if things went badly. Our defence team wanted the Colombian state to take responsibility for our safety or fly us home. The government wanted to do neither. More meetings were planned to sort something out, and meanwhile we would have to stay put. On the 7pm news on Caracole TV we featured in the headlines. They said that we would not leave the prison until we had guarantees about our safety.

A terrible accident totally removed our story from the news. A 50-ton earth-moving machine fell down an embankment on to a bus full of students. Seventeen were killed and about thirty-five more were badly injured, including four or five adults.

On Thursday 29 June we learned that the latest development was that a colonel in the police had drawn up a plan for our security, if we were to stay in Bogotá, but not in prison (a stay in prison in protective custody was not acceptable to us). In a second worst case scenario we could have to remain in Bogotá for up to a year before going home. In a worst-case scenario, the appeal by the *Fiscal* General would be upheld by the judicial tribunal and we could be sentenced to twenty years.

The colonel was to present his plan to our legal team. If it was accepted then we would leave La Modelo to take up residence in our new home – a house where we would be protected by the state. We would be free in the sense that we could leave the protected area when we wanted to, but at our own risk.

The state wanted us out of the prison and responsible for our own survival over the coming months – in a city in which their police and military tended to have links with the paramilitary death squads – especially the 13th Brigade of the army, the military police. It appeared that they in particular deeply resented the 'not guilty' verdict.

It struck me that the judge had played it in such a way that he came out of the trial with his good reputation intact, but we could still end up with the long sentence that Osario wanted. I was probably inclined to be sceptical: how did a fair-minded judge get to be so senior in a state run by a corrupt oligarchy? I hoped I was on a wrong line of thinking on this!

The situation was evolving, hopefully towards putting us on a plane home. Monday at around 4pm was to be a tense time for us: if the *Fiscal* General did not lodge an appeal, then Caitríona could book the next available flight home for all of us. If he did lodge an appeal, there was still the possibility that within a week or so, the judge would rule that we could sign for bail in the Colombian Consulate in Dublin. That had legal problems attached, the main one being what happened if the *Fiscal's* appeal was successful and we got twenty years? If he lodged an appeal, and the judge did not rule that we could sign in Dublin, then we would end up in some 'safe' place in Bogota. In that case we wanted the Colombian state to take responsibility for our safety, as that situation could go on for months.

An investigation had been ordered by Judge Acosta into possible perjury charges against the two army witnesses. A year was the time allowed for an appeal, and in our case the appeals tribunal of three judges might rule that the outcome of the perjury charges must be obtained first – before the year can start – because it had a major bearing on the credibility of the evidence.

Before I could raise my doubts about Judge Acosta, both Caitríona and Pedro, my lawyer, said that they believed he was a fair and honourable man, who would not pull any strokes. That satisfied me that my doubts were groundless.

A new month and the future was still very uncertain on 1 May. The stress of waiting was mounting, and I was sure that it was the same outside among our legal team and among our supporters in Colombia and Ireland. We did not expect any developments over the weekend and probably not until about Wednesday or Thursday of the next week.

Caitríona and Therese came in on a visit. This time it was a social rather than a working visit, and we were able to relax and go into the little bits of news about the case here and events in Ireland. Even though we would get the major news from Ireland, the human detail was missing and that was what we were able to talk about. They also described some of the human detail of their time here in Bogotá, such a playing 'spot the spook'. There were quite a few with short haircuts and shiny shoes, but they were not the real spooks, just the watchers. One sixty-year-old Englishman who stayed in their hotel turned up within hours of them doing a rapid change of hotel; he booked into the next room to theirs!

They told us about a reception the Dutch Ambassador invited them to, at which he made a great public fuss of them and they had a pleasant time and met a lot of people. There were about 500 at the reception, all wearing formal clothes, while our two had to come in what they had in their bags.

They met the AP correspondent there and tackled him about his writing that the IRA was putting up the money for our bail, which was completely untrue. A lot of well-placed people there expressed amazement that we had won the case. In supposedly well-informed circles, they had been completely fooled by the media bias and army statements. What the Dutch Ambassador had done was extremely significant. Ireland did not have an embassy in Bogotá, and the Dutch looked after the affairs of EU member states that were not directly represented. His gesture clearly underlined to the Colombian government that the EU were giving us the diplomatic protection that we were entitled to as EU citizens.

Caitríona and Therese had brought in meals of very spicy steak with tomato and potato, prepared by the hotel chef. After they had a meal with us they left about 11.30am after a very pleasant visit.

Martha, her sister Carmen and her daughter Sindy arrived for the final visit at about 12 noon. It had worked out well and we had a good visit. They brought in two plastic boxes of food for the three of us Irish. One box was a salad of lettuce, cabbage, tomato and cucumber, the other contained rice and meat and fried bananas. We were already fed, but the women insisted we eat the stuff they brought. That worked out well because neither Martin nor Niall were keen on lots of salad, while I loved it.

Later in the evening, after the visits were over, I phoned Anne. She had tried to get in but was not allowed as she had arrived about 2pm. Donni Nelsi in the shop had told her that she might get a special half hour visit on a weekday to receive stuff being handed out by a prisoner. I arranged that for Wednesday. It would not be as good as a relaxed time to talk about things, but at least she would get the bag of stuff.

The next day Martin was saying that he had changed his mind about a United Ireland: now that he could not smoke in the pubs in the South, the black North seemed not so bad after all. The rain was hammering on the sheets of tin outside the cell window. The sheets had been corrugated iron but had been flattened out to cover a bigger area and were now laid out to cover leaks in the roof of Piso 1. The noise of the tropical downpour drowned out conversation.

Niall came into the cell with news from Caitríona. She and Pedro were going to the judge's office to see would the *Procurador* put in an appeal as well as the *Fiscal* General. Pedro thought it would be very significant if he did not. The deadline was 4pm – that was in two hours.

They had even better news. Bertie Ahern and the Irish

Ambassador to Mexico, Art Agnew, had both sent letters to Colombia supporting our position on three major points:

1. They wanted our speedy return to Ireland.

2. A hotel would not be a safe place for us to stay if the appeal went ahead – a house would be required.

3. Our campaign – Caitríona representing it – would have the final say on what was acceptable.

We considered this very important because it not only backed up what we wanted, but meant that the Irish government was putting in writing its support.

Writing was extremely important in Colombia; anything not in writing carried very little weight. The judge would get copies of these letters entered as evidence in his consideration of the terms of our bail, and they could be the deciding factor. We now had about two hours to wait to find out if the *Procuradora* had lodged an appeal. His job was to ensure that the whole trial was properly and fairly carried out. But during the trial he showed a lack of interest in the proceedings and at the end called for the maximum sentence to be imposed on us. If he appealed it would not be like the *Fiscalía's* appeal on points of law; his appeal would have to be an accusation that the judge or defence did not follow correct or fair procedures. It would probably amount to putting the judge himself under an inquiry for improper behaviour.

I worried about them saying that they would be at the judge's office for 4pm. It was not a good idea to let the Colombian government, the military, or the American Embassy know your movements in advance. Hopefully no harm had been done. Niall would try calling the mobile number at about 4.15pm to give them time to be out of the office.

The news arrived: the bastards had appealed! Caitríona would be in on a visit tomorrow and she would explain why Pedro thought it very important that he did not appeal. It was probably to do with intimidating the judge by the threat of putting him under investigation into why he had reached a 'not guilty' verdict.

The stress on Caitríona and Therese was obvious, and we were under a lot of mental stress ourselves as things dragged on. I was sure that our lawyers were feeling it too: they were in even more physical danger than we were, and they had to be at their very best mentally if they were to get us out of prison on bail.

Martin was on the phone and said to me and Niall that there had been announcements in Ireland about Bertie's and Brian Cowen's letters, and that the government were making a very public call for our safe and speedy return to Ireland. That was better than I had hoped for. He said that Steve McCabe and other North American lawyers had sent a strong letter to Uribe outlining their concerns about what was happening and also calling for our speedy return to Ireland. Caitríona said on the visit that the appeal by the *Procurador* was not unexpected and did not indicate a new move by the government.

Diego arrived in here. He had been here some months ago, still recovering from a grenade explosion that blew off both his hands. I had become friendly with him. He was an ELN guerrilla, an Afro-Colombian. I was always drawing or painting and he soon started to learn to write again, using the stumps of his wrists to hold the biro. One day he asked me why the Catholics were fighting the Protestants in Ireland. I told him that the war in Ireland was about ending British colonialism and the British had succeeded in presenting it internationally as a religious fight with them acting as peacekeepers. The war in Colombia was also being misrepresented by propaganda as being about control of drugs. I had asked him to write his life story, about the village where he grew up, why he joined the guerrillas and what happened to him.

He came over and I shook the stump of his wrist. I asked him was he still writing but he told me that the guards had destroyed all that he had written and he had not re-done the work as they would destroy it again. It was a great pity as he had more or less completed his book. I was delighted to see him again. He was in a very hot and rough place, far from Bogotá and even further from Antoquia, making visits rare.

At least while he was here he should get a few visits. His family were all refugees, driven out by the paramilitaries, along with all the people in the village that he came from. I was talking to him up on the roof in the patio all day. Unlike the cold mornings, and hot afternoons in Cómbita, his prison was hot from early morning and reached over 40° centigrade in the afternoon.

The North American rules in Diego's prison forbade books, writing materials and even newspapers. The discomfort and extreme boredom was part of the system, so that they would fight with each other – rats in an overcrowded cage. It was a way of destroying their unity and comradeship and eventually even the personality of the individual prisoner. It was sadistic, and a cold, inhuman type of sadism; it was not for the sadists' pleasure in inflicting pain, but for well-defined political goals. As a nation the US had large numbers of the best human rights people and lawyers on Earth, so I wondered why it was that their country had such an awful record over the past fifty years in Latin America.

Work was proceeding on entering letters and papers for the judge, but the really important papers were the appeals entered by the *Fiscalía* and *Procuraduría* – and our lawyers would not be able to read these until 4pm that day when we would know the precise grounds on which they were making their appeals and have some idea of how serious the situation was. This briefing was really just keeping us up to date, the next one would contain more important material. We would get a general overview of the appeals by phone, but discussing our legal alternatives would require the privacy of a visit. Nothing was private that was said on the telephone in Colombia.

In the Colombian press there had been two serious articles so far. One in last Sunday's *El Espectador* was said by Anne to be favourable. The other was in a newspaper called *El Mundo* published in Medellín, and was an attack on the judge. '3 IRA walk free' was the headline.

I did not want to throw cold water on the good mood so I did not mention my own quiet reservations about how things were going. My reasoning went that since Osario, the *Fiscal* General, was a government appointee, not a judge, he must have reported to and taken direction from the government.

Osario must have reported to Uribe's government ministers that if he did not lodge an appeal, then we were legally free and would leave the country as soon as a flight was available. They must have considered the question of whether or not they wanted us to leave the country and they made the appeal to prevent this. As the political implications of the case affected the peace process in Ireland, the

British Embassy was most likely asked for its opinion, too. The United States Embassy was directly involved in the case, so they were also asked for their opinion. The consensus was to continue with the legal process. Mine was a bleak analysis; I hoped it was a wrong one.

I noticed that I was getting a little bit of a cough in the mornings. I needed to get away from Martin's smoking and I really should have looked for a change of cell, but as we were near a crunch situation about bail, I would wait. On Thursday 13 May – in six more days – the judge might have sent us back to Ireland on bail or he might have sent our case to the appeals tribunal with us in a 'safe house' in Bogotá. Either way I hoped to escape from the dreaded cigarette smoke.

Amongst the stuff that was downloaded and left in to us yesterday was one page that said the legal judgment in our case was the most significant in Colombia in the past 100 years. The struggle between the judiciary, or at least an enlightened section of it, and the combined forces of the executive and armed forces had been going on for some time. Our case was another battle in a war within a war.

Caitríona came in to give us an update on what was happening. She hoped to get to see the appeals in the judge's office around 4pm and in the meantime she was doing interviews with both Caracol TV and *Cromous* magazine. The *Cromous* interview was about the campaign rather than the actual trial. Our presence in Colombia had introduced new elements of struggle to them in both legal and publicity terms. Caitríona thought that a good number of middle-class people were surprised and happy that we had won in court, and they wanted to know how we did it. It was seen clearly as a reverse for the Uribe government and some are pleased to see that happen.

Our lawyers said that there had been no surprises in the appeals and that the documents from the Irish government to the Colombian Foreign Office had arrived in to the judge's office, so that was another worry over.

One of the guards came to the three of us with an official form and a letter. The letter was one written by a lawyer from Defensoría del Pueblo saying that since the verdict was given, we were at greater risk of attack by hostile elements. The guard said that we must write on the form just what and when and who we feared attack from. He emphasised that each of us must sign and fingerprint the bottom of the form. We discussed the matter among ourselves after he had gone, and we decided not to write anything or sign the form.

When we had been in La Picota prison there was a paramilitary who signed a form saying that he felt threatened by Robinson after the shooting, and he was put in a cell and isolated there. We got in touch with our lawyers and sent the form to the judge along with an explanation from our lawyers.

Therese was in on a visit the next day and told us that they had spent the weekend in the old colonial city of Cartagena on the Caribbean coast. One new bit of information was that the *Procuradora* did not in the end put in an appeal.

On the news it showed eighteen paramilitaries from Colombia who had been captured near Caracas in Venezuela. Many of them were ex-Colombian army soldiers. The Venezuelan President Hugo Chavez said that their mission had been to help in a coup d'etat, or *Golpe de Estado*, as it was called. Uribe was almost choking when he had to condemn the paramilitaries. Santos could not bring himself to condem them, and said that if Venezuela had a problem with paramilitaries, it was because they did not take strong enough action against the FARC and ELN who crossed the border from Colombia. There would be glum faces in the American Embassy tonight!

The head of *Fiscalía*, Dr Luis Camilo Osario, announced to Associated Press that not only would we have to stay in Colombia for two years waiting for the tribunal to decide on the appeal, but also for a further three years while it went to a higher court! Who is going to pay for rent and food in a 'safe house' for the next five years?

A very shifty looking spokesperson for the US State Department said that it was irresponsible of the Venezuelan government to accuse the US of being part of the plot to overthrow them. He looked like a man who was unsure whether or not the Venezuelans had proof. The links between the Colombian army and the paramilitaries seemed to be dramatically exposed by the identities of the captured men, who numbered eighty in total. Some of the captured men were shown on TV and at least one was telling all he knew. Santos publicly denied that the Colombian authorities helped identify the men captured.

Gerry Kelly of Sinn Féin and Caitríona came in on a visit and told us to be ready because they would pay the bail the next morning and collect us later in the day. After all the waiting it was a relief to have something happening, but also a worry that it might go wrong for us. I found it difficult to get to sleep that night.

Chapter 20

Freedom Ride?

AFTER BREAKFAST WE started to pack our things. It was a matter of deciding what to take and what to leave behind for the lads. I gave Diego my pens and paints, brushes and art paper. He had learned to write better than most people who had the use of both hands, and he would learn to paint well if given the opportunity in prison. His chances of surviving without hands were not good, but he was a fighter and would try. I gave my extra clothes and blankets to Freddy and José.

The other prisoners were about to throw buckets of water over us, as was the custom, but they decided against it knowing that we faced a very uncertain future outside the front gate. Going out in wet clothes would not help in the crucial first minutes. The media was waiting for us, and the DAS, and possibly the paramilitaries had a sniper in place.

There were farewell speeches from José on behalf of the FARC, and from Freddy and from two or three others. We made our farewell speeches in return. After that there was a kind of anti-climax because everything was said and done and we could only wait.

We were sitting making small talk when the guards finally came to take us to reception. We were handcuffed and told to follow the guards out through the heavy steel door and down the stairs. These were the same stairs that the paramilitaries had thrown the bomb down at us nearly three years ago. The wall phone was still there at the bottom of the stairs but it looked to be broken and disused.

It felt unreal when the handcuffs were removed and we were given the final fingerprinting and videoed for the last time. Our bags were searched. We were strip searched and handed our 'property' – mail and items of clothes. We emerged from the front door of the building, blinking in the sunlight. We were free!

There was a car waiting to take us to a safe house. We got in and drove out the gates of La Modelo Prison. We were delighted to leave it behind us.

We had a long journey home, and needed the help of many good people. The story of that journey cannot be told for many years because that might endanger those people. There are intelligence services who would dearly love to know how it was done, and to punish those who helped us escape from tyranny.

When all three of us were back safely in Ireland we asked for legal advice as to what was our situation. We were advised that deportation back to Colombia would probably not be legally possible and that we should announce our presence, wait a while to get the reaction, and then decide our next step.

I was asked would I do a TV interview to announce that we were back in Ireland. I was brought to a house where the TV cameras were set up, and the interview with Charlie Bird took place on Friday 5 August 2005.

"I'm back," I said, "and I would hope that I'll be left in peace."

I was described as fifty-eight, thin, pale and obviously nervous. Asked if I was on the run, I answered: "I wouldn't be giving this interview... The Taoiseach asked that we be sent back when we were waiting on the appeal – so I hope that they will continue in that vein."

"Was there a deal between the government and Sinn Féin?"

"No, not that I'm aware of. There hasn't been any deal of any sort. We returned as soon as we were able to return."

"Who helped you return?"

"That would endanger those involved. If it's a case that the guards or someone wants to talk to us – or wants to talk to me – that's all right."

The headline on Saturday's *Irish News* was "Relief and Fury at Shock Return of Colombia Three". That was fairly typical of what the media had to say.

In Belfast there were spontaneous celebrations, while the Irish right-wing politicians, the Unionists and the British were furious. There were lurid media reports of our return causing a crisis in the Dublin government, angry reaction by the United States and the imminent collapse of the peace process if we were not deported back to Colombia, or at least jailed for the seventeen years in Ireland. Unionist politicians claimed that our return was arranged by the Dublin government as part of a secret deal with Sinn Féin. It seemed to me that the issue had divided opinion on a gut pro- and anti-imperialist line as few other issues had done.

There was one further stage before the journey was over. It was a walk of ten or twenty metres. Garrett Sheehan, our legal adviser, had said that each of us should walk into a Garda station in Dublin and ask them if they had any questions they wanted answered. On 18 August 2005, as I walked into the station, I was acutely aware that if Garrett had got it wrong then I could find myself on a plane back to Colombia and almost certain death, and if he had got it right then the journey was over.

He got it right! In spite of the fury of the Minister for Justice and his Colombian counterparts, extradition back to Colombia was neither legally nor politically possible.

Acknowledgements and thanks

FIRST I WANT to thank all the Colombian people who made our survival possible. We could not have returned home without their help, and indeed might not be alive to tell the story but for them. They were people from different walks of life, but all very generous and kind, and willing to help us at great risk to themselves and their loved ones. They did it for patriotic reasons, as a part of the struggle to free their own country from tyranny.

The lawyers of the José Alvear Restrepo Colectivo deserve special thanks as they risked their lives to represent us, and they continue living under the threat of death as long as they remain defenders of human rights in Colombia. Pedro Mahecha represented me, José Luis Velasco represented Martin McCauley, and Eduardo Matyas represented Niall Connolly. Peter Madden gave extremely good legal advice from Ireland.

I want to thank all the thousands who helped the 'Bring Them Home' campaign. People raised money by collections, by sponsored mountain walks, by parachute jumps, by music and singing, by a whole range of imaginative fund-raising events. That money enabled family visits, phone contact and most importantly, it enabled the defence to have a very good team of international observers present at every stage of the trial. I particularly want to thank Caitríona Ruane who did great work in managing the Campaign, and her sister Therese who was ever ready to step into her place if Caitríona was arrested or refused entry to Colombia.

I want to thank the members of the international observers team. Without their consistent presence, I think that we would be still in prison. They were:

Irish Observers
Niall Andrews, Member of the European Parliament (Fianna Fáil)
Seán Crowe, TD (Sinn Féin and a negotiator for Belfast Agreement)
Finian McGrath, TD (Independent, Dublin)

Senator Mary White, Senator (Fianna Fáil, former national executive member)

Barry McElduff MLA (Sinn Féin, West Tyrone)

Desmond Bonass, Trade Unionist (Dublin Council of Trade Unions)

Ronan Munro, BL Criminal Lawyer (Dublin)

Pat Daly, Criminal Law Solicitor, Tutor in Criminal Law

Paul Hill, Guildford Four (fifteen years in miscarriage of justice)

US Observers

Steve McCabe, Lawyer (New York and Supreme Court USA, Brehon Law Society President)

Natalie Kabasakalian, Court Attorney (Appellant Division, Supreme Court USA)

Patrick Fowler, Social Worker, Human Rights Activist

Cody McCone, Lawyer (New York, Brehon Law Society member)

Frank Durkan, Lawyer (New York, Brehon Law Society member)

Australian Observers

Paul Lynch, Member of the Australian Parliament

Shaun Kerrigan, Lawyer (Human Rights, Industrial, Immigration and Refugee, Criminal Law)

Ian Latham, Barrister (Discrimination, Employment and Criminal Law, Australian Labour Party councillor)

Brett Gay, Member of Australian National Executive and Council of Trade Unions Movement

Along with them I want to thank the Irish Embassy in Mexico. The presence of Art Agnew and Síle Maguire undoubtedly made a difference both in our prison treatment and in the court.

Mike Ritchie, Dr Laurence McKeown, Ros O'Sullivan, Dr Seán Ó Domhnaill, and Dr Keith Borer gave evidence for the defence. Danny Morrison, Catherine Murphy and Michelle Devlin were in Bogotá prepared to give evidence but were not called. They all deserve the deepest thanks.

I want to thank the prisoners who helped us survive in the sometimes frightening conditions of Colombian prison life, especially El Comandante Alfredo, Robinson, Tito and Yesid Arteta.

Thanks also to Martin, Niall and their families, as well as to my brother Gerry for keeping our collective morale up during difficult times.

Anne Barr was brilliant for her constant visits to me, especially when it was very dangerous and difficult, such as in La Modelo in the first weeks and in Cómbita, all the time. Rose Dugdale worked long and hard at maintaining a constant flow of information and detailed political discussion papers with me about what was going on in the outside world. Maureen Fanning and Eileen Sheils, among many others, never tired in organising support.

Special thanks are due to Margie O'Rourke who typed up the hand-written diaries that I had sent out of prison, and to Leo Cooper, Morgan Llywelyn, and Christy Moore who encouraged me to start writing the book and advised me how to go about it.

Lastly I want to thank Brandon Books for their friendly help and advice.

Jim Monaghan

MANCHÁN MAGAN

Angels and Rabies:
A Journey Through the Americas

"Each chapter is gripping because truly insane things happen around the author: war breaks out in Ecuador; a famous Hollywood actress falls into his arms. Then there are the near death experiences . . . The book kicks into top gear when the protagonist, realising that the Amazon jungle is just around the corner, takes off on a bicycle to surrender himself to its mighty embrace. The ensuing adventure is the highlight of the book. It is a warm, well written and entertaining book which will keep readers happy this summer and maybe even inspire a few to book their passage to Colombia." *Village*

"Frightening, funny and lovable." *The Sunday Times*

"[Magan's] writing is unashamedly sensual and he has an engagingly confessional narrative voice; his adventures are as poignant as they are hair-raising. And while exposing the chaotic workings of his own soul, Magan reveals the underbelly of the colourful cultural and sociological jigsaw of these two great continents."
Sunday Telegraph

"This travelogue exudes an attitude that is unmistakably rock 'n' roll. Fuelled by the same wild abandon as Jack Kerouac, Magan journeys through the Americas with nothing but adventure on his mind." *Hot Press*

"A cross between Joseph Conrad and Frank Zappa." Gerry Ryan

"His writing is intimate and immediate, perceptive and humorous."
Books Ireland

ISBN 9780863223495; paperback original

MANCHÁN MAGAN

Manchán's Travels: A Journey Through India

"A road trip unlike any we've ever seen. Magan's writing is as unique as his TV style; endearing and honest, his personality shining through. He succeeds in bringing the Indian landscape, the country, to life, but his real talent lies in the people. At heart, this is a story about the personalities the brothers encounter and Manchan succeeds in bringing them all, zany as they may be, to life. The title – *Manchan's Travels* – suggests this is the first in a long series of travelogues. They are most welcome." *Irish Independent*

"An irresistible read. From beginning to end, I chortled, chuckled, gasped and held my breath. Well done! Let's have more of it. What a tale. Miss it at your peril." Gerry Ryan, RTE 2FM

"Crazy, entertaining and ultimately thought-provoking...The best part of this book is not the unique stories told (though they are fascinating and present you with an India you'll never get in your Lonely Planet), but the way the Westmeath man recounts his experiences. Mocha proves to be deeply funny without even trying, and he lays his soul so bare you could die of embarrassment at times. Mocha 'on the road' makes for one unforgettable aventure." *Irish World*

"As off-beat as it is entertaining, taking a look at the often surreal nature of life in modern India." *Traveller*

"Magan has a keen eye for the hypocrisies of elite urban India and artfully evokes the 'fevered serenity' of the Himalayas." *Times Literary Supplement*

ISSBN 978086322 3686; paperback original

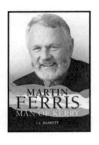

J. J. BARRETT
Martin Ferris: Man of Kerry

"An amazing insight into the world of a man on a mission." *Irish Post*

"[The] graphic and fluid biography of a man who has since beaten his sword into a ploughshare." *Irish Independent*

"The story of how Martin went on to contribute to the story of his county and his country is a compelling one, which nobody is better fitted than Jo Jo to write." Tim Pat Coogan

ISBN 9780863223518; paperback

SEAN O'CALLAGHAN
To Hell or Barbados
The ethnic cleansing of Ireland

"An illuminating insight into a neglected episode in Irish history... its main achievement is to situate the story of colonialism in Ireland in the much larger context of world-wide European imperialism." *Irish World*

ISBN 9780863222870; paperback

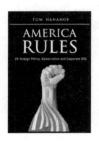

TOM HANAHOE
America Rules: US Foreign Policy, Globalization and Corporate USA

The disturbing, definitive account of globalization and the new American imperialism. Rather than serving as a global protector, the United States has shown contempt for the ideas of freedom, democracy and human rights.

ISBN 9780863223099; paperback original

DENNIS COOKE
Persecuting Zeal: A Portrait of Ian Paisley

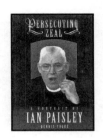

"This highly qualified author writes with an admirable mixture of clarity, charity and scholarship... I conclude with one word of advice: read this book." Tim Pat Coogan

ISBN 9780863222429; paperback

HENRY SINNERTON
David Ervine: Uncharted Waters

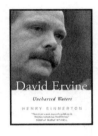

"Revealing . . . Ervine is an impressive advocate of modern unionism." *Irish Examiner*
"[A] valuable contribution to the understanding of the troubles." *Irish World*

ISBN 9780863223129; *paperback*

ADRIAN HOAR
In Green and Red: The Lives of Frank Ryan

"The work is of a high standard, well documented, with index, a list of sources and copious notes... there is hardly a dull moment in the account from beginning to end." *Irish Independent*

ISBN 9780863223327; *hardback*

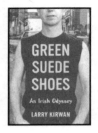

LARRY KIRWAN
Green Suede Shoes

The sparkling autobiography of the lead singer and songwriter of New York rock band, Black 47.

"Lively and always readable. He has wrought a refined tale of a raw existence, filled with colorful characters and vivid accounts." *Publishers Weekly*

ISBN 9780863223433; paperback original

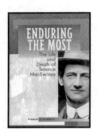

FRANCIS J. COSTELLO
Enduring the Most
The Life and Death of Terence MacSwiney

"Francis J. Costello's comprehensive biography is most welcome... It will surely remain the definitive work." *Sunday Independent*

"Worth reading for several reasons: it is a transatlantic and fresh revision; it offers a psychology that explains a history; it illuminates an aspect of our present as well as our past." *The Irish Times*

ISBN 9780863222207; paperback

JOE GOOD
Enchanted by Dreams
The Journal of a Revolutionary

A fascinating first-hand account of the 1916 Rising and its aftermath by a Londoner who was a member of the Irish Volunteers who joined the garrison in the GPO.

ISBN 9780863222252; paperback original

MÍCHEÁL Ó DUBHSHLÁINE
A Dark Day on the Blaskets

"A wonderful piece of drama-documentary... entertaining and captivating. It's an evocative story, a portrait of a young woman and her times, and an engrossing description of a beautiful place at a turning point in its history." *Ireland Magazine*

"A fascinating insight into Blasket Island life, life on the mainland, and life in Dublin in the early part of the last century." *Kerryman*

ISBN 9780863223372; paperback

GEORGE THOMSON
Island Home

"Imbued with Thomson's deep respect for the rich oral culture and his aspiration that the best of the past might be preserved in the future. It is when the deprived and the dispossessed take their future into their own hands, he concludes, that civilisation can be raised to a higher level."
Sunday Tribune

ISBN 9780863221613; paperback

STEVE MACDONOGH
The Dingle Peninsula

A comprehensive illustrated survey of the archaeology, folklore and history of one of Ireland's most fascinating regions.

"Far and away the best of the many books written about the area. A visitor who travels to Dingle without it is seriously deprived." *The Examiner*

ISBN 9780863222696; paperback original

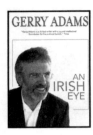

GERRY ADAMS

An Irish Eye

A unique book reflecting the Sinn Féin president's involvement in events between 2004 and 2007.

"Overall, Adams comes across as an intelligent man with a inexorable passion for writing, history and politics." *Sunday Business Post*

"Intelligent writing... Mr Adams is a fine writer and an equally fine orator." *Irish World*

ISBN 9780863223709; paperback original

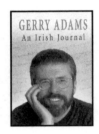

An Irish Journal

"Gives an almost personal feel for the peace process as it develops, from Sinn Féin's first meeting with Britain's new prime minister Tony Blair to the build-up to the Good Friday agreement." *Sunday Tribune*

ISBN 9780863222825X; paperback original

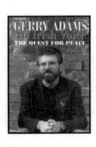

An Irish Voice

"[A]s these articles show, he is a thinker of considerable stature... *An Irish Voice* is a good read. For the humour as much as the philosophy or the politics." Tim Pat Coogan

ISBN 9781902011011; paperback original

GERRY ADAMS

Before the Dawn: An Autobiography

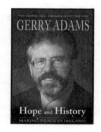

"One thing about him is certain: Gerry Adams is a gifted writer who, if he were not at the center of the war-and-peace business, could easily make a living as an author, of fiction or fact."
New York Times

ISBN 9780863222894; paperback

Hope and History: Making Peace in Ireland

"A fascinating account of his journey through the peace process, from the first tentative discussions with a priest called Father Reid, to his present position sharing the pages of *Hello!* with The Corrs, the international stage with Nelson Mandela." *Daily Mirror*

ISBN 9780863223303; paperback

The New Ireland

A political manifesto from the leading figure in Irish Republicanism, published on the occasion of the centenary of the founding of Sinn Féin and pointing the way in the struggle for Irish unity in the twenty-first century.

ISBN 9780863223440; paperback original

GERRY ADAMS
Cage Eleven

"Quite brilliant... a tribute to a particular kind of survival by a group of people who have committed their lives to a deeply held political belief about their country." *Books Ireland*

ISBN 9780863222924; paperback

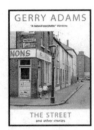

The Street

"The warmth of Adams's writing comes from the affection of a man for the remembered things of his past... Adams can write well."
Times Literary Supplement

ISBN 9780086322931; paperback

Selected Writings

"Adams writes fluently and observantly... He displays a hard-edged compassion for the silent poor, the old and the down-and-out."
Financial Times

ISBN 9780863222337; paperback original